Wildflo

OF SOUTHERN

WESTERN AUSTRALIA

MARGARET G. CORRICK   BRUCE A. FUHRER

ROSENBERG

This third edition first published in Australia in 2009
by Rosenberg Publishing Pty Ltd
Reprinted 2013
PO Box 6125, Dural Delivery Centre NSW 2158
Phone: 612 9654 1502 Fax: 612 9654 1338
Email: rosenbergpub@smartchat.net.au
Web: www.rosenbergpub.com.au

National Library of Australia Cataloguing-in-Publication data

Corrick, Margaret.
Wildflowers of southern Western Australia / Margaret Corrick and Bruce Fuhrer.
3rd ed.
ISBN: 9781877058844 (pbk.)

Includes index.
Bibliography.

Wild flowers--Western Australia--Identification.
Wild flowers--Western Australia--Pictorial works.

Other Authors/Contributors: Fuhrer, B.
A. (Bruce Alexander), 1930-

582.13099412

Cover photos by show: (front top) Coastal heathland near Albany with *Pimelea ferruginea*
(front bottom) Mulga woodland in Paynes Find/Yalgoo area, (back top) *Ptilotus exaltatus* near Mullewa,
(back bottom) Kwongan east of Lake King showing *Melaleuca* and *Verticordia.*
The two top photos are by Bruce Fuhrer and the two bottom ones are by Margaret Corrick.

Printed in China by Everbest Printing Co Limited

CONTENTS

ACKNOWLEDGMENTS AND CREDITS

The Photographs

All photography was done in the field. Most photographs are supported by vouchers lodged at the National Herbarium of Victoria.

Photographic credits

All photographs are by Bruce Fuhrer except the following: plates 46(b), 157, 160(b), 170, 188, 189, 222(b), 243, 280, 285, 286, 322, 368, 418, 427, 485, 488, 510, 542, 586, 628(a), 629, 719, 742, 749 by Margaret and Bill Corrick, and plates 9, 10, 64, 148, 158, 201, 268c, 279, 320, 369, 370, 377, 379, 380, 381, 385, 434, 525, 535, 546, 547, 554, 576, 607, 673 by Mary and Basil Smith. The photographs on pages 10 and 11 are by Alex George.

Acknowledgments

With the publication of this book, the Department of Ecology and Evolutionary Biology at Monash University aims to make Bruce Fuhrer's photographs available to a wider public than the University community where they have been an important adjunct in a variety of study programs. The initiative of Associate Professor Neil Hallam and the Department is gratefully acknowledged. Annabel Carle has assisted in the organisation of the project in many ways, and we particularly thank Linda Dembinski for her cheerful, competent word processing.

We thank Dr Jim Ross, formerly Chief Botanist of the National Herbarium of Victoria, for access to the collections and for facilities enabling us to check voucher specimens. Our thanks also to Helen Cohn and Jill Thurlow of the Herbarium Library for assistance in locating elusive literature.

Many other people helped us in a variety of ways. Botanists and technical staff from several other Australian herbaria assisted with identification of voucher specimens; local residents, field naturalists, students and native plant enthusiasts have offered hospitality, guided us to particular plants, or accompanied us on field trips. We extend our grateful thanks to the following: David Albrecht, Christine & Will Ashburner, Robyn Barker, Don & Barbara Bellairs, Eleanor Bennett, Ian Brooker, Christine Cargill, Barry Conn, Cathryn Coles, Lyn Craven, the late Eileen Croxford, Stuart Duncan, Roger Elliot, the late Don Foreman, the late George Gardner, Jeff Jeanes, Clare Land, Nicholas Lander, Brendan Lepschi, Jim McCulloch, Bob Makinson, Neville Marchant, Bruce Maslin, Barbara Rye, the late George Scott, Philip Short, Mary & Basil Smith, Richard & Garry Sounness, Gary Swinton, Roslyn St Clair, Neville Walsh and Paul Wilson. In conclusion we especially thank Cathie Hair for her help with proof-reading and our spouses, Irene and Bill, for their support and encouragement.

For help in preparation of the third edition we thank Anne Fletcher, Resources Manager, Monash School of Biological Sciences, for preparation of publishing contracts and Alex George for advice and for providing additional photographs.

PREFACE

This book illustrates 755 of the flowering plants of southern Western Australia; the areas covered are shown in the accompanying map of the Botanical Districts of the State. Of the plants illustrated 656 are endemic in W.A. and many are very restricted in their distribution, whilst others extend widely in the State or to other States.

The book is intended for all those who enjoy the unique, diverse flora of W.A. The majority of species illustrated were found on roadsides, many in National Parks and reserves, accessible by conventional vehicle. Wherever possible technical botanical terms have been avoided except where precision or brevity necessitate their use; a glossary is provided to cover these terms.

Many wildflower books of this type are divided into sections according to habitat, but the authors felt that to group plants together in families placed in alphabetical order would make the book easier to use and provide an opportunity for an overview of the diversity within some of the larger families. Sixty-eight families are represented, with a short introduction to each including its size and distribution. Since first publication of the book in 1996 advances in plant taxonomy, particularly in molecular studies and cladistics, have led to proposals for revised classifications at generic and family level. For reasons of economy and lack of agreement between authorities we have retained the family names and layout of plates used in the original edition of the book. We have updated species names but have not been able to retain the alphabetical sequence within genera. Old names have been cited in synonymy and are fully indexed.

The captions to species are not comprehensive descriptions of the plants illustrated; where possible the photograph is left to speak for itself. Each caption states botanical name, common name (if available), size of plant, habitat and distribution. Photographs are not all reproduced to the same scale but measurements are stated. Where leaves do not appear, a brief description and measurements are given, with length stated before width; where leaves appear clearly, length measurement only is given. Flower size is almost always stated. All measurements should be liberally interpreted, as situation and seasonal conditions will affect both the size of the plant and its flowers. Habitat notes are provided in each caption. The only common names used are those recommended by Bennett (1993).

The captions give distribution by numbers taken from Hnatiuk (1990). The larger-scale map, after Beard (1979), shows the Botanical Regions with Hnatiuk's numbers superimposed. Every effort has been made to update distributions but these should not be regarded as exclusive of extensions or changes in range. The data were up to date at time of writing. 'Florabase', the website of the WA Herbarium, is continually updated and is recommended as a reference for more recent changes.

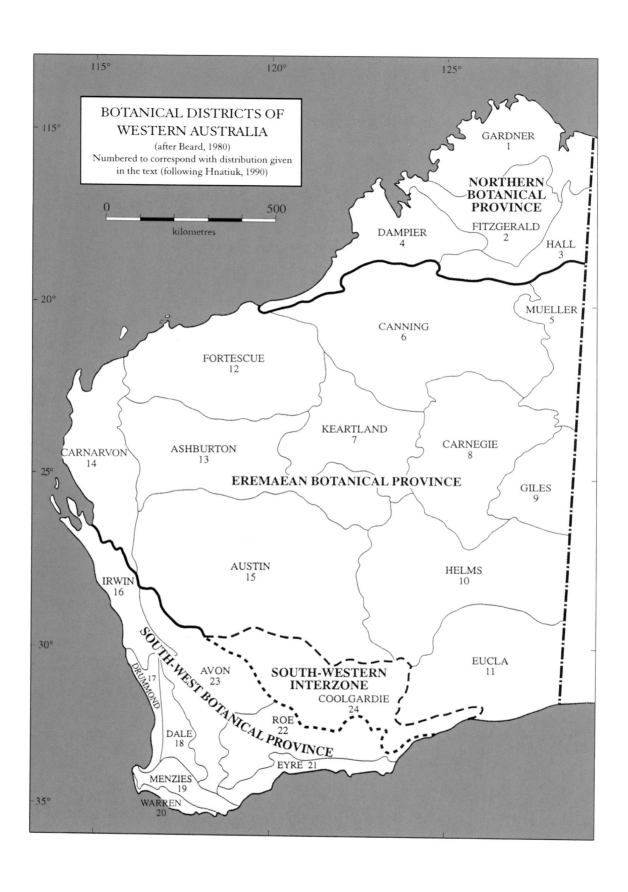

BOTANICAL DISTRICTS OF
WESTERN AUSTRALIA
(after Beard, 1980)
Numbered to correspond with distribution given
in the text (following Hnatiuk, 1990)

0   500
kilometres

GARDNER
1

NORTHERN
BOTANICAL
PROVINCE

FITZGERALD
2

DAMPIER
4

HALL
3

MUELLER
5

CANNING
6

FORTESCUE
12

KEARTLAND
7

CARNEGIE
8

CARNARVON
14

ASHBURTON
13

EREMAEAN BOTANICAL PROVINCE

GILES
9

AUSTIN
15

HELMS
10

IRWIN
16

SOUTH-WEST BOTANICAL PROVINCE

DRUMMOND
17

AVON
23

SOUTH-WESTERN
INTERZONE

COOLGARDIE
24

EUCLA
11

ROE
22

DALE
18

EYRE 21

MENZIES
19

WARREN
20

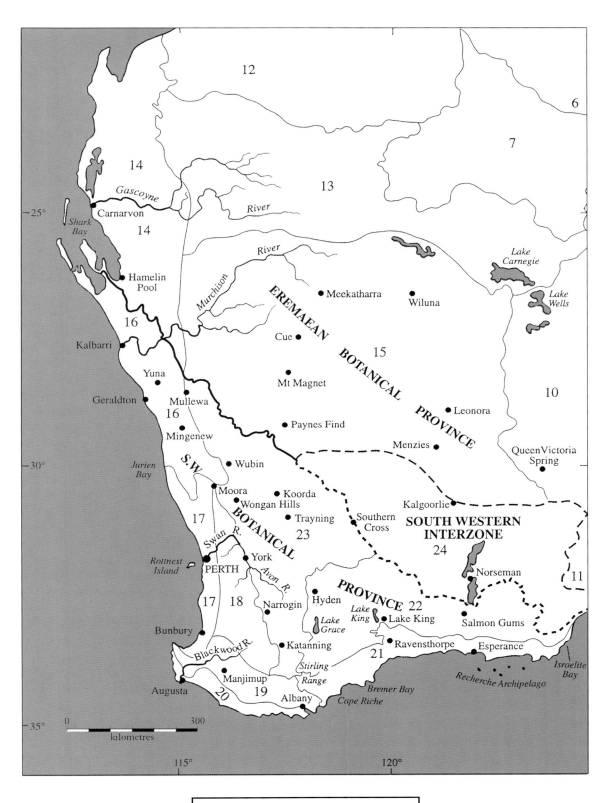

ENLARGEMENT OF SOUTH-WEST
BOTANICAL PROVINCE, SOUTHWESTERN
INTERZONE AND PORTION OF EREMAEAN
BOTANICAL PROVINCE
(after Beard, 1980, as adapted by Blackall and Grieve, 1988)

SELECTED REFERENCES

Australian Plant Census: www.cpbr/gov.au/chah/apc/indexx.html

Australian Plant Name Index: www.anbg.gov.au/cgi-bin/apni

Beard, J.S. (1988). *A New Phytogeographic Map of Western Australia.* WA Herbarium Research Notes 3:37–58.

Blackall, W.E. & Grieve, B.J. (1980–98). *How to know Western Australian Wildflowers.* published in several parts. University of WA Press, Nedlands.

Brooker, M.I.H. & Kleinig, D.A. (2002). *Field Guide to Eucalypts*, Vol. 2, South-Western and Southern Australia. Bloomings Books, Melbourne.

Cavanagh, Tony and Pieroni, Margaret (2006). *The Dryandras.* Australian Plant Society Inc.(SGAP Vic.), Hawthorn and Western Australia Wildflower Society, Nedlands.

Chinnock, R.J. (2007). *Eremophila and Allied Genera: A Monograph of the Eremophilas.* Rosenberg Publishing, Kenthurst

Collins, K. & K. & George, A.S. (2008). *Banksias.* Bloomings Books, Melbourne.

Elliot, R. & Jones, D.L. (1980–). *Encyclopaedia of Australian Plants Suitable for Cultivation.* Vols 1–8 & Supplement. Lothian, Melbourne.

Flora of Australia (1981–). Vols 1–. Australian Government Publishing Service, Canberra/ Australian Biological Resources Study and CSIRO, Melbourne.

Florabase, the website of the WA Herbarium, includes full lists of species, distribution maps and many photographs. http://florabase.dec.wa.gov.au/

George, E.A. (Berndt) (2002). *Verticordia – The Turner of Hearts.* University of WA Press, Nedlands.

Hoffman, N. & Brown, A. (1998). *Orchids of South-west Australia*, 2nd edn, revised. University of WA Press, Nedlands.

Hopper, S.D. (1993). *Kangaroo Paws and Catspaws.* Department of Conservation & Land Management, Como, WA.

Lowrie, A. (1987–89). *Carnivorous Plants of Australia*, Vols 1, 2 and 3. University of WA Press, Nedlands.

Marchant, N.G. et al. (1987). *Flora of the Perth Region*, Parts 1 & 2. WA Herbarium, Department of Agriculture, Como, WA.

Meney, K.A. and Pate, J.S. (eds) (1999). *Australian Rushes.* University of WA Press, Nedlands.

Nevill, Simon (2001). *Travellers Guide to the Parks and Reserves of Western Australia.* Simon Nevill Publications, South Fremantle, WA.

Nuytsia (1970–). Bulletin of Western Australian Herbarium. Continuing series containing papers on the Australian Flora. Western Australian Herbarium, Como, WA.

Olde, P. & Marriott, N. (1994–95). *The Grevillea Book*, Vols 1–3. Kangaroo Press, Kenthurst.

Wheeler, Judy et al. (2002) *Flora of the South West,* Vols.1 and 2. University of WA Press, Nedlands.

INTRODUCTION

A one-sentence summary of Western Australia might read as follows:

A vast area, mostly very old geologically, relatively flat, generally infertile, tropical in the north, temperate in the south, subject to drought, with a large, diverse flora and fauna including many species peculiar to the region.

To fill in the details would take many books, and even then there would be large gaps where we simply do not know the whole story; it will be decades before we know that. Here only a brief overview can be given, outlining the main features.

The South-West

The South-West is home to one of the richest floras in the world. South and west of a line lying roughly between Shark Bay and Israelite Bay, there are about 8000 species of flowering plants, of which some 80% grow nowhere else. Some large groups are wholly or mostly confined to the region and have clearly evolved here, e.g. dryandra (92 spp.), synaphea (c. 60 spp.), cottonheads (*Conostylis*, c. 50 spp.), wax flower (*Chamelaucium*, c. 30 spp.) and one-sided bottlebrush (*Calothamnus,* c. 45 spp.). Others appeared before the region became isolated but have speciated here more than elsewhere, e.g. featherflower (*Verticordia*, more than 90 of 100 spp.), darwinia (40+ of 55+ spp.), triggerplants (150 of 200+ spp.) and gastrolobiums (33 of 34 spp.). This proliferation occurred after the isolation of the region from eastern Australia in the early Cretaceous age some 100 million years ago. The ancient origin is shown by the relationship to the floras of other lands that made up the supercontinent Gondwana which completed its break-up some 65 million years ago. Families such as Proteaceae, Epacridaceae, Rutaceae, Restionaceae and Myrtaceae are well represented in South America and South Africa, but at the generic level they have little in common with Australia. Casuarinaceae is found as fossils in Africa but is now extinct there, occurring in Australia, south-eastern Asia, New Caledonia and some islands of the Pacific.

This is a relatively flat area, the major feature being the Darling Plateau or Western Shield of ancient granitic rocks, overlain in many places by recently formed sandstone or laterite and large areas of sand. The soil variety is extraordinary, even in small areas, and it is this that most strongly affects the distribution of plants.

The region has a 'mediterranean' climate, that is, a cool, wet winter with rain from east-moving mid-latitude depressions, and a warm to hot, dry summer when almost no rain falls over a five-to-six-month period. The plants are strongly adapted to the seasonal climate as well as to drought and fire, all events that developed long before humans reached these shores.

Kwongan: This Aboriginal term is now widely used for the low heath-like vegetation common over large areas of the south-west where rainfall is 250–400 mm. It is usually on soils of low fertility, yet here is the richest development of the flora. Several families are especially dominant, viz. Proteaceae, Myrtaceae, Fabaceae and Epacridaceae. It is common to find dozens of species in a small area. Compact growth, small tough leaves and a profusion of small flowers characterise many species, although when not flowering many assume a confusing sameness of form. Thorns are virtually absent, but are replaced by pungent leaves or stem tips. Herbaceous plants are not well represented in kwongan, although there are some spectacular ones such as leschenaultia, pop flower (*Glischrocaryon*) and triggerplants. Throughout the region, kwongan is commonly associated with taller shrubs, especially mallee eucalypts.

Kwongan covers large areas of the south-west, in particular north of Perth between the lower Murchison and Moore rivers, in the south from Dumbleyung and the

Kwongan near Lake King including *Verticordia*

Stirling Range to Israelite Bay, and to the east and south-east of Southern Cross. Particularly rich areas are the Kalbarri, Stirling Range and Fitzgerald River National Parks, and Mount Lesueur, near Jurien.

Woodlands: On the heavier loam and clay soils are woodlands dominated by eucalypts and wattles. The tall salmon gum (*Eucalyptus salmonophloia*) is especially attractive, its pink bark turning deeper shades during autumn. Wandoo (*E. wandoo*) is also widespread, and other common eucalypts are york gum (*E. loxophleba*), morrell (*E. longicornis*), gimlet (*E. salubris*) and mallet (especially *E. astringens*). There is usually an open understorey of shrubs such as grevillea, wattle, olearia, cassia, phebalium and templetonia. The ground flora is sparse, although orchids are sometimes common. The wattle Raspberry Jam (*Acacia acuminata*) is common on red loam, either dominant or mixed with York Gum or Wandoo, with a sparse shrubby understorey but with more herbs than other formations, including many orchids in late winter and spring.

Wandoo woodland south-west of York

Mallee: Large areas of the south-west, especially in the south-eastern wheatbelt, have heavier clay-loam soils on which mallee eucalypts form the dominant vegetation. Many species of eucalypt occur here, a number being summer-flowering.

Granite outcrops (including islands off the south coast such as the Recherche Archipelago): These are the 'bones' of the ancient underlying rocks, exposed by erosion. Having soil quite different from that of surrounding areas, and with additional water from run-off, they support a different suite of plants. Trees and tall shrubs such as sheoak, wattle, grevillea, thryptomene, teatree (*Leptospermum*) and melaleuca are common on the immediate surrounds. Shallower soil pockets on the rocks are home to an amazing variety of plants, many of them tiny 'belly plants' that require close inspection to appreciate. Remarkable among these are the pincushions (*Borya*), whose needle-like leaves turn orange in dry

Granite rocks at Billyacatting Hill

periods and either become dormant or fall. Those that become dormant have the capability to restore themselves and continue growing when adequate moisture is again available. These outcrops are home to many orchids.

Salt lakes: These occur throughout the drier parts of the south-west. Some are old, but a number have formed since clearing for agriculture began in the last century. In the most saline parts, samphire, bluebush and saltbush predominate. Towards the margins, salt stars (*Gunniopsis*), bindieye (*Sclerolaena*), disphyma, berry saltbush (*Rhagodia*) and ephemeral and perennial daisies are found; further away there may be scattered shrubs such as templetonia, wattle, teatree and hakea, and trees such as mirret (*Eucalyptus celastroides*) and Kondinin Blackbutt (*E. kondininensis*).

Salt lake south-west of Mount Ney

Jarrah-Marri forest: Towards the south-west corner, where rainfall is above 650 mm and lateritic soils predominate, taller forests dominated by Jarrah (*Eucalyptus marginata*) and Marri (*Corymbia calophylla*) are the common vegetation. Usually there are the only two tall tree species present, but in a few wetter areas they are joined by blackbutt (*E. patens*) and bullich (*E. megacarpa*). Below these, smaller trees are bull banksia, sheoak, parrot bush (*Dryandra*) and snottygobble (*Persoonia*). There is a rich ground storey of many shrubby species, especially of Proteaceae, Fabaceae, Mimosaceae, Epacridaceae and Dilleniaceae. Orchids, triggerplants and sundews abound.

Jarrah open forest at Roleystone Reserve

Karri forest: In the wettest area, receiving 1000–1450 mm of rain a year, deep loam soils support the high Karri forest. Growing to 80 metres tall, it occurs either in pure stands or sometimes mixed with Marri or tingle. Along the larger creeks and rivers is a fringe of River Banksia, paperbark and Wattie (*Taxandria juniperina*). The Karri understorey is dominated by sheoak, hazel (*Trymalium spathulatum*), chorilaena, wattle, tree hovea, waterbush (*Bossiaea*), bracken (*Pteridium*) and lepidosperma, as well as the creepers coral vine (*Kennedia coccinea*), clematis and hardenbergia. The ground flora is limited, although dampiera is common and after fire a colourful species of velleia germinates profusely. A rainforest relic, *Podocarpus drouyniana* (emu plum) is common here and in the southern Jarrah forest.

There are only a few major rivers in the south-west, and most have their headwaters in salt lakes of the wheatbelt and adjacent pastoral districts. Their vegetation is thus controlled by the water content, and the paperbarks, sheoaks, flooded gums (*Eucalyptus rudis*) and sedges (*Juncus, Lepidosperma*) along their banks are species that can tolerate some degree of salinity. The smaller freshwater streams of the far south-west are usually lined with Wattie.

Near the coast and for a short distance inland are freshwater swamps, mostly seasonal because of the winter rainfall. They vary greatly botanically, some along the south coast being extremely rich in species including sedges, heaths and myrtles. The Restionaceae is another example of a Gondwanan link, the family being well represented in South Africa.

The south-western coast is a succession of dunes and cliffs (mostly granite, limestone or sandstone), subject to frequent, sometimes strong, salt-laden winds. The vegetation is mostly low and shrubby, containing characteristic species of daisybush (*Olearia*), banjine (*Pimelea*), wattle, scaevola, teatree, sedge (*Lepidosperma*), spinifex grass, tail flower (*Anthocercis*) and many other shrubs and small trees.

The South-Western Interzone

Beyond the South-West region, where rainfall is lower and less regular, the vegetation changes as it passes into that of the deserts. Much of this South-Western Interzone lies on Archaean rock more than 2000 million years old, overlain extensively by much younger sand and laterite. The region is largely one of low relief and little drainage, where tall shrubland and open woodland predominate. Wattles, grevilleas, hakeas, mallee eucalypts and others make up the taller shrubs, interspersed with open eucalypt woodland. The 'broombush' habit—shrubs of a funnel-like form with erect branches and narrow leaves—can cause much confusion to those unfamiliar with the flora, species of wattle, melaleuca, sheoak, hakea, grevillea and poverty bush commonly being very similar in appearance until one inspects the leaves and flowers. Here, the granitic domes common in the south-west are also conspicuous, both for their rounded rock formations and the distinctive vegetation that grows on and around them.

Remarkable in the Interzone are the Eastern Goldfields, a large area centred on Kalgoorlie, supporting one of the wonders of the Western Australian flora. Here, in an unreliable rainfall that averages only 200 millimetres a year, tall woodlands of eucalypts have evolved that look more fitted to a region of much higher rainfall. And unlike the eucalypt forests of the wetter parts of the State, they contain many species, some with colourful flowers. Below the trees is a layer of shrubs such as poverty bush, boree (*Melaleuca*), cassia, grevillea, sheoak, hopbush (*Dodonaea*), greybush (*Cratystylis*) and scaevola. The soil is mainly loam, and spinifex is absent except in a few sandy areas. As elsewhere inland, after good rain there is a profusion of ephemeral everlastings, mulla mullas and a wide variety of annuals.

The Nullarbor

Eastwards, the South-Western Interzone passes into the vast limestone Nullarbor Plain. Laid down as marine sediments in the Eocene and Miocene (20–50 million years ago) and exposed as the sea level fell some 12 million years ago, the Plain is extraordinary for its flatness. It rises gradually from the spectacular cliffs of the Great Australian Bight, up to 100 metres high, to about 250 metres above sea level where it merges with the desert. There are no hills, only slight depressions (called dongas) to provide any variation. The Plain has a desert climate with low, irregular, mainly winter rainfall; summer is warm to hot and dry. What rain there is soaks in quickly (some through large subterranean caves). Much of the Plain is covered with saltbush and bluebush (now widely eaten out by sheep and rabbits and replaced by introduced weeds) and speargrass (*Austrostipa*). The few tall shrubs that appear in places are mainly Western Myall (*Acacia papyrocarpa*) and, towards the edges, myoporum and sheoak (*Casuarina*).

The North-West

North-western Australia has the oldest known rocks and the oldest fossils. The massive ironstones that make up the Hamersley Range are Proterozoic, over 1500 million years old, overlying the even older Archaean granites. Here are the highest mountains in the State, the highest Mt Meharry at 1245 metres. From a distance the relief is quite subdued, but where erosion has worn away the rock there are colourful ramparts and deep gorges. By contrast, the Cape Range leading to North West Cape consists of rocks, mainly limestones, formed 'only' some 10–25 million years ago. The coastal plains are wide and flat, of much more recent formation.

The north-west is a dry land, its rain falling mainly in summer from cyclones and thunderstorms, but much less than in the Kimberley. The rain is irregular and in some years little falls. On average, no part receives more than 300 millimetres, although local falls may be heavy—Whim Creek has the record for the State's wettest day: 1350 millimetres! Hence the plants of the north-west are all adapted to surviving long dry periods. Only along the few permanent waters of the gorges and rivers is there anything lush, mainly river gums and paperbarks with a ground layer of sedges, grasses and small herbs. Lying north of the Tropic of Capricorn, the region has a very hot summer with the sun directly overhead, shade temperatures usually being in the high 30s and 40s. Winter is mild to warm, though inland nights can be quite cool.

In the Hamersley Range (the main feature of the Pilbara), the hills carry an open woodland or shrubland in which eucalypts and wattles are common, though there are others such as poverty bush (*Eremophila*), grevillea, hakea and cypress (*Callitris*). Between the trees, spinifex is dominant, flowering if summer rain falls. After good rain there is a widespread germination of herbs such as daisies, goodenias, mulla mullas (*Ptilotus*) and Sturt Pea, which turn vast areas into seas of colour.

South of the Hamersley Range lie many smaller ranges and mountains, some now no more than residual rock outcrops, with a similar vegetation but floristically a little less diverse. Prominent among them is Mt Augustus, which has several plants of its own including a native foxglove (*Pityrodia*).

Hamersley Range, Mount Bruce

The Cape Range rises at its highest point to just over 300 metres high. Its surface is very rugged limestone; creeks that flow only after heavy rain have carved deep canyons, exposing soft underlying rocks. There is virtually no permanent surface water, but beneath the range are several caves in which unique small terrestrial and aquatic animals have evolved. The range is covered with an open vegetation of shrubs and mallees scattered among spinifex. It is an interesting area where the State's tropical, temperate and arid floras overlap. Here is the northern-most occurrence of southern banksias, hibbertias and dampieras, the southernmost cabbage palm and plumbago. The Range also has its own plants, found nowhere else, such as the unusual shrubby Yardie Morning Glory (*Ipomoea yardiensis*), two grevilleas and a stackhousia. Sturt Pea in this area always has a dark red, not black, 'boss' to the flower.

Between the ranges of the north-west and stretching southwards are vast plains dominated on loam soil by mulga (*Acacia aneura*), and on sand by spinifex. The mulga plains provide perhaps the most spectacular displays of winter annuals after good rains, with sheets of white and yellow interspersed with other colours such as pink, purple and red.

The wide coastal plain is generally quite flat and sandy, supporting grasslands of spinifex, love grass (*Eragrostis*) and now the introduced Buffel Grass (*Cenchrus*) with scattered trees and shrubs such as eucalypts, wattles, grevilleas and cassias. The coast itself is of long, sandy beaches, wide tidal flats and a few rocky headlands.

Off the north-west coast lie the largest islands in the state. Dirk Hartog Island off Shark Bay is some 79 kilometres long. Its backbone is Quaternary Eolianite (less than 2 million years old), and over much of the island this is overlain by recent sands. Wattle scrub dominates the vegetation, but between is an array of other shrubs and perennial herbs, with a good showing of annuals in the rare good rainfall year. Some 260 species have been recorded for the island. To its north lie Bernier and Dorre Islands, gazetted as a nature reserve. These low, narrow islands carry a sparse cover of spinifex and low shrubs. North of Exmouth Gulf is Barrow Island, a limestone island similar geologically to the Cape Range and with a similar but poorer flora. By contrast, the Dampier Archipelago farther north-east consists of ironstone of an age similar to the Hamersley Range. Here erosion has reduced some hills to huge piles of boulders, devoid of plants except the occasional native fig. Otherwise, spinifex and scattered shrubs are the principal vegetation. None of the islands has fresh surface water. Their fauna obtain their needs from the moisture in the vegetation that they eat.

Scattered across the inland are vast saline depressions, commonly called salt lakes although they hold water only after heavy rain. Some, such as Lake Auld and Lake Austin, are the 'fossil' remains of ancient rivers. The salt is not derived from the underlying rock but has been brought on the wind from the sea, accumulating over many thousands of years. In some lakes the floors are bare, in others covered with low succulent-leaved shrubs such as samphire (*Tecticornia* etc.), saltbush (*Atriplex*) and bluebush (*Maireana*). Around the margins and on rises there is an array of low plants such as frankenia, scaevola and sporobolus.

The Kimberley

In the far north of Western Australia is the Kimberley, the most rugged region of the State. Although not high (Mt Broome at 935 metres is the highest mountain in the region), it is a maze of ranges and hills and a deeply dissected coastline, to the south passing almost imperceptibly into the Great Sandy Desert and past the Eighty Mile Beach to the Pilbara. The underlying rocks are ancient Archaean granites (more than 2000 million years old) that rarely outcrop. Over them lie massive sandstones and dark volcanics of Proterozoic age (1500 million years old), Devonian limestones (360–395 million years old) and much younger Mesozoic gravelly plateaus (c. 100 million years old). All are dissected by innumerable creeks and rivers, many, in the wet season, flowing over falls and through gorges to discharge huge quantities of fresh water into the Timor Sea and the Bonaparte Gulf. Mingling of these waters with the sea is assisted by twice-daily tides of up to 10 metres.

The Kimberley lies between 13° and 19° south of the Equator, hence has a tropical climate. It is almost always warm or hot during the day, and nights are mild to warm, although away from the coast it may become quite cool towards dawn. Most rains fall in summer, from thunderstorms, cyclones and the occasional monsoonal depression. They may be heavy, causing flooding over large areas. The north-western Kimberley receives up to 1500 mm and this grades to about 400 mm on the southern desert fringe. Winter rain is rare.

By far the most typical vegetation is savanna woodland, dominated by eucalypts but with more variety in the associated trees than elsewhere in the state. Wattle, terminalia, kapok tree (*Cochlospermum fraseri*), boab (*Adansonia*), kurrajong (*Brachychiton*), grevillea, quinine tree (*Petalostigma*) and whitewood (*Atalaya*) are just some of the tree species. Cabbage palms (*Livistona*) occur in places. Below the trees, shrubs form a usually open layer, but between all is a dominant layer of grasses. Spear grasses, sorghum (up to three metres tall) and spinifex (*Triodia*) are common, flowering after summer rain and later causing discomfort to people and stock with their sharp seeds. Along the rivers, cadjeput paper barks, river gums, bauhinia, Leichhardt tree (*Nauclea*), terminalia and screwpines (*Pandanus*) are common.

The Kimberley has no vast areas of rain forest as are found in Queensland and many tropical regions. The winter drought accounts for that. There are a few small pockets of high forest where there is permanent water, but a kind of 'dry' rain forest known as vine thicket occurs in small patches throughout the north and north-west Kimberley. It is always on volcanic rocks and is a dense tangle of small trees, shrubs and lianes of genera characteristic of lands to the north rather than the southern Gondwanan flora; such plants probably migrated here as Australia drifted north. A number of Kimberley plants such as Boab, kurrajong, bombax and Kapok Bush are deciduous in the dry season, flowering before the new leaves appear.

Billabongs, small lakes and seasonal swamps abound in the region, supporting a wide range of aquatic and marsh herbs. Common among them are marshworts (*Nymphoides*), bladderworts (*Utricularia*), waterlilies (*Nymphaea*), sundews (*Drosera*) and triggerplants (*Stylidium*).

The mangroves are a strange world on tidal shores. They are a closed, evergreen woodland, although in places they are reduced to a narrow fringe, sometimes only one tree wide. Only 15 species make up the mangroves; rarely do more than six or seven species occur at one place, and then commonly in bands. Most have inconspicuous flowers, and fruits designed to anchor themselves in the mud and take root rapidly so as to avoid being washed away. Some species have special roots to provide either additional support (prop roots) or supplementary oxygen (pneumatophores). At high tide they are surrounded by seawater, at low tide by exposed, slimy mud.

In the south-western Kimberley, wide sandy plains are covered by a low open woodland and tall shrubland known as pindan, in which wattles are dominant, with a grassy understorey. Passing southwards, as the rainfall diminishes there is a corresponding fall in the lushness and variety of the vegetation. To the south-west the transition is to the rugged Pilbara, and to the south the desert.

The Deserts

About two-thirds of Western Australia is termed desert, but it is by no means the desolate, bare region that the term commonly brings to mind. Most of the desert is formed of sedimentary rocks laid down in the sea more than 100 million years ago. More than 15 million years ago the region was covered with rain forest, but it became progressively more arid, leaving fossil river systems, and grasslands became dominant. Very little of the desert is bare—chiefly some of the large saline 'lakes'. Elsewhere, even the driest parts have at least a sparse cover of plants, and most have a good vegetation of mulga or spinifex. Mulga covers loamy plains and rocky hills in the central and southern deserts, and spinifex the sandy and gravelly plains and low rises. In the north, the Great Sandy Desert is characterised by huge areas of sand ridges, mostly long parallel dunes with wide intervening swales. The dunes themselves have an interesting flora of shrubs such as wattle, grevillea, clerodendrum and bird flower (*Crotalaria*), together with perennial herbs and soft spinifex, and even a few low trees such as bloodwoods. In the swales spinifex predominates, commonly with an open shrubland especially of wattle and grevillea. There are occasional outcrops of the underlying Cretaceous and Jurassic sandstones as small hills carrying scattered shrubs such as wattle, poverty bush and cassia.

The Gibson Desert, named after an early explorer who perished there, is essentially a region of undulating gravel plains with the occasional lateritic breakaway rising a few metres, and a scattering of sandy plains. These overlie Cretaceous and Jurassic sandstones. The gravelly plains carry an open spinifex grassland with scattered shrubs such as wattle, poverty bush and cassia.

The southernmost desert is the Great Victoria. Here, overlying Mesozoic sandstones are vast areas of red sand dunes and wide plains which, surprisingly for such a low rainfall, have a low open woodland dominated by the Bara or Marble Gum (*Eucalyptus gongylocarpa*) and Ooldea Mallee (*Eucalyptus youngiana*). Mulga is common on patches of loamy soil.

In the far eastern central desert rise many ranges of Proterozoic rocks, some such as the Rawlinson and Walter James being very colourful, and among the most spectacular arid scenery in Australia. Stunted eucalypts and shrubs such as wattle, cassia and poverty bush grow among the ubiquitous spinifex.

Unlike the floras of deserts in other countries, succulence is rare here. Such an adaptation appears only in herbs such as zygophyllum and samphire and in the leaves of plants such as bluebush, saltbush and parakeelya (*Calandrinia*).

ALEXANDER S. GEORGE

1 *Disphyma crassifolium*

2 *Gunniopsis intermedia*

AIZOACEAE stoneflowers, pigface

This large, cosmopolitan family of mostly succulent or fleshy-leaved plants comprises many species that are particularly well adapted to arid or saline coastal and inland areas. World-wide the family contains about 2300 species with about 60 species in Australia. Many exotic species are valued in horticulture.

The introduced genus *Mesembryanthemum*, together with several native genera including *Carpobrotus* and *Disphyma*, are well known for their colourful, daisy-like flowers which consist of several rows of enlarged, petal-like staminodes. Other genera such as *Gunniopsis* and *Tetragonia* have small, star-like flowers with a single row of often fleshy perianth parts. The fleshy leaves and fruits of many Australian species were a dependable source of Aboriginal food and were eaten both raw and steamed.

1 **Disphyma crassifolium** (Linnaeus) Bolus
Round-leaved Pigface
Prostrate, spreading perennial; leaves fleshy, almost cylindrical 0.5–5 cm long; 0.4–1 cm thick, varying in colour from green to shades of purple and red; flowers 2–5 cm across.
Habitat: coastal on cliffs and saline depressions and inland on salt pans.
Dist: 10, 11, 15, 21, 22, 23, 24; also SA, Qld, NSW, Vic, Tas.

3 *Gunniopsis quadrifida*

2 **Gunniopsis intermedia** Diels
Yellow Salt Star
Semi-prostrate annual herb to 30 cm high, usually forming a dense mound to 0.5 m across; leaves 2–7 cm long; flowers 2–3 cm across.
Habitat: saline flats and sandy rises near salt lakes.
Dist: 15, 22, 23, 24.

3 **Gunniopsis quadrifida** (F.Mueller) Pax
Sturt's Pigface
Rounded, divaricate shrub to 60 cm high; leaves to c. 80 mm long; flowers 3–4 cm across.
Habitat: margins of salt lakes and clay pans.
Dist: 10, 11, 15, 22, 23, 24; also NT, SA, Qld, NSW.

4 *Macarthuria australis*

4 **Macarthuria australis** Huegel ex Endlicher
Shrub 30–60 cm high with erect, wiry stems; leaves, if present, linear, to 4 cm long, reduced to scales up stems; flower c. 4 mm across, with sweet honey scent. Sometimes placed in the family Molluginaceae.
Habitat: in sand or gravel, in low woodland.
Dist: 16,17,18.

5 **Tetragonia cristata** C.A.Gardner ex A.Prescott
Annual succulent herb; leaves 1–5 cm x 3–20 mm wide, densely crystalline or papillose; flowers 6–8 mm across.
Habitat: red sand, clay or rocky soil, often in acacia shrubland.
Dist: 14, 15.

5 *Tetragonia cristata*

6 *Ptilotus drummondii* var. *minor*

7 *Ptilotus exaltatus*

8 *Ptilotus grandiflorus* var. *grandiflorus*

AMARANTHACEAE

The Amaranthaceae is an almost cosmopolitan family whose flowers have one whorl of perianth segments which are usually membranous and/or dry and often colourful. The family is horticulturally important for such ornamental species as *Celosia cristata* (Cockscomb) and *Gomphrena globosa* (Globe amaranth). Some species of *Amaranthus* have become widespread weeds. The genus *Ptilotus* contains about 100 species of which only one extends beyond Australia; many are highly ornamental but most have proved difficult to bring into cultivation.

6   *Ptilotus drummondii* (Moquin) F.Mueller var. *minor* (Nees) Benl
Narrowleaf Mulla Mulla
Erect, many-stemmed shrub to 40 cm high; leaves mostly basal, often absent; flower heads sub-globose, to 2 cm long; perianth streaked with pink but soon fading to yellowish white. One of several varieties differing mainly in size and shape of inflorescence.
Habitat: sandy or rocky soils in shrubland and mallee.
Dist: 13, 14, 15, 16, 17, 23.

7   *Ptilotus exaltatus* Nees
Tall Mulla Mulla
Robust ephemeral or perennial herb to 1 m high; basal leaves to 20 x 7 cm, stem leaves smaller; flower spikes up to 15 x 4–5 cm.
Habitat: widespread in the more arid regions on lateritic plains, mulga woodland, sand ridges and rocky outcrops.
Dist: 1, 2, 3, 4, 5, 6, 7, 8, 9, 10, 12, 13, 14, 15, 16, 17, 18, 19, 20, 21, 22, 23, 24; also NT, SA, Qld, NSW, Vic.

8   *Ptilotus grandiflorus* F.Mueller var. *grandiflorus*
Annual or biennial herb, erect or decumbent to 0.45 m high; leaves up to 60 mm long; flowers in terminal spikes to 30 mm long; petals absent but with conspicuous pink sepals; often abundant in favourable seasons.
Habitat: inland in sandy or rocky soil.
Dist: 14, 15, 16, 24.

9   *Ptilotus helichrysoides* (F.Mueller) F.Mueller
Compact, densely silky-hairy shrub to 1.5 m high; leaves lanceolate, to 1 cm long, crowded along stems; flower heads 1–2 cm across.
Habitat: rocky, lateritic hillsides. Uncommon.
Dist: 10, 15, 24.

10 **_Ptilotus macrocephalus_** (R. Brown) Poiret
Featherheads
Robust perennial to 1 m tall; leaves linear, 5-12 cm
long often with wavy margins; flower heads 4-20 cm
long, elongating as the flowers open.
Habitat: red sandy soil in open acacia woodland.
Dist: 1, 2, 4, 6, 7, 8, 9, 10, 12, 13, 14, 15, 16, 17, 23, and
all states.

P. nobilis is similar but its leaves are obovate and much
broader.

9 *Ptilotus helichrysoides*

11 **_Ptilotus spathulatus_** (R.Brown) Poiret
Prostrate perennial; stems 5–20 cm long; basal leaves
spathulate, 2–5 cm long; stem leaves smaller; flower
heads 3–7 cm long.
Habitat: clay and clay-loam in open woodland,
grassland and saltbush communities, also in sandy
red earth in mallee communities.
Dist: 10, 15, 16, 17, 18, 19, 20, 21, 22, 23, 24; also
SA, NSW, Vic, Tas.

11 *Ptilotus spathulatus*

10 *Ptilotus macrocephalus*

12 *Eryngium pinnatifidum*

13 *Platysace compressa*

APIACEAE carrot, parsley, fennel

The Apiaceae is a large family of herbs and, rarely, shrubs comprising c. 3000 species world-wide of which c. 167 occur in Australia. The family has a characteristic umbrella-like inflorescence, although the irregular branching of some Australian species makes this less obvious.

Members of the family are rich in special resins which impart distinctive odours and flavours.

Many species are important culinary herbs such as *Petroselinum crispum* (parsley) or vegetables, including *Daucus carota* (carrot). *Conium maculatum* (hemlock), introduced into the Eastern States, is a weed of disturbed sites and is noteworthy for its poisonous properties. It is said to have been responsible for Socrates' death.

12 ***Eryngium pinnatifidum*** Bunge
Blue Devils
Low-growing annual or biennial herb; stems erect, to 60 cm tall; basal leaves 16–25 cm long with a few long, prickly lobes; stem leaves shorter and usually opposite; flower heads 1.5–2 cm long with 5–8 sharply pointed bracts 5–7 mm long.
Habitat: moist and dry situations in a variety of soils in woodland and kwongan.
Dist: 16, 17, 18, 19, 20, 21, 23.

14 *Xanthosia rotundifolia*

Two species of *Eryngium* occur in WA; world-wide it is a large genus and a number of very ornamental species such as *E. maritimum* (Sea holly) are cultivated.

13 **Platysace compressa** (Labillardière) C.Norman
Tapeworm Plant
Divaricate, leafless shrub to 60 cm high; stems flattened, margins winged; flowers cream, 1–2 mm across, in loose clusters; fruit ribbed with alternate broad and narrow wings. Width of the flattened stems is very variable; they are particularly broad in plants from near the south coast.
Habitat: in kwongan in gravel or rocky soil, often granitic.
Dist: 18, 19, 20, 21.

14 **Xanthosia rotundifolia** de Candolle
Southern Cross
Erect perennial herb to 60 cm high; leaves serrate or toothed, to 6 cm long; inflorescence usually with four branches arranged in a cross; flowers surrounded by petal-like bracts c. 1.5 cm long.
Habitat: gravelly, lateritic soil in open woodland or kwongan.
Dist: 18, 19, 20, 21.
Xanthosia has 11 species in WA. Some are early colonisers after fire and become quite rare beyond the first year after a fire.

15 *Alyxia buxifolia*

APOCYNACEAE

The Apocynaceae is an important pan-tropical family containing many decorative species such as *Nerium* (Oleander), *Plumeria* (Frangipani) and *Mandevilla*. Of the 14 genera represented in Australia most are restricted to northern subtropical and tropical regions.

15 **Alyxia buxifolia** R.Brown
Dysentery Bush
Woody shrub to 2 m high, leaves 1–3 x 5 mm, leathery, shiny; flowers about 1 cm long, fragrant; fruit a bright orange, red or yellowish drupe 8–15 mm long.
A. buxifolia is the most widespread species of the *Apocynaceae* in Australia.
Habitat: mainly coastal cliffs and also inland.
Dist: 14, 15, 16, 17, 22, 23, 24; and all states.

ASCLEPIADACEAE

The Asclepiadaceae is a family of trees, shrubs and climbers most common in the tropics and sub-tropics with some extensions into temperate regions. Of c. 2000 species world-wide, c. 75 occur in Australia. Several curious, ornamental members of the family are widely cultivated including *Hoya*, *Stapelia*, *Ceropegia* and *Stephanotis*. Many species contain milky sap. The fruit matures into a characteristic follicle that opens longitudinally to release the seeds which are surmounted by a tuft of silky hairs.

Leichhardtia australis, a creeper scattered in the drier areas of WA, the Northern Territory and Queensland, was an important Aboriginal food source. Young follicles were eaten raw, older ones cooked and most parts of the plant were considered good food.

16 *Sarcostemma viminale subsp. australe*

17 *Asteridea asteroides*

20 *Brachyscome iberidifolia*

16 ***Sarcostemma viminale* subsp. *australe***
(R.Brown) P.I.Forster
Milk Bush, Caustic Bush
Many-stemmed shrub 1–2 m high with milky sap,
sometimes trailing stems; leaves very small, scale-
like; flowers creamy or green, c. 5 mm across, in
inconspicuous clusters along the stems. The sticky
sap was used by the Aborigines to decorate the body
and cure skin sores.
Habitat: diverse, often in rocky places.
Dist: 14, 15, 16 and widespread further north; also
NT, SA, Qld and NSW.

ASTERACEAE   daisies, sunflower

The Asteraceae family, also known by the alternative
name Compositae, is among the largest and most widely
distributed families in the world; it comprises a variety
of growth forms including minute annual and ephemeral herbs, biennial and perennial herbs of all sizes, as
well as shrubs, trees and a few climbers. The major economic importance of the family is in horticulture; there
would be scarcely a garden in the world without a daisy
flower of some sort. Several species such as *Lactuca sativa*
(lettuce), *Cichorum endiva* (endive), *Cynara scolymos* (artichoke) and *Helianthus tuberosus* (Jerusalem artichoke)
are cultivated as vegetables and several species are used
as culinary or medicinal herbs. *Helianthus annua* (sun-
flower) and *Carthamus tinctoria* (safflower), are important sources of edible oil. Many of Australia's most troublesome weeds also belong to this family. Roots of
Asteraceae, notably *Microseris* sp. (Yam) were eaten by
Aborigines, and the fluffy seeds of some species were
used for bodily decoration.

The Asteraceae flower-head consists of a number of tiny
flowers (florets) usually sitting on a fleshy receptacle
and surrounded by involucral bracts, either soft and
green or stiff and papery, and often colourful. The individual florets vary in form and function. They have
a tubular corolla formed from fused petals. In the typical daisy flower one petal of all or some florets is enlarged into a strap-like ligule, forming the colourful
ring of 'petals' in species such as *Olearia*. The seeds
(achenes) are usually surmounted by a ring (pappus)
of hairs, bristles or scales; characters of the pappus and
achene are important diagnostic features but both are
very small and often difficult to see without a microscope.

17 ***Asteridea asteroides*** (Turczaninow) Kroner
Perennial herb 7–15 cm high; leaves 2–3.5 cm long;
flower heads 2–3 cm across.
Habitat: in kwongan or shrubland in sand or grav-
elly sand.
Dist: 16, 21, 22, 23.

18 **Bellida graminea** A.J.Ewart
Rosy Bellida
The only member of the genus, a dwarf, tufted,
annual herb; leaves 2–7 cm long; flower heads c.
1 cm across with prominent red or purple-tipped
pappus bristles; fruit with distinctive horizontal
sculpturing.
Habitat: dry acacia scrub north of the wheatbelt,
particularly around Paynes Find and the goldfields.
Dist: 15, 16, 23, 24.

18 *Bellida graminea*

19 **Brachyscome ciliaris** (Labillardière) Lesson
Variable Daisy
At least 70 species, annual or perennial herbs, are
currently recognised as belonging to *Brachyscome*.
About 20 occur in WA including members of the
B. ciliaris complex, forms of which are found in all
states. The form illustrated is common near Norseman and Balladonia. Most members of the complex produce dimorphic fruits, i.e. fruits from the
outer (ray) florets have a broad, flat wing, but those
from the disc (inner) florets have no wing.
Habitat: sand or gravelly soil in woodland.
Dist. of complex: 9, 10, 11, 12, 13, 14, 15, 16, 18, 20,
21, 22, 23, 24 and all states.

20 **Brachyscome iberidifolia** Bentham
Swan River Daisy
Much-branched annual herb, leaves to c. 3 cm long,
pinnate with narrow segments; flower heads to
2 cm across, white, blue or purple; popular as a
garden plant and first cultivated in Europe in the
late 1830s.
Habitat: very diverse including Jarrah forest and
banksia woodland.
Dist: 13, 14, 15, 16, 17, 18, 19, 20, 21, 22, 23, 24; also
NT and SA.

19 *Brachyscome ciliaris*

21 **Brachyscome oncocarpa** Diels
Swollen-fruited Daisy
Erect, much-branched annual 10–30 cm high;
flower heads c. 1 cm across.
Habitat: sandy soil in woodland and open
shrubland, mainly north of the wheatbelt.
Dist: 14, 15.

21 *Brachyscome oncocarpa*

22 *Brachyscome tatei*

22 **Brachyscome tatei** J.Black
Perennial, usually succulent herb to 8 cm high, forming compact clumps.
Habitat: top of sea cliffs along the Great Australian Bight.
Dist: 11.

23 **Xerochrysum** sp.
Erect, perennial herb to 2m tall; leaves linear, to 15 x 20 mm; flowers 4–8 cm across when fully open. This very showy species has previously been known as *Helichrysum macranthum* Bentham and *Helichrysum bracteatum* (Ventenat) Willldenow var. *albidum* A.P.de Candolle
Habitat: very diverse, including laterite and granitic soil in Jarrah forest and shrublands.
Dist: 16, 17, 18, 20, 21, 23.

24 **Calotis multicaulis** (Turczaninow) Druce
Many-stemmed Burr-daisy
Branching annual to 30 cm high; leaves hairy, 2–3 cm long; flowers 1–2 cm across, white or bluish; fruits woolly with broad ciliate wings and pappus of minutely barbed awns.
Habitat: red sandy soil in open woodland or shrubland, also on bluebush plains.
Dist: 6, 9, 10, 11, 12, 13, 14, 15, 16, 24; also NT, SA, Qld and NSW.

The genus *Calotis* is endemic in mainland Australia and contains about 26 herbaceous species, most of which occur in semi-arid regions of eastern Australia. Most species have fruits with a pappus of rigid barbed awns and yellow flowers are more common.

25 **Cephalipterum drummondii** A.Gray
Pompom Head
Slender, erect annual; leaves 1–5 cm long, lower ones broad, upper linear lanceolate; inflorescence c. 2.5 cm across; white, cream, pale pink or, rarely, bronze.
Habitat: sand or gravelly soil in woodland or open

23 *Xerochrysum* sp.

24 *Calotis multicaulis*

25 *Cephalipterum drummondii*

shrubland, particularly north of the wheatbelt.
Dist: 9, 10, 11, 15, 16, 23, 24; also SA.

26 **Cephalosorus carpesioides** (Turczaninow)
P.S.Short [syn. *Angianthus phyllocephalus* (A.Gray)
Bentham]
The only member of its genus; an annual herb to c.
30 cm tall; leaves c. 3 cm long; flower heads up to
1.5 cm across surrounded by broad, leafy bracts.
Habitat: ironstone gravel between Northampton
and Carnamah.
Dist: 16.

27 **Cratystylis conocephala** (F.Mueller) S.Moore
Grey Bush
Spreading dioecious shrub to 1.5 m high; leaves
broadly obovate, c. 1 cm long, grey-woolly; flower
heads 1–2 cm long, yellow.
Habitat: calcareous soil in mallee shrubland or
chenopod steppe; the dominant plant on parts of
the Nullarbor Plain.
Dist: 11, 21, 24; also NT, SA, NSW, Vic.

26 *Cephalosorus carpesioides*   28 *Dithyrostegia amplexicaulis*

28 **Dithyrostegia amplexicaulis** A.Gray [syn.
Angianthus amplexicaulis (A.Gray) Bentham]
Annual herb to 16 cm high; leaves 10–12 mm long,
stem-clasping; inflorescence subtended by two dis-
tinctive, overlapping bracts.
Habitat: margins of salt lakes.
Dist: 15, 24.

27 *Cratystylis conocephala*

30 *Hyalochlamys globifera*

31 *Hyalosperma glutinosum* subsp. *venustum*

29 ***Gilberta tenuifolia*** Turczaninow
[syn. *Myriocephalus gracilis* (A.Gray) Bentham]
Slender Myriocephalus
Erect, slender annual to 16 cm high; leaves terete,
to 1.5 cm long; flower heads c. 5 mm across,
commonly reflexed.
Habitat: in sand or gravelly lateritic sand in
shrubland and woodland, also in granitic sand.
Dist: 15, 16, 23, 24.

30 ***Hyalochlamys globifera*** A.Gray [syn. *Angianthus
globifer* (A.Gray) Bentham]
Tiny annual, 5–25 mm high, often forming extensive mats.
Habitat: margins of temporary pools, damp depressions, often associated with granite outcrops.
Dist: 14, 15, 16, 22, 23, 24.

31 ***Hyalosperma glutinosum*** Steetz subsp. ***venustum***
(S.Moore) Paul G.Wilson [syn. *Helipterum
venustum* S. Moore]
Charming Sunray
Hyalosperma has nine species and all until recently
were incorporated in *Helipterum*. The genus is endemic in temperate Australia. *H. glutinosum* has two
subspecies: subsp. *venustum*, depicted here, is a small
annual herb to 20 cm high with flower heads
2–2.5 cm across, conspicuous and showy.
Habitat: sandy soil in acacia woodland.
Dist: 15, 16, 23, 24.
Subsp. *glutinosum* has smaller flowers to 1.5 cm
across and is widely distributed over much of the
southern Australian mainland.

33 *Lawrencella davenportii*

32 *Kippistia suaedifolia*

32 **Kippistia suaedifolia** F.Mueller
Fleshy Minuria
Compact dwarf shrub to 60 cm high; leaves terete,
5–25 mm long, semi-succulent; flower heads
5–7 mm across; closely related to and formerly in-
cluded in the genus *Minuria*.
Habitat: margins of saline lakes and claypans.
Dist: 15, 22, 23, 24; also NT, NSW, Vic.

33 **Lawrencella davenportii** (F.Mueller) Paul G.Wilson
[syn. *Helichrysum davenportii* F.Mueller]
Sticky Everlasting
Annual herb to 40 cm tall; leaves 0.3–14 cm long,
up to 1 cm wide, usually sticky with glandular hairs;
flower heads to c. 4.5 cm across, lamina of bracts white
to pink; lower part of pappus bristles pink, upper
part white.
Habitat: sandy soil in mulga woodland or mallee
shrubland.
Dist: 9, 10, 13, 14, 15, 16, 21, 23; also NT, SA.

29 *Gilberta tenuifolia*   35 *Myriocephalus guerinae*

34 **Myriocephalus appendiculatus** Bentham
White-tip Myriocephalus
Annual herb; stems erect or spreading, sometimes
branched; leaves to 2.5 cm long, base stem-clasping; flower heads to c. 1.5 cm across. Very similar to
and probably conspecific with *M. nudus* (A. Gray)
Bentham which has yellow-tipped bracts surrounding the flower heads.
Habitat: sandy soil in depressions in woodland, near
streams, in dried out clay pans and on margins of
saline flats.
Dist: 13, 14, 15, 16, 17, 22.

34 *Myriocephalus appendiculatus*

35 **Myriocephalus guerinae** F.Mueller
Annual herb to 25 cm high; leaves to 5 cm long;
flower heads 1–2.5 cm across. A common component of the extensive fields of everlastings that carpet
the ground after good rains in the northern wheatbelt
and arid areas.
Habitat: acacia woodland and mallee.
Dist: 14, 15, 16, 23.

36 **Olearia humilis** Lander
Erect shrub to 1 m high; leaves 2–3 mm long; flower
heads c. 2 cm across.
Habitat: shrubland or open woodland in red sand,
loam or clay, often on lateritic hills, sometimes on
granite outcrops.
Dist: 15, 23.

Olearia is a genus of about 100 species of small to
medium shrubs found in Australia, New Guinea
and New Zealand.

36 *Olearia humilis*

37 *Olearia magniflora*

38 *Olearia muelleri*

37 ***Olearia magniflora*** (F.Mueller) F.Mueller ex Bentham
Splendid Daisy Bush
Open, sparsely branched shrub to 1 m high; leaves 3–26 mm long, often toothed apically; flower heads 3.5–6 cm diam; one of the largest flowered species in the genus.
Habitat: mallee woodland restricted to the extreme east of WA.
Dist: 24; also SA, NSW, Vic.

38 ***Olearia muelleri*** (Sonder) Bentham
Goldfields Daisy
Shrub to 1.5 m high, usually twiggy with short branches, leaves obovate, 5–14 x 2–8 mm, toothed or entire; flower heads 13–31 mm across; rays white or pinkish to pale mauve.
Habitat: sand or gravelly sand in mallee woodland or shrubland.
Dist: 11, 15, 16, 21, 22, 23, 24; also SA, NSW and Vic.

39 *Olearia ramosissima*

39 **Olearia ramosissima** (A.P. de Candolle) Bentham
Shrub to 1.3 m high; leaves ovate or elliptic, 0.5–5 mm long, often reflexed; flower heads 2–2.5 cm across, rays white, blue or mauve.
Habitat: mallee shrubland in sandy loam. (In eastern states it is an understorey shrub in eucalypt forest, usually on rocky hillsides.)
Dist: 22, 23, 24; also NSW and Qld.

40 **Olearia rudis** (Bentham) F.Mueller ex Bentham
Azure Daisy Bush
Shrub to 1 m high, aromatic, often glutinous; leaves 2–5 cm long; flower heads 3–4 cm across.
Habitat: in various soils, in shrubland, often in mallee eucalypt associations.
Dist: 16, 17, 19, 20, 21, 23; also SA, NSW and Vic.

41 **Podolepis canescens** Cunningham ex
A.P. de Candolle
Bright Podolepis
Wiry annual to 85 cm high with a few basal leaves and scattered stem-clasping leaves to 8 cm long; flower heads to 2.5 cm across.
Habitat: open woodland or shrubland in sandy soil.
Dist: 9, 11, 14, 15, 16, 17, 18, 20, 21, 22, 23, 24; also NT, Qld, NSW and Vic.

42 **Podolepis capillaris** (Steetz) Diels [syn. *Siemssenia capillaris* Steetz)
Delicate, much-branched perennial herb; leaves linear, to 12 mm long; flower heads to 1 cm across, usually smaller; both yellow and white flowered plants occur in WA but in other states they are usually white. The achenes lack a pappus and the species is probably better placed in the separate genus *Siemssenia*.
Habitat: mallee and arid woodlands.
Dist: 9, 10, 12, 13, 15, 16, 17, 21, 22, 23, 24; also NT, SA, Qld, NSW and Vic.

40 *Olearia rudis*

41 *Podolepis canescens*

42 *Podolepis capillaris*

43 *Podolepis gardneri*

45 *Rhodanthe charsleyae*

44 *Podotheca gnaphalioides*

43 ***Podolepis gardneri*** Davis
Much-branched annual to 24 cm high; stems glabrous, reddish; leaves 2–3 cm long, mainly along lower stems; flowers to 2.5 cm across.
Habitat: sandy soil in open woodland.
Dist: 14, 15.

44 ***Podotheca gnaphalioides*** Graham
Golden Long-heads
Semi-prostrate herbaceous annual 30–45 cm high; leaves 3–6 cm long; flower-heads to 5 cm long.
Habitat: open woodland, often forming carpets, or scattered in shrubland.
Dist: 14, 15, 16, 17, 18, 19, 23, 24.

45 ***Rhodanthe charsleyae*** (F.Mueller) Paul G.Wilson
[syn. *Helipterum charsleyae* F.Mueller]
Erect, annual multi-stemmed herb up to 60 cm high; leaves to 7 cm long; flower heads 5–10 mm across.
Habitat: clay loam or sandy soil in open woodland, in clay pans and creek margins.
Dist: 8, 9, 10, 12, 13, 15, 24; also NT, SA and Qld.
R. battii (F.Mueller) Paul G.Wilson is similar but has blackish anthers and emits a foetid odour when crushed; it is confined to southern arid areas of WA.

46 ***Rhodanthe chlorocephala*** subsp. ***rosea*** (Hooker) Paul G.Wilson [syn. *Helipterum roseum* (W.J.Hooker) Bentham]
Pink Everlasting
Annual herb to 50 cm high; leaves 1–6 cm long, glabrous, green or grey-green; flower heads 3–6 cm across, bracts white or pink. A very showy and widely cultivated plant, introduced to horticulture in England in 1838. The size and colour of flowers is very variable and many intermediates occur between the two extreme forms illustrated.
Habitat: sandy soil in open woodland or shrubland.
Dist: 11, 13, 14, 15, 16, 17, 23, 24.

46(a) *Rhodanthe chlorocephala* subsp. *rosea*

46(b) *Rhodanthe chlorocephala* subsp. *rosea*

47 **Rhodanthe chlorocephala** subsp. **splendida** (Hemsley) Paul G.Wilson [syn. *Helipterum splendidum* Hemsley]
Splendid Everlasting
Annual glabrous herb to 60 cm high; leaves grey-green, 1–3 cm long; flower heads to 6 cm across. A very showy species capable of carpeting large areas following rain.
Habitat: red sand or sandy clay usually in acacia woodland.
Dist: 16, 23, 24.

48 **Rhodanthe citrina** (Bentham) Paul G.Wilson [syn. *Waitzia citrina* (Bentham) Steetz]
Annual herb to 40 cm high; leaves basal and cauline, 5–40 mm long; flower heads to 2 cm across, clustered; a widespread, common species.
Habitat: inland in open Jarrah forest, woodland or shrubland, or in scrub in coastal sand.
Dist: 10, 13, 14, 15, 16, 17, 18, 19, 20, 21, 22, 23, 24; also NT, SA and NSW.

48 *Rhodanthe citrina*

47 *Rhodanthe chlorocephala* subsp. *splendida*

52 *Senecio gregorii*

53 *Senecio pinnatifolius* var. *maritimus*

49 ***Rhodanthe humboldtiana*** (Gaudichaud) Paul G.Wilson [syn. *Helipterum humboldtianum* (Gaudichaud) A.P.de Candolle]
Annual herb to 50 cm high; leaves up to 4 x 1 cm, cauline, grey-green with soft hairs, margins undulate; flower heads to 1 cm across in large terminal clusters to 8 cm across.
Habitat: sand, often with limestone, in open woodland.
Distr: 11, 14, 15, 16, 24.

50 ***Rhodanthe manglesii*** Lindley [syn. *Helipterum manglesii* (Lindley) Bentham]
Pink Sunray
Annual herb to 60 cm high; leaves 6–46 x 3–34 mm, ovate to orbicular, cauline and stem-clasping; flower heads to 3 cm across, pink to white, often recurved.
Habitat: sandy soil in open forest or woodland and on granite outcrops.
Dist: 16, 17, 19, 21, 23, 24.

51 ***Schoenia cassiniana*** (Gaudichaud) Steetz [syn. *Helichrysum cassinianum* Gaudichaud]
Annual herb to 40 cm high; leaves 1.5–12 cm long,

51 *Schoenia cassiniana*

linear-lanceolate, mainly basal with a few smaller leaves scattered up the stem; flower heads 2–3 cm across in flat-topped clusters of usually 5–10 heads, pink or occasionally white; pink flowers fade almost white with age.

Habitat: in sandy soil in open acacia woodland or scrub.

Dist: 5, 9, 13, 14, 15, 16, 23, 24; also NT and SA.

52 **Senecio gregorii** F.Mueller
Fleshy Groundsel
Glabrous annual herb 20–40 cm high; leaves fleshy, broadly linear, 3–9 cm long; flowers to 1.5 cm across; prolific after rain.

Habitat: sandy soil in a wide variety of arid habitats.

Dist: 8, 9, 10, 13, 14, 15, 16; also NT, SA, Qld, NSW and Vic.

53 **Senecio pinnatifolius** var. **maritimus** (Ali) I.Thompson [syn. *S. lautus* subsp. *maritimus* Ali]
Coastal Groundsel
Sprawling plant with fleshy leaves. Flowers with c.13 ray florets. Recent studies have shown that the closely related *S. lautus* is a New Zealand endemic.

Habitat: coastal cliffs and dunes, usually associated with limestone.

Distr.: 11, 17, 19, 21; also SA, Vic. Tas.

54 **Trichanthodium exilis** (W.V. Fitzgerald) Short [syn. *Gnephosis exilis* W.V.Fitzgerald]
Annual herb; stems 2–20 cm long; leaves 4–11 mm long, sometimes semi-succulent; flower heads to 1 cm long.

Habitat: margins of salt lakes and adjoining sand ridges, particularly on the Monger Lake System including Lake Moore.

Dist: 15, 23.

49 *Rhodanthe humboldtiana*

54 *Trichanthodium exilis*

50 *Rhodanthe manglesii*

55 *Waitzia nitida*

56 *Waitzia suaveolens*

55 **Waitzia nitida** (Lindley) Paul G.Wilson [syn. *W. aurea* (Bentham) Steetz]
Annual to 30 cm high; leaves narrowly ovate to linear, 3–5 cm long, upper leaves and branches cottony-woolly; pappus bristles with distinctive golden tips.
Habitat: sand or gravelly sand in open woodland or shrubland.
Dist: 15, 16, 17, 18, 21, 22, 23, 24.

56 **Waitzia suaveolens** (Bentham) Druce
Fragrant Waitzia
Erect annual 30–60 cm high; leaves narrow, 2–4 cm long; flower heads c. 2 cm across.
Habitat: woodland, shrubland or mallee in sandy soil from Geraldton to the south coast and east to Esperance.
Dist: 14, 15, 16, 17, 21, 22, 23.
Var. *flava* Paul G.Wilson has straw colour or pale yellow flowers and occurs from Balladonia to Norseman and west to the Stirling Range.

BORAGINACEAE heliotropes, forget-me-nots

The Boraginaceae is a large family of herbs, shrubs and trees centred mainly in the Mediterranean region of Europe. Of c. 2000 species world-wide, c. 63 occur in Australia. Most species have glandular-hairy leaves. *Halgania* and *Trichodesma* both have showy blue flowers. Introduced species of *Echium* (Paterson's Curse or Salvation Jane) have become widespread weeds in the warmer parts of southern Australian states. *E. plantagineum* is widespread in south-western Western Australia and extends from Kalbarri to the south coast and well inland.

57 *Halgania andromedifolia*

57 **_Halgania andromedifolia_** Behr and F.Mueller
Lavender Halgania
Erect shrub to 2 m high; mature leaves up to 3 cm
long, the upper surface glabrous, lower surface
densely hairy; flowers c. 2.5 cm across.
Habitat: alkaline sand or gravel in mallee
shrubland.
Dist: 11, 21, 22, 23, 24; also SA.

58 **_Halgania_** sp.
Shrub 30–90 cm high; leaves to 2.5 cm long, toothed
near apex, hairy and rough; flowers c. 1.2 cm across.
Habitat: sandy or sandy loam in mallee woodland
or shrubland.
Dist: 16, 23.

59 _Halgania littoralis_

59 **_Halgania littoralis_** Gaudichaud
Shrub up to 60 cm high; leaves to 6 cm long, cov-
ered with soft, appressed hairs; flowers c. 2 cm
across.
Habitat: near-coastal in stony soil.
Dist: 14, 16.

60 **_Heliotropium asperrimum_** R.Brown
Rough Heliotrope
Perennial herb, erect or semi-decumbent 0.3–1 m
high; leaves 2.5–9 cm long; leaves, stems and calyces covered with a mixture of simple and glandular hairs; flowers c. 6 mm across with a strong,
rather sickly sweet perfume.
Habitat: open woodland, usually in stony soil.
Dist: 14, 19, 21, 24; also SA, NT, NSW, Vic.

60 _Heliotropium asperrimum_

58 _Halgania_ sp.

61 *Trichodesma zeylanicum*

62 *Brunonia australis*

61 ***Trichodesma zeylanicum*** (Burmann f.) R.Brown
Rough Bluebell

Erect, perennial herb to 1 m high, covered with short stiff hairs; leaves 3–8 cm long; flowers up to 2 cm across.

Habitat: diverse, coastal cliffs and dunes to arid inland.

Dist: 13, 14, 16, 23, 24 and widespread in more northern areas; also NT, SA, Qld and NSW.

BRUNONIACEAE Native Cornflower

The Brunoniaceae is a family of one monotypic genus endemic in Australia and widespread in all states. It is closely related to the Goodeniaceae, having a similar cup at the top of the style and enclosing the stigma. The single species is very variable in size and hairiness and can be perennial or annual.

62 ***Brunonia australis*** Smith ex R.Brown
Native Cornflower

Herb to 35 cm tall, silky hairy to almost glabrous; leaves oblanceolate to obovate, 3–15 cm long in a basal rosette; flower heads to 3 cm across on naked stems. Widespread in all states south of the 17th parallel.

Habitat: in sandy or loamy soil in a wide variety of habitats, especially shrubland and woodland.

Dist: 14, 15, 16, 17, 19, 20, 22, 24, 25, 26; and all states.

CAESALPINIACEAE cassia

The Caesalpiniaceae is a large family with world-wide distribution in the tropics and subtropics; about 50 species occur in Western Australia and many of these are found in the far north and the more arid inland. The largest and most widespread of the Western Australia genera is *Senna*, formerly included within a broad concept of *Cassia*. Many very ornamental exotic species are widely cultivated including *Gleditsia* (Honey locust), *Cercis* (Judas tree) and *Bauhinia* (Orchid tree).

63 ***Labichea lanceolata*** Bentham subsp. ***lanceolata***
Tall Labichea

Large open shrub to 4 m high; leaves very variable, either unifoliate or trifoliate, the central or solitary leaflet 4–12 cm long. It occurs mainly to the north of Perth [Plate 63(a)]. Subsp. *brevifolia* has three- to six-foliate leaves with a shorter central leaflet and ranges from east of Perth south to Israelite Bay [Plate 63(b)].

Habitat: diverse, including kwongan, creek beds, granite outcrops and lateritic soil.

Dist: 12, 16, 17, 18.

Labichea is an endemic genus of 14 species of shrubs

with flowers superficially similar to *Senna* but with only two fertile anthers.

64 ***Petalostylis cassioides*** (F.Mueller) Symon [syn. *P. millefolium* Pritzel]

Prostrate or decumbent shrub to 30 cm high, softly hairy; leaves to 10 cm long with up to 25 pairs of leaflets each c. 2–7 mm long; flowers 3–4 cm across; a very variable species.

Habitat: red sandy soil in open acacia woodland or shrubland, commonly with spinifex. An erect form with larger leaves and leaflets occurs in rocky creekbeds.

Dist: 2, 5, 7, 8, 9, 12, 13, 14, 15, 24; also NT.

Petalostylis is a small endemic genus in which two species are currently recognised. The flowers are distinctive in having a large boat-shaped petal-like style.

65 ***Senna artemisioides*** (A.P.de Candolle) Randell
Silver Cassia

Another widespread, variable shrub with several recognised subspecies; subsp. *filifolia* Randell, depicted here, was 1.5 m high with flowers c. 1.5 cm across, generally smaller than those of *S. glutinosa*.

Habitat: red sand in open shrubland.

Dist: 8, 9, 10, 11, 12, 13, 15, 21, 24; also NT, SA, Qld, Vic.

66 ***Senna glutinosa*** (A.P.de Candolle) Randell
Sticky Cassia

A highly variable shrub ranging widely across arid Australia; five subspecies are recognised, distinctions between them being based on rather complex combinations of leaf characters. Illustrated is subsp. *chatelainiana* (Gaudichaud) Randell which is confined to WA and is a shrub 2–4 m high; leaves pinnate up to 10 cm long with 4–6 pairs of leaflets 10–20 x 2–4 mm; flowers 1.5–2.5 cm across.

Habitat: sandy soil in arid shrubland.

Dist: 14, 15, 16, 23.

63(a) *Labichea lanceolata* subsp. *lanceolata*

63(b) *Labichea lanceolata* subsp. *brevifolia*

65 *Senna artemisioides*

66 *Senna glutinosa*

64 *Petalostylis cassioides*

67 *Senna pleurocarpa* var. *angustifolia*

68 *Isotoma hypocrateriformis*

67 **Senna pleurocarpa** (F.Mueller) Randell var. **angustifolia** Symon
Native Senna
Shrub 1–3 m high; leaves pinnate, 10–25 cm long with 8 or 9 pairs of leaflets. The flowers are followed by flat oblong pods. Var. *pleurocarpa* has shorter leaves with broader pinnae and is widespread in northern areas of the state and extends to NT, SA and Qld.
Habitat: in red sand in shrubland or woodland.
Dist: 10, 15, 22, 23, 24.

CAMPANULACEAE

The Campanulaceae is a world-wide family of herbs and a few shrubs, generally not of economic importance although many are popular in horticulture. Australian members of the family are herbs and several have been brought into cultivation including *Isotoma*, *Lobelia*, *Wahlenbergia* and *Pratia*. Many species have milky sap; that of *Isotoma* can cause temporarily impaired vision on contact with the eyes and some species are poisonous to stock. Some genera, including *Lobelia* and *Isotoma*, have the stamens fused into a tube through which the style protrudes as the flower matures.

68 **Isotoma hypocrateriformis** (R.Brown) Druce
Woodbridge Poison
Slender, annual herb, erect, usually unbranched; leaves to 2.5 cm long; flowers to c. 3 cm across, white, blue, pink or mauve.
Habitat: in Jarrah forest or woodland, sometimes in disturbed sites.
Dist: 16, 17, 18, 19, 20, 21, 22, 23.

69 **Lobelia rarifolia** E.Wimmer
Annual, glabrous herb 20–40 cm high; leaves usually entire, 4–7 mm long; flowers 1.5–2 cm long.
Habitat: moist areas in open forest or shrubland.
Dist: 18, 21, 22.

70 **Lobelia rhytidosperma** Bentham
Wrinkle-seeded Lobelia
Lanky annual herb to c. 30 cm; leaves toothed or lobed; flowers to 2 cm across, the blunt corolla lobe with notched yellow patch is distinctive.
Habitat: moist, sandy areas in shrubland or woodland.
Dist: 16, 17, 19, 20, 23.

71 **Wahlenbergia capensis** A.P. de Candolle
Cape Bluebell
Roughly hairy, erect annual 15–50 cm high; leaves

71 *Wahlenbergia capensis*

69   *Lobelia rarifolia*

to 1.5 cm long; flowers c. 2 cm across; introduced from South Africa.

Habitat: sandy soils of the coastal plain between Kalbarri and Perth and scattered areas to the south.

Dist: 16, 17, 18, 19, 21.

CASUARINACEAE   sheoak

The Casuarinaceae is a distinctive, mainly Australian family of monoecious and dioecious trees and shrubs, with a few species extending to the Pacific islands and south-east Asia. The leaves are reduced to tiny teeth on the jointed, green, needle-like branches. All flowers lack petals; male flowers are arranged in spikes, female flowers are in globular to ovoid heads. The fruits are cone-like. About 32 species occur in Western Australia, of which 5 are in the genus *Casuarina* (2 being naturalised eastern Australian species) and 27 are now placed in the genus *Allocasuarina*. The general common name 'Sheoak' was applied to the larger tree species by early settlers because of the similarity of the timber to English oak. It was used for shingles and bullock yokes and is now chiefly valued for wood crafts and specialised cabinet-making.

70 *Lobelia rhytidosperma*

72 *Allocasuarina pinaster*

72 ***Allocasuarina pinaster*** (C.A.Gardner) L.A.S. Johnson [syn. *Casuarina pinaster* C.A.Gardner] Compass Bush
Shrub 1—3 m high; branchlets leaf-like, 4—5 cm long, pungent; leaves reduced to 4 brown scales at base of branchlet. Female plants have a main axis with upswept almost parallel branches and the whole plant usually leans towards the south; male plants are smaller with spreading branches.
Habitat: in sand over laterite in kwongan.
Dist.: 21, 22.

CELASTRACEAE

The Celastraceae is a world-wide family of trees, shrubs and climbers, mainly tropical or subtropical. Of c. 1000 species only c. 33 occur in Australia, mainly in the north and east of the continent. Several exotic members of the family such as *Celastrus*, *Maytenus* and *Euonymus* are cultivated for their evergreen leaves and attractive fruit. Two endemic species of *Psammomoya*, both small, leafless shrubs, are the only representatives of the family in south-western Western Australia.

73 *Psammomoya choretroides*

73 ***Psammomoya choretroides*** (F.Mueller) Diels and Loesener
Shrub to 40 cm high with many slender leaf-less four-angled stems; flowers 4—5 mm across.
Habitat: in sandy soil in kwongan.
Dist: 16, 22, 23, 24.

CENTROLEPIDACEAE

The Centrolepidaceae is a small, mainly Australian family of sedge-like annuals and perennials with greatly reduced unisexual flowers combined into condensed heads; the male flower consists of a solitary stamen and the female flower a single style and ovary containing one ovule. *Aphelia* can be recognised by the inflorescence composed of two opposite rows of six or more bracts.

74 ***Aphelia brizula*** F.Mueller
Grass-like annual herb up to 65 mm high; flower heads 4-6 mm long.
Habitat: usually soil pockets in granite rocks; wide-spread from Badgingarra to east of Esperance.
Dist: 16, 17, 18, 19, 21, 22, 23.

74 *Aphelia brizula*

CEPHALOTACEAE Pitcher Plant

This family contains the single species *Cephalotus follicularis*; botanically it is close to the Saxifragaceae but its ability to obtain nitrogen from insects is reminiscent of the Droseraceae (sundews) and Lentibulariaceae (bladderworts). Another, unrelated pitcher plant, *Nepenthes mirabilis*, occurs on Queensland's Cape York Peninsula.

75 **Cephalotus follicularis** Labillardière
Albany Pitcher Plant
Small perennial herb to 60 cm high; normal leaves 5–7 cm long, fleshy. The pitchers, up to 5 cm long, are modified leaves and contain liquid in which insects drown and decompose making nitrogen available for absorption by the plant.
Habitat: dense vegetation on the banks of streams and swamps.
Dist: 19, 20, 21.

CHENOPODIACEAE

saltbush, bluebush, samphire

The Chenopodiaceae is a large cosmopolitan family of mostly herbs and shrubs, often with fleshy leaves or with leaves apparently absent and replaced by succulent, jointed stems. The family is common in arid, often saline habitats, particularly round inland salt lakes and also in coastal marshes. Many species are important as stock feed and some produce berries which were eaten by Aborigines. Most have inconspicuous flowers although a few have ornamental fruits or foliage. Several species of *Maireana* are conspicuous for their fruits which are often surrounded with colourful wings or immersed in wool.

76 **Atriplex holocarpa** F.Mueller
Pop Saltbush
Compact annual or short-lived perennial herb to 30 cm high; leaves triangular to narrowly rhombic, 15–30 mm long; flowers minute, enclosed within two fused spongy bracteoles c. 6 mm across. When mature these form colourful bladder-like fruits in shades of red and green.
Habitat: widespread throughout southern Australia in various soils and vegetation types; abundant on floodplains and sandy flats following flooding.
Dist: 10, 11, 13, 14, 15, 16, 22, 23, 24; also NT, SA, Qld, NSW, Vic.

75 *Cephalotus follicularis*

76 *Atriplex holocarpa*

77 *Enchylaena tomentosa*

78 *Maireana carnosa*

79 *Sclerolaena eurotioides*

82 *Dicrastylis fulva*

80 *Chloanthes coccinea*

77 ***Enchylaena tomentosa*** R.Brown
Ruby Saltbush
Prostrate to erect shrub to 1 m high; leaves
7–20 mm long, varying from very woolly to shortly
villous, glabrous or sometimes glaucous; flowers inconspicuous, immersed in a swollen, depressed
globular green, yellow or red perianth.
Habitat: widely distributed in saline and sub-sa-
line soil, both coastal and inland.
Dist: WA in all regions; also NT, SA, Qld, NSW,
Vic.

78 ***Maireana carnosa*** (Moquin) Paul G.Wilson
Cottony Bluebush
Erect perennial to 30 cm high; leaves fleshy to
10 mm long; flowers and fruits densely covered in
long, fine wool.
Habitat: heavy soil, usually round salt lakes.
Dist: 6, 7, 8, 10, 12, 13, 14, 15, 16, 23, 24; also NT,
SA, Qld.

79 ***Sclerolaena eurotioides*** (F.Mueller) A.J.Scott
Fluffy Bindii
Perennial herb c. 30 cm high; leaves 5–10 mm long,
semi-terete, silky hairy and fleshy; flowers in leafy
spikes, fruit papery and covered with long, silky
hairs and with 2–4 spines.
Habitat: dry, inland slightly salty sand.
Dist: 6, 10, 13, 14, 15, 16.

CHLOANTHACEAE

native foxglove, lambswool, lambstail

This is an endemic Australian family which in some
classifications is placed as a tribe in the Verbenaceae. It
can be recognised by its simple, opposite leaves, flowers
with two bracteoles at the base of the pedicel, corolla with
five-fused petals and dry fruits with albuminous seeds.
Many species are densely tomentose or clothed with much-
branched hairs. All ten genera and most of the 102 species
occur in WA, mainly in dry Eremaean habitats.

80 ***Chloanthes coccinea*** Bartling
Low, decumbent shrub up to 80 cm high; leaves
1–3 cm long; flowers to 3.5 cm long.
Habitat: kwongan or mallee woodland in well-
drained sand.
Dist: 22, 23.

81 ***Cyanostegia angustifolia*** Turczaninow
Tinsel Flower
Erect shrub 1–2 m high; leaves 2–4 cm x 1–4 mm,
resinous and usually folded lengthwise; flowers c. 1.5
cm across, calyx large, papery and paler than the deep
blue or purple corolla. This species can be distin-

guished from others in the genus by the narrow, usually folded leaves.

Habitat: sandy soil in kwongan or shrubland.

Dist: 18, 22, 23, 24.

82 ***Dicrastylis fulva*** Drummond ex Harvey

Shrub to 1.2 m high; branches densely covered with brownish hairs; leaves 1–4 cm long; flowers c. 2–3 mm across, arranged in dense corymbose panicles.

Habitat: shrubland in yellow sandy soil, particularly round Kalbarri and Geraldton.

Dist: 14, 15, 16, 23.

81 *Cyanostegia angustifolia*

83 ***Lachnostachys bracteosa*** C.A.Gardner

Dense shrub to 50 cm high; leaves narrowly linear, 10–15 mm long, decurrent, the margins strongly revolute; flowers 6–7 mm long, in dense spikes 2–5 cm long. Closely related to *L. eriobotrya* but distinguished by the decurrent leaves and solitary, terminal flower spikes.

Habitat: in sandy soil in kwongan, uncommon and restricted to areas around Lake King and Lake Cronin.

Dist: 22.

83 *Lachnostachys bracteosa*

84 ***Lachnostachys eriobotrya*** (F.Mueller) Druce

Lambswool

Tall, spreading shrub 1–2 m high; leaves 2.3–5.0 cm long; flowers 4–5 mm long in dense panicles.

Habitat: in kwongan and shrubland in sand.

Dist: 15, 16, 17, 18, 23, 24.

85 ***Lachnostachys ferruginea*** W.J.Hooker var. ***ferruginea*** forma ***ferruginea***

Soft, much-branched spreading shrub to 70 cm high; flowers 6–9 mm long tightly packed in dense spikes. The whole plant is covered with a dense mat of woolly hairs which are often rusty coloured.

Habitat: open woodland or shrubland.

Dist: 22, 23.

84 *Lachnostachys eriobotrya*

86 ***Lachnostachys ferruginea*** W.J. Hooker var. ***ferruginea*** forma ***reticulata*** Munir

Rusty Lambstail

Very similar to forma *ferruginea*, this taxon is restricted to Tarin Rock Reserve. It is distinguished by the reticulate veining on the underside of the leaf which is clearly visible through the loose covering of hairs.

Habitat: shrubland.

Dist: 22.

A third form, forma *acutifolia* Munir, has oblong-lanceolate, somewhat acute leaves and is restricted to the vicinity of Kulin.

85 *Lachnostachys ferruginea*

86 *Lachnostachys ferruginea*

87 *Dicrastylis globiflora*

89 *Physopsis spicata*

88 *Physopsis lachnostachya*

90 *Pityrodia atriplicina*

91 *Pityrodia axillaris*

92 *Pityrodia bartlingii*

87 **Dicrastylis globiflora** (Endl.)Rye [syn. *Mallophora globiflora* Endlicher]
Woody shrub to 45 cm high; stems slender, densely covered with a greyish, powdery indumentum; leaves 4–15 mm long, densely hairy; flowers 5–7 mm long, tightly clustered in woolly globular heads.
Habitat: in sandy soil in kwongan or shrubland.
Dist: 15, 21, 22, 23, 24.

88 **Physopsis lachnostachya** C.A.Gardner
Shrub to 120 cm high; leaves leathery, ovate 10–18 mm long, the margins strongly recurved, undersurface densely covered with yellowish brown hairs; inflorescence spicate with three flowers to each bract, compared with one flower per bract in *P. spicata*. The ovate, rather than oblong, leaves and the yellowish hairs on stems and undersurface of leaves are also distinctive.
Habitat: lateritic sand or gravel in kwongan, confined to a small area in Roe district.
Dist: 22.

89 **Physopsis spicata** Turczaninow
Hill River Lambstail
Spreading shrub to 75 cm high; leaves oblong, 1.5–3.5 cm long, the margins recurved and undersurface white woolly; inflorescence a dense woolly spike 4–8 cm long; flowers 7–9 mm long, solitary in the axil of a bract; corolla yellowish, almost hidden by the grey densely woolly calyx.
Habitat: in sand in kwongan or shrubland from Badgingarra to about Dongara.
Dist: 16, 17.

90 **Pityrodia atriplicina** (F.Mueller) Bentham
Much-branched shrub 1–2.5 m high; leaves broadly elliptic or almost orbicular, 1–2.5 x 1–2.5 cm; stems and leaves densely covered with short ashy-grey hairs.
Habitat: in sand in shrubland.
Dist: 14, 16.

91 **Pityrodia axillaris** (Endlicher) Druce
Woolly Foxglove
Spreading undershrub to 30 cm high; leaves obovate, 2–4 x 1–1.5 cm, woolly hairy; flowers 2.5–3 cm long.
Habitat: in sand or gravel in shrubland, mainly between Pindar and Morawa.
Dist: 23, 24.

92 **_Pityrodia bartlingii_** (Lehmann) Bentham
Woolly Dragon
Erect shrub 30–90 cm high; leaves 3–4 cm long, rugose with strongly recurved margin; flowers 15–23 mm long, varying from white to purple or pink, with brown or purple dots in the throat.
Habitat: sandy kwongan and woodland.
Dist: 16, 17, 18, 19, 22, 23, 24.

93 **_Pityrodia loxocarpa_** (F.Mueller) Druce
Open shrub 1–2.5 m high with numerous spindly intertwined stems; leaves 2–4 cm long, mostly basal; flowers 12–20 mm long.
Habitat: coastal sand over limestone, in shrubland.
Dist: 5, 9, 12, 13, 14, 15, 16, 20; also NT.

93 *Pityrodia loxocarpa*   94 *Pityrodia oldfieldii*

94 **_Pityrodia oldfieldii_** (F.Mueller) Bentham
Oldfield's Foxglove
Densely tomentose open shrub, to 1.5 m high; young stems and leaves often gold or reddish; leaves 2–4.5 cm long; flowers 18–23 mm long.
Habitat: in sand in kwongan.
Dist: 16.

95 **_Pityrodia terminalis_** (Endlicher) A.S.George
Native Foxglove
Compact, erect shrub to 1 m high; entire plant white-hoary, or grey woolly-felted; leaves 1.5–3 cm long; flowers 1.8–2 cm long, varying from white to pink or deep red. The deep carmine-red form [95(b)] occurs in the northern part of the species' range and is considered to be conspecific with the white form from the Lake Grace area [95(a)].
Habitat: kwongan, common on road verges.
Dist: 15, 16, 17, 22, 23, 24.

95(a) *Pityrodia terminalis*   96 *Pityrodia verbascina*

96 **_Pityrodia verbascina_** (F.Mueller) Bentham
Golden Bush
Erect woolly-hairy shrub to 2.1 m high; stems densely covered in brownish-red or brownish-yellow hairs, often golden on young growth; leaves variable in shape, usually 3–7 x 1–3 cm; flowers 9–12 mm long, pinkish white with pink spots in throat.
Habitat: sandy soil in kwongan or shrubland, particularly along road verges in Geraldton–Kalbarri area.
Dist: 16.

95(b) *Pityrodia terminalis*

97 *Bonamia rosea*

98 *Duperreya sericea*

CONVOLVULACEAE morning glory

The Convolvulaceae is a family of herbs and shrubs with a world-wide distribution in tropical and subtropical regions with a few in temperate areas. Many species have trailing or twining stems; some introduced species have become troublesome weeds. The swollen roots of some *Ipomaea* species were used as food by Aborigines.

97 **Bonamia rosea** (F.Mueller) H.Hallier
Felty Bell-flower
Erect shrub with lax stems up to 1 m long, often growing through and supported by surrounding shrubs; leaves and stems densely covered with brownish hairs; flowers 1–2 cm across, yellow, pink or white.
Habitat: sandy soil in kwongan or shrubland.
Dist: 13, 14, 15, 16; also SA and NT.

Bonamia, named after Francois Bonami, an 18th-century French botanist, is a small genus of about 50 species of which nine are endemic in Australia; most are found in northern subtropical areas.

98 **Duperreya sericea** Gaudichaud [syn. *Porana sericea* (Gaudichaud) F. Mueller]
Tall, slender climber with soft, grey, silky-hairy leaves 3–4 cm long; flowers 2 cm across; often forms a tangled mass over other shrubs.
Habitat: sandy or loamy soil in shrubland.
Dist: 14, 15, 16, 17.

CUPRESSACEAE cypress, native pine

The Cupressaceae is a world-wide family of evergreen trees and shrubs with the majority of the 140 species in the northern hemisphere. Australia has 17 species with nine in Western Australia.

Many exotic species are cultivated widely as ornamentals, but the Australian species are not often grown. *Callitris* species are resistant to termite attack and were used in building by the early settlers. *C. glaucophylla*, which occurs in all states and in large stands in parts of the eastern states and the NT, was widely used by the Aborigines. It is still a valuable source of timber for housing in termite infested areas.

99 **Actinostrobus arenarius** C.A.Gardner
Sandplain Cypress
A conical small tree or large shrub 3–5m high; leaves scale-like, ovate or triangular, c. 2 mm long. Among the three species in the genus this is

distinguished by its glaucous foliage and cones.
Habitat: in deep sand in kwongan.
Dist: 16, 17, 23.

100 ***Actinostrobus pyramidalis*** Miquel
Swamp Cypress
Medium shrub to small tree, more widely distrib-
uted than *A. arenarius* and with bright green, not
glaucous, foliage.
Habitat: in winter-moist sand, in shrubland.
Dist: 16, 17, 18, 19, 21, 22, 23, 24.

101 ***Callitris roei*** (Endlicher) F.Mueller
Erect tree to 5 m high; leaves scale-like, 1–3 mm
long; female cones 1–1.5 cm across with a curved
protuberance in the centre of each scale.
Habitat: in gravelly clay in shrubland and mallee
scrub.
Dist: 18, 21, 22, 23.

99 *Actinostrobus arenarius*

CYPERACEAE   sedge, rush

The Cyperaceae is a large family of grass- or rush-like
herbs found in moist habitats throughout the world
from the alps to rainforests or sea shores. World-wide
there are about 4000 species in 90 genera. Australia has
about 650 species in 47 genera. Many species have restricted local uses for weaving, thatching, food, perfume
or medicine. *Cyperus papyrus* is widely used as an ornamental plant and was the source of ancient Egyptian
paper. *Eleocharis dulcis* is eaten as the Chinese water
chestnut and Aborigines ate the tubers of *Cyperus
bulbosus*. Members of the family are often difficult to
identify and are usually overlooked among the rich floral displays of south-western Western Australia.
Mesomelaena is a genus of five species restricted to Western Australia. Illustrated is the largest and most distinctive species.

100 *Actinostrobus pyramidalis*

102 ***Mesomelaena tetragona*** (R.Brown) Bentham
Semaphore Sedge
Perennial, erect herb 30–80 cm high; leaves basal,
to 60 cm long; inflorescence terminating a long,
leafless stem and surrounded by three bracts of
which two are very long and angled as in the sig-
nalling arms of a semaphore.
Habitat: widespread in sand or lateritic soil in
woodland and shrubland.
Dist: 16, 17, 18, 19, 20, 21.

101 *Callitris roei*

102 *Mesomelaena tetragona*

103 *Hibbertia cuneiformis*

104 *Hibbertia hypericoides*

106 *Hibbertia stellaris*

105 *Hibbertia recurvifolia*

DILLENIACEAE hibbertia

This family occurs throughout the tropics, only the genus *Hibbertia* extending into temperate regions in Australia. The family contains c. 530 species worldwide. About 130 species in four genera occur in Australia with *Hibbertia* (guinea flower), of c. 110 species, being the largest and most widespread genus and abundant in many plant communities. Many are particularly showy plants in south-western WA bushlands. Most *Hibbertia* species are small shrubs with plentiful although short-lived, bright yellow or occasionally apricot flowers. Two eastern Australian species (*H. scandens* and *H. dentata*) are widely cultivated as ornamentals.

103 ***Hibbertia cuneiformis*** (Labillardière) Smith
Cutleaf Hibbertia
Erect shrub to 2 m high; leaves obovate, 2–3 cm x 5–11 mm, occasionally with a few serrations towards the apex; flowers solitary, 2.5–4 cm across.
Habitat: coastal dunes and Karri forest.
Dist: 17, 19, 20, 21.

104 ***Hibbertia hypericoides*** (A.P. de Candolle) Bentham
Yellow Buttercup
Spreading shrub to 1 m high; leaves 6–15 x 1-4 mm, narrowly oblong to obovate; flowers 15–25 mm across; very common in the south-west.
Habitat: diverse, sandy and granitic soils in kwongan, Jarrah forest and banksia woodland.
Dist: 16, 17, 18, 19, 20, 23.

105 ***Hibbertia recurvifolia*** Bentham
Small erect shrub to 1 m high; leaves 5–9 x 1 mm with recurved tips; flowers 1–1.5 cm across.
Habitat: gravelly soil, usually near granite outcrops.
Dist: 21, 22, 23.

106 ***Hibbertia stellaris*** Endlicher
Orange Stars
Dwarf, rounded, twiggy shrub; stems often reddish; leaves 15–25 x 0.5–2.5 mm, linear to narrowly spathulate; flowers 0.5–2 cm across; plants from northern areas have yellowish flowers.
Habitat: sandy soil in winter-wet depressions.
Dist: 17, 18, 19, 20, 21.

DIOSCOREACEAE

The Dioscoreaceae is a large family of herbs or vines with world-wide distribution in tropical regions. *Dioscorea* is the only genus in the family in Australia. Of the four native species, three are restricted to tropical and subtropical regions. The rootstock formed an important food item for many tropical Aboriginal groups, but the presence of toxins necessitated an elaborate process of grinding and washing similar to that applied to the seed of *Cycas*.

107 ***Dioscorea hastifolia*** Endlicher
  Warrine, Native Yam
  Slender, dioecious climber; leaves 2.3–5.0 cm long; flowers very small, pale yellow; male flowers in spikes 1–3 cm long, female flowers in racemes c. l cm long; capsules 0.5–1.0 cm long and prominently winged, becoming pinkish when mature.
  Habitat: shallow soil and rocky situations in the Darling Range, east to York and north towards Shark Bay.
  Dist: 14, 16, 17, 18, 23.

DROSERACEAE sundews

The Droseraceae is a world-wide family all of whose species are carnivorous, supplementing their nutrition by trapping and ingesting small insects. The family is well represented in Australia with about 100 species of *Drosera* and one species of *Aldrovandra*.

South-western Western Australia is particularly rich in *Drosera* species; they vary considerably in size and habit, ranging from the pygmy sundews with rosettes of tiny leaves and small flowers, to tall, erect or long trailing plants. In order to capture insects, the leaves are either covered with sticky glands on the upper surface or (in *Aldrovandra*) modified into bi-valved traps. The leaf glands digest the trapped insects by secretion of enzymes assisted by bacterial action. Roots are fibrous or tuberous.

The early settlers used dye from some species as ink. Many species are cultivated, mainly as glasshouse novelties.

108 ***Drosera barbigera*** Planchon
  Small perennial herb to 10 cm tall with a basal rosette of narrow leaves up to 1.5 cm long; flowers 2 cm across.
  Habitat: seasonally wet situations in kwongan and woodland.
  Dist: 16, 22, 23.

107 *Dioscorea hastifolia*

108 *Drosera barbigera*

109(a) and 109(b): *Drosera macrantha*

109 ***Drosera macrantha*** Endlicher
Bridal Rainbow
Tuberous climbing herb with delicate climbing or trailing stems to 1.5 m long; leaves orbicular in scattered groups of three; flowers 1.5–3 cm across, white, pink or rarely red.
Habitat: very common in sandy soil in forest, shrubland and kwongan.
Dist: 15, 16, 17, 18, 19, 20, 21, 22, 23, 24; also SA, Vic, Tas.
The second picture [109(b)] shows the modified glandular leaves; the sticky globules at the ends of the leaf hairs capture insects which are digested by enzymes. The small bug, a species of *Cyrtopeltis*, appears to be immune to the sticky digestive globules and feeds on the trapped insects.

110 ***Drosera menziesii*** R.Brown ex A.P. de Candolle
Pink Rainbow
Erect scrambling or climbing tuberous herb, stems red, up to 1 m long; leaves usually in scattered groups of three; flowers 2–3 cm across. A variable species but the red stems and red fimbriate sepals are distinctive.
Habitat: widespread and common in winter wet sand and clay soils.
Dist: 16, 17, 18, 19, 20, 21, 22, 23.

110 *Drosera menziesii*

EPACRIDACEAE heaths

The Epacridaceae is a predominantly Australian family, extending northward to Indonesia and Malesia and eastward to New Zealand and the Pacific Islands; one species occurs in South America. Of approximately 430 Australian species, over 180 occur in Western Australia and most favour open heathland habitats with acidic soils. The family is frequently referred to as the southern or Australian heaths because of their resemblance to European heaths and heathers which are in the closely related family Ericaceae. Epacridaceae leaves are usually small, rigid and often pungent, the flowers are tubular and in most species surrounded by several rows of enveloping bracts. In many species the flowers develop into edible, often colourful fruits which were widely used as food by the Aborigines and early settlers.

111 *Andersonia caerulea*   112 *Andersonia echinocephala*

111 ***Andersonia caerulea*** R.Brown
Foxtails
Erect, sparsely branched shrub to 50 cm high; leaves 1–15 mm long, usually spirally twisted and with a wavy edge; flowers 5–12 mm long. A very variable species both in habit and leaf form.
Habitat: sandy soil in kwongan or in open forest with heath understorey.
Dist: 18, 19, 20, 21, 22.

112 ***Andersonia echinocephala*** (Stschegleew) Druce
Upright shrub 1–3 m high, leaves 0.5–3 cm long, twisted and undulate; flowers in 'heads' 1.5–2 cm across surrounded by pale greenish cream or occasionally pale pink floral leaves.
Habitat: confined to higher rocky slopes of Stirling Range.
Dist: 21.

113 *Andersonia grandiflora*

113 ***Andersonia grandiflora*** Stschegleew
Red Andersonia
Prostrate, cushion-like shrub to 0.3m high, leaves up to 1.5 cm long, tapering to a fine point and spirally twisted; flowers c. 1 cm long.
Habitat: sandy soil, often among rocks, in the Stirling Range.
Dist: 21.

114 ***Astroloma microdonta*** F.Mueller ex Bentham
Sandplain Cranberry
Dwarf shrub to 1m high; leaves c. 15 x 2 mm with margin finely toothed and hairy; flowers to 1 cm long.
Habitat: sandy gravel soil in shrubland or kwongan.
Dist: 16.

114 *Astroloma microdonta*

115 *Astroloma xerophyllum*   116 *Conostephium pendulum*

117 *Cosmelia rubra*   118 *Croninia kingiana*

121 *Lysinema ciliatum*   120 *Oligarrhena micrantha*

115 **Astroloma xerophyllum** (A.P.de Candolle) Sonder
Shrub 0.5–1 m high; leaves c. 1 cm long, concave and with prominent veins; flowers to 1 cm long.
Habitat: sandy soil in kwongan.
Dist: 16, 17, 23.

116 **Conostephium pendulum** Bentham
Pearl Flower
Shrub to 1 m high; leaves 2–3 cm long with a pungent tip; flowers to 2 cm long; common in near-coastal regions north and south of Perth.
Habitat: sandy soil in woodland and Jarrah forest.
Dist: 16, 17, 19.

117 **Cosmelia rubra** R.Brown
Spindle Heath
Erect, sparsely branched shrub to 1 m high; leaves 1–2.5 cm long; flowers to 2.5 cm long.
Habitat: swampy areas.
Dist: 19, 20, 21.

118 **Croninia kingiana** (F.Mueller) J.Powell [syn. *Leucopogon kingianus* (F.Mueller) C.A.Gardner]
Erect shrub to 1 m high with ascending branches; leaves to 1 cm long, tapering to a slender, spreading apex, underside prominently veined; flowers to 1.5 cm long, white, cream or pale yellow.
Habitat: sandy soil, in banksia woodland, or kwongan.
Dist: 16, 17, 18, 19, 20, 23, 24.

119 **Leucopogon verticillatus** R.Brown
Tassel Flower
Erect shrub 1–4 m high; leaves 5–15 cm long; corolla to 10 mm long; tube pink with white lobes, bearded inside. This is the largest species of *Leucopogon*.
Habitat: Karri, Jarrah and Marri forest.
Dist: 18, 19, 20, 21.

120 **Oligarrhena micrantha** R.Brown
Dwarf, compact, erect heath-like shrub; leaves scale-like, 1–2 mm long, closely appressed to the stem; flowers 1–2 mm long, crowded, white to yellow.
Habitat: southern kwongan, usually near the coast, in sandy soil.
Dist: 21.

121 ***Lysinema ciliatum*** R.Brown
Curry flower
Slender, erect shrub 30–80 cm high; leaves stem-clasping, 4–8 mm long, flowers curry scented; corolla tube 1–1.5 cm long. This is the most common and most widespread species of the genus.
Habitat: in sandy soil in kwongan and woodland.
Dist: 16, 17, 18, 19, 21, 22, 23, 24.

122 ***Needhamiella pumilio*** (R.Brown) L.Watson
Small, compact shrub 8–20 cm high; leaves keeled with ciliate margins, 2–3 mm long; flowers c. 5 mm long and 3–4 mm across.
Habitat: sandy soil in kwongan, usually near the coast, often in wet depressions.
Dist: 17, 19, 20, 21.

119 *Leucopogon verticillatus*

122 *Needhamiella pumilio*

EUPHORBIACEAE

The Euphorbiaceae is a large and very diverse family of world-wide, mainly tropical distribution. It includes trees, shrubs and herbs; flowers are generally small, almost always unisexual and frequently on separate plants; some species have milky sap. Some exotic species are of economic importance; *Hevea brasiliensis* is the source of most of the world's natural rubber; *Manihot esculenta,* the manioc, cassava or tapioca plant, is the source of a staple foodstuff in many tropical countries; several species yield oils, including castor oil from *Ricinus communis.* Of the genera illustrated, *Stachystemon* is endemic in WA. *Monotaxis* and *Ricinocarpos*, except for one species in New Caledonia, are all Australian. *Ricinocarpos* is usually a showy shrub with white, yellow or pink flowers; white-flowered forms are widely known as Wedding Bush. *Phyllanthus* is a large, diverse world-wide genus, occurring mainly in tropical and subtropical regions.

123 *Monotaxis bracteata*

123 **Monotaxis bracteata** Nee [syn. *Monotaxis lurida* (Mueller Argoviensis) Bentham]
Small monoecious shrub to 50 cm high; leaves 10–25 mm long; male and female flowers clustered in heads c. 1 cm across.
Habitat: kwongan, in red sandy soil.
Dist: 14, 15, 16, 23, 24.

124 **Phyllanthus calycinus** Labillardière
False Boronia
Monoecious or dioecious shrub to 1 m high; leaves 5–20 mm long; female flowers solitary, 3–6 mm long, enlarging in fruit, male flowers smaller, two or three together with perianth 1.5–3 mm long; flower colour usually white to cream, occasionally pink.
Habitat: in sand or gravelly soil in forest or woodland.
Dist: 14, 16.

125 **Ricinocarpos glaucus** Endlicher
Wedding Bush
Erect monoecius shrub to 1 m high; leaves 1.5–5 x 1–3 mm with revolute margins; flowers 1.5–3.0 cm across, fragrant, varying from white to yellow; male flowers are larger and in denser clusters than female flowers.
Habitat: in sandy soil in the coastal plain, kwongan and granitic soil on the Darling Scarp.
Dist: 16, 17, 19, 20, 21, 22, 23.

125 *Ricinocarpos glaucus*

124 *Phyllanthus calycinus*

126 **Ricinocarpos velutinus** F.Mueller
  Erect, rounded shrub 1–2 m high; leaves 2–6 cm long covered with short, velvety hairs; flowers 1.5–2 cm across.
  Habitat: red sand in acacia-sheoak woodland or shrubland.
  Dist: 15, 16, 23, 24.

127 **Stachystemon polyandrus** (F.Mueller) Bentham
  Monoecious, erect shrub to 50 cm high; leaves to 3 mm long, confined to new growth; old stems bare and twiggy; flowers c. 6 mm long, in loose terminal clusters.
  Habitat: in sandy soil in kwongan.
  Dist: 21, 22.

FABACEAE

The Fabaceae family is also recognised by its alternative name Papilionaceae. In some classifications, Caesalpiniaceae, Mimosaceae and Fabaceae are regarded as subfamilies of Leguminosae.

The Fabaceae is one of the largest and economically most important plant families in the world due to the high nutrient levels contained in the many species used as food by humans and grazing animals. A number of species are used for timber and many are widely grown as ornamentals. World-wide the family contains about 500 genera with 12 000 species; Australia has about 140 genera comprising 1100 species. Over 90 native genera are found in south-western Western Australia, of which 22 are represented here.

Overall the family exhibits great species diversity and is a major contributor to the floral displays of heathland and forest habitats.

128 **Aotus genistoides** Turczaninow
  Erect shrub to 1 m high; leaves 1–2 cm long in irregular whorls of three, margins recurved and underside covered with pale, appressed hairs; flowers 8–10 mm wide.
  Habitat: sand, commonly rocky, in sheltered forest. Dist: 19, 20.
  The leaves with recurved margins and in groups of three are typical of the genus *Aotus*, of which there are about ten species in WA.

Bossiaea has about 40 species in WA which show considerable variation in both leaves and flowers. All species have united stamens, flat pods at least twice as long as wide with several seeds, and valves which completely separate at maturity.

126 *Ricinocarpos velutinus*

127 *Stachystemon polyandrus*

128 *Aotus genistoides*

129 *Bossiaea cucullata*   131 *Bossiaea eriocarpa*

130 *Bossiaea aquifolium* subsp. *laidlawiana*

132 *Bossiaea linophylla*

133 *Bossiaea ornata*

129 *Bossiaea cucullata* J.H.Ross
Erect, leafless shrub to 1.5 m high; similar to *B. walkeri* but differing in being of much more floriferous habit and having differently shaped and coloured flowers.
Habitat: margins of salt lakes.
Dist: 22, 23.

130 *Bossiaea aquifolium* Bentham subsp. *laidlawiana* (Tovey and Morris) J.H.Ross
Water Bush
Shrub or small tree to 8 m high; leaves opposite, 0.8–2.2 cm long, margin slightly angular, usually with 11–25 pungent points; flowers 10–18 mm wide.
Habitat: clay loam soil, occasionally also with gravel. An important understorey shrub in Karri forest, sometimes found with Jarrah–Marri or with all three together.
Dist: 19, 20.
Subsp. *aquifolium* has leaves more angular with sinuate margins and 5–11 pungent points; it is a common understorey shrub in Jarrah–Marri forest.

131 *Bossiaea eriocarpa* Bentham
Common Brown Pea
Shrub to 60 cm high; leaves oblong, alternate, distichous, to 2.5 cm long; flowers 10–15 mm across; pod flat, oblong, covered with silky hairs.
Habitat: sandy soil in woodland and kwongan.
Dist: 17, 18, 19, 20.
A very variable species and sometimes confused with narrow-leaved forms of *B. ornata* which can be distinguished by its ovate, rather than oblong, leaves.

132 *Bossiaea linophylla* R.Brown
Soft, usually densely branched shrub to 3 m high; branches often pendulous; leaves to 2.5 cm long; flowers profuse, 7–8 mm across.
Habitat: in sand or gravel in southern Jarrah forest.
Dist: 19, 20, 21.

133 *Bossiaea ornata* Bentham
Broad Leaved Brown Pea
Shrub to 1 m high, very variable from a lax, few-stemmed plant to a multi-stemmed erect shrub; leaves narrowly to broadly ovate, 2–5 cm x 3–20 mm; flowers up to 2 cm across.
Habitat: in lateritic soil in Jarrah forest.
Dist: 17, 18, 19, 20.

134 *Bossiaea preissii* Meisner

Low, spreading shrub to 0.5 m high; branches spine-tipped; leaves 7–10 x 2–4 mm; flowers (including calyx) 12–15 mm long; sometimes confused with *B. spinosa* which has distinctive, much enlarged, almost petal-like upper calyx lobes.
Habitat: grey or white sand in kwongan, sandy or gravelly loam in woodland.
Dist: 21, 22.

135 *Bossiaea pulchella* Meisner

Spreading shrub to 1.5 m high; leaves alternate, 2–10 mm long; flowers c. 10 mm wide.
Habitat: lateritic sand and gravel in Jarrah forest.
Dist: 17, 18, 19.

134 *Bossiaea preissii*

136 *Bossiaea rufa* R.Brown

Lax, many-stemmed shrub to 2 m high, often almost leafless, stems flattened and winged; leaves, when present, obovate to narrowly elliptic, 7–29 x 2.2–10 mm; flowers 8.6–11.7 mm wide on pedicels 5–10 mm long.
Habitat: moist situations in sandy alluvial or peaty soil or among rocks along stream banks and near swamps. Flowers November to January.
Dist: 17, 18, 19, 20, 21.
B. praetermissa (not illustrated) is similar but is usually a smaller plant with smaller flowers which appear in September to October.

135 *Bossiaea pulchella*   136 *Bossiaea rufa*

137 *Bossiaea walkeri* F.Mueller

Cactus Bossiaea
Shrub 2–3 m high, erect or spreading; stems flattened, glaucous and usually leafless; juvenile leaves oval, 2–3 cm long, occasionally present; flowers have the standard much shorter than the wings and keel.
Habitat: inland, mallee woodland, commonly near salt lakes.
Dist: 15, 16, 22, 24; also NSW, SA, Vic.

137 *Bossiaea walkeri*

138 *Gastrolobium bracteolosum*

139 *Gastrolobium latifolium*

140 *Callistachys lanceolata*

141 *Chorizema aciculare* subsp. *aciculare*

138 ***Gastrolobium bracteolosum*** (F.Mueller)
G. Chandler & Crisp [syn. *Brachysema bracteolosum* F.Mueller]
Spreading semi-prostrate shrub to 3 m across; often scrambling over neighbouring shrubs to form large clumps; leaves 5-11 cm x 5-10 mm; flowers 1.5-3 cm long.
Habitat: sand or sandy clay over laterite.
Dist: 19, 21.

139 ***Gastrolobium latifolium*** (R.Brown)
G. Chandler & Crisp [syn. *Brachysema latifolium* R.Brown]
Prostrate creeper forming dense patches; leaves to c. 5 cm long, leathery and with prominent central nerve, undersurface covered with pale silky hairs; flowers 2-3 cm long.
Habitat: sandy clay in mallee shrubland.
Dist: 21, 22.

Callistachys is at present regarded as a monotypic genus but a variant with ovate or elliptic silky leaves extends along the south coast from east of Albany to Cape le Grand and intergrades with the typical form around Albany.

140 ***Callistachys lanceolata*** Ventenat [syn. *Oxylobium lanceolatum* (Ventenat) Druce]
Native Willow, Wannich
Tall shrub to 4 m high; leaves 5–14 cm x 6–25 mm; flowers 12–14 mm across in terminal racemes.
Habitat: clay loam and sand in moist situations, particularly beside streams.
Dist: 16, 17, 18, 19, 20, 21; also Vic (naturalised).

Chorizema (flame peas), so named for the brilliant colours of the flowers, comprises 25 species of which all but one occur in south-western WA. The leaves usually have conspicuous reticulate veining on the upper surface and flat, recurved or spiny margins. The pods are usually turgid with 4–32 ovules.

141 ***Chorizema aciculare*** (A.P. de Candolle)
C.A.Gardner subsp. ***aciculare***
Needle-leaved Chorizema
Erect or spreading shrub 0.5–1 m high; leaves 8–28 mm long, margins revolute, obscuring the undersurface; flowers 10–14 mm across, pink or orange; subsp. *laxum* differs in having slightly longer leaves with loosely revolute margins with underside partly visible and pale yellow or orange, rarely pink, flowers.
Habitat: grey, yellow or white sand in woodland or coastal mallee kwongan.
Dist: 21, 22, 23.

142 *Chorizema glycinifolium* (Smith) Druce
Small shrub with sprawling branches to 80 cm long; leaves very variable, 15–75 x 1–15 mm; lower leaves often short, broad and upper leaves long, narrow; flowers 10–12 mm across, orange, pink or red with yellowish markings.
Habitat: usually sandy loam, sandy clay or gravel in kwongan or swampy places.
Dist: 17, 18, 19, 21, 22, 23.

143 *Chorizema retrorsum* J.M.Taylor and Crisp
Scrambling shrub with branches to 3 m long; leaves ovate to oblong, 3.5–10 x 0.8–4.5 cm, margins undulate and with spine-tipped teeth including at least some retrorse spines. This is one of five species in the genus with superficially similar leaves. The other four are smaller plants, never scrambling, and rarely have retrorse spines on the marginal teeth.
Habitat: tall eucalypt forest with dense understorey; various soils including red loam, sandy loam, gravel and clay.
Dist: 17, 18, 19, 20.

144 *Chorizema rhombeum* R.Brown
Erect or sprawling shrub with branches to 60 cm long; leaves variable, from broadly rhombic to narrowly ovate, to 4 cm x 4–14 mm; flowers 13–16 mm across.
Habitat: in Jarrah forest or kwongan on a wide variety of soils.
Dist: 17, 18, 19, 20, 21.

Daviesia (bitter-pea, rattle-pea) is a large genus of shrubs with over 90 species in WA. Many species are prickly or leafless and often densely covered with rather small flowers. The triangular, inflated pods are distinctive and usually rattle when the seeds develop.

142 *Chorizema glycinifolium*

144 *Chorizema rhombeum*

145 *Daviesia audax*

143 *Chorizema retrorsum*

146 *Daviesia benthamii* subsp. *benthamii*

147 *Daviesia costata*

148 *Daviesia euphorbioides*

145 ***Daviesia audax*** Crisp
Erect shrub to 2 m high; leaves to 7 cm long; flowers 5–6 mm across.
Habitat: shrubland in sandy or gravelly lateritic soil.
Dist: 22.

146 ***Daviesia benthamii*** Meisner subsp. ***benthamii***
Shrub 2 m high; leaves reduced to spine-tipped phyllodes decurrent along the branches; flowers c. 5 mm across. This is the only subspecies occurring in WA. Subsp. *humilis* is a smaller plant occurring in SA, Vic and NSW.
Habitat: shrubland in sand or sandy clay.
Dist: 10, 13, 14, 15, 16, 18, 21, 22, 23, 24; also SA.

147 ***Daviesia costata*** E.Cheel
Sprawling multi-stemmed shrub to 70 cm high; leaves 1–30 cm long, often reduced to scales towards tips of flowering branches; flowers c. 10 mm wide; calyx with 10 prominent ribs.
Habitat: open Wandoo or Jarrah forest or shrubland on gravelly, lateritic soil or yellow-brown sand.
Dist: 18, 23.

148 ***Daviesia euphorbioides*** Bentham
Wongan Cactus
Leafless cactus-like shrub, branches erect or ascending, terete, thick and pithy; leaves replaced by small scales on the branchlets; flowers 6–8 mm across. A rare species restricted to small areas between Cadoux and Wongan Hills.
Habitat: in sandy loam in kwongan.
Dist: 23.

149 ***Daviesia incrassata*** Smith
Spreading shrub to 1 x 1 m, leafless, with short rigid branchlets ending in a pungent point; flowers c. 8 mm across.
Habitat: sand or sandy gravel in shrubland.
Dist: 16, 17, 18, 19, 21, 22, 23.

150 ***Daviesia obovata*** Turczaninow
Broad-leaf Daviesia
Shrub 0.25–1 m high; leaves elliptic to obovate, to 5 cm long; flowers c. 1.5 cm across, surrounded by conspicuous reticulate veined bracts that enlarge as the flower fades and eventually completely enclose the developing pod.
Habitat: sandy soil in shrubland in the Stirling Range.
Dist: 21.

151 ***Daviesia pachyphylla*** F.Mueller
Ouch Bush
Small open shrub to 1.5 m high; branches usually arching; leaves l–2 cm long, thick, fleshy and tapering to a hard pungent point; flowers c. 7 mm across.
Habitat: sandy soil in kwongan.
Dist: 21, 22.

Euchilopsis is an endemic genus of one species restricted to south-western WA. The small, hairy, inflated pods hang on a slender stem with a recurved calyx.

152 ***Euchilopsis linearis*** (Bentham) F.Mueller
Swamp Pea
Prostrate to ascending many-stemmed shrub; leaves 1–2.5 cm long; flowers 1.5 cm across on slender pedicels 1–2 cm long.
Habitat: winter wet depressions in sands of the coastal plain in banksia woodland or shrubland.
Dist: 17, 18, 19, 20.

150 *Daviesia obovata*

149 *Daviesia incrassata*

152 *Euchilopsis linearis*

151 *Daviesia pachyphylla*

154 *Eutaxia parvifolia*

155 *Gastrolobium oxylobioides*

156 *Gastrolobium spinosum*

153 *Eutaxia baxteri*

159 *Gompholobium ovatum*

Eutaxia is an endemic Australian genus of c. 10 species with c. 8 in south-western WA. It is easily distinguished by the flat or incurved regularly decussate leaves.

153 ***Eutaxia baxteri*** Knowles and Westcott
Slender to spreading shrub to 2.5 m high; leaves to 2 cm long; flowers c. 1.5 cm across.
Habitat: often associated with outcrops and soils derived from granite, also in coastal shrubland from about Esperance to Busselton.
Dist: 17, 19, 20, 21, 22.

154 ***Eutaxia parvifolia*** Bentham [syn. *Eutaxia densifolia* Turczaninow]
Small dense shrub to 1.5 m high; leaves to 1 cm long; flowers c. 7--8 mm across.
Habitat: clay or stony loam soil, often in wet situations, mainly north and west of Albany.
Dist: 18, 20, 21, 22, 23.

The genus ***Gastrolobium*** now contains over 100 species, the majority of which occur in Southern WA. Most species are highly toxic to stock due to the presence of a monofluoroacetic acid. The sodium salt of this is used as the pesticide '1080'. Most native herbivores in areas where the plants grow are immune but losses of introduced stock by early graziers led to a program of eradication. Consequently many species are rare or endangered. Recent taxonomic studies have resulted in the incorporation of several genera into *Gastrolobium*. (See pp. 58 & 68).

155 ***Gastrolobium oxylobioides*** Bentham
Champion Bay Poison
Spreading shrub to 0.5 m high with long arching branches; leaves 2–5 cm x 3–10 mm; flowers c. 1 cm across.
Habitat: northern sandplains.
Dist: 16, 17, 18.

156 ***Gastrolobium spinosum*** Bentham
Prickly Poison
Erect or spreading shrub 1–2 m high; leaf shape very irregular, broadly to shallowly triangular or ovate 1–4.5 x 1–4 cm, base cordate, margin pungently toothed; flowers 9–14 mm across, colour variable, orange or yellow with dark red markings; a widely distributed and very variable species; poisonous to stock but some forms more toxic than others.
Habitat: diverse including Jarrah and Wandoo woodland in gravel and sand, mallee in white clay and shrubland in sandy soil.
Dist: 10, 16, 17, 19, 21, 22, 23, 24.

Gompholobium derived from the Greek *gomphos* (a club) and *lobos* (pod), referring to the club-shaped pod. *Gompholobium* is a genus of about 40 species endemic in Australia except one species in New Guinea. The majority occur in south-western WA and are shrubs or lax, semi-twining undershrubs. Flower colour varies from pale yellow to orange, pink, red or mauve-purple; the pods are glabrous, inflated and rather brittle. The small genus formerly known as *Burtonia* is now included in *Gompholobium*.

157 *Gompholobium capitatum*

157 ***Gompholobium capitatum*** Cunningham
Yellow Pea
Slender shrub 30 cm–1 m high; leaves pinnately divided into 5–7 terete segments, each 7–22 mm long; flowers c. 1.5 cm across.
Habitat: sandy soil in heath and open forest.
Dist: 17, 18, 19, 20.

158 ***Gompholobium hendersonii*** Paxton [syn. *Burtonia hendersonii* (Paxton) Bentham]
Red Bonnets
Well-branched shrub to 1.5 m high; leaves narrow, c. 5 mm long, in groups of three; flowers c. 1 cm across.
Habitat: sand or gravelly soil in mallee shrubland or heath.
Dist: 21, 22, 23, 24.

158 *Gompholobium hendersonii*

159 ***Gompholobium ovatum*** Meisner
Lax, spreading shrub to 80 cm high; leaves 2–3 x 1–3 cm; flowers to 2.5 cm across; one of the few species of *Gompholobium* with simple leaves.
Habitat: lateritic soil in forest.
Dist: 17, 19, 20.

160(a) *Gompholobium polymorphum*

160 ***Gompholobium polymorphum*** R.Brown
Twining or straggling shrub, stems to 40 cm long; leaves trifoliate; leaflets 10–30 mm long; flowers c. 2 cm across, yellow, orange, pink or red; a highly variable species; the pale form [plate 160(b)] was photographed on the Darling Scarp. Plate 160(a) shows a deep orange-red form from the Stirling Range.
Habitat: widespread in moist loam or sandy soil in forest and shrubland.
Dist: 16, 17, 18, 19, 20, 21, 22.

160(b) *Gompholobium polymorphum*

161 *Gompholobium scabrum*

162 *Gompholobium venustum*

163 *Mirbelia floribunda*

164 *Hovea elliptica*

161 ***Gompholobium scabrum*** Smith   [syn. *Burtonia scabra* (Sm.) R.Brown]
Painted Lady
Erect, much-branched shrub to 3 m high; leaves 1–1.5 cm long in groups of three. *G. villosa* from the Stirling Range is very similar but has a densely woolly calyx in contrast to the glabrous or slightly pubescent calyx of *G. scabrum*.
Habitat: sandy soil in heath or forest.
Dist: 16, 17, 18, 19, 20, 21, 22, 23.

162 ***Gompholobium venustum*** R.Brown
Handsome Wedge-pea
Slender, straggly shrub; branches to 1 m long; leaves pinnate with stalks to 2.5 cm long and with 9–21 leaflets 1–2 cm long; flowers c. 1.5 cm across in loose heads, varying from blue or reddish purple to pink.
Habitat: heathland and Jarrah forest in sandy or rocky soil.
Dist: 17, 19, 20, 21, 22, 23.

Hovea named by Robert Brown in honour of the Polish collector A.P. Hove who sent many plants to the Royal Gardens, Kew. It is an endemic genus of c. 20 species of which eight occur in south-western WA; most are small to medium shrubs with purple, rarely (in WA) blue, mauve or white flowers. In most species the standard is conspicuously larger than the other petals; the pods are ovate, glabrous or hairy, turgid and usually broader than long.

163 ***Mirbelia floribunda*** Bentham
Purple Mirbelia
Much branched shrub to 30 cm high;
leaves 3–7 mm long with hooked tip; flowers 1 cm across.
Habitat: sandy soil in Kwongan or woodland.
Dist: 16, 17

164 ***Hovea elliptica*** (Smith) A.P.de Candolle
Tree Hovea
Slender shrub to 3 m high, often single-stemmed; leaves 2.5–10 x 1–3.2 cm; flowers 12–17 mm wide.
Habitat: Karri, Jarrah and Marri forest in sand and clay loam, granite outcrops and stabilized dunes.
Dist: 19, 20, 21.

165 ***Hovea pungens*** Bentham
Devil's Pins
Erect shrub to 1.8 m high; leaves 5–30 x 1–3 mm, the margins strongly recurved, apex pungent;   flowers 12–16 mm across; similar and often confused with *H. stricta* (q.v.)

Habitat: granite and lateritic sand and gravel, coastal limestone and clay and loamy soils in heath, Jarrah forest and woodland.

Dist: 17, 18, 21, 23, 24.

166 *Hovea stricta* Meisner

Erect shrub to 1 m high, usually few-branched and often single-stemmed; leaves 10–40 x 1.5–7.5 mm, the margins strongly revolute, apex occasionally pungent; flowers 11–17 mm wide. This species is very similar to *H. pungens* but can be distinguished by its usually slightly wider leaves which arch upward and have a distinct petiole in contrast to the outward arching, almost sessile leaves of *H. pungens*. Most importantly the seeds of *H. stricta* are a uniform yellowish or olive brown but those of *H. pungens* are brown with distinct pale mottling.

Habitat: in sand in kwongan.

Dist: 16, 17.

167 *Hovea trisperma* Bentham

Common Hovea

Sub-shrub to 60 cm high; stems 1–several, often sprawling; leaves 1–13 x 0.5–3.5 cm, variable, even on the same plant; flowers 11–25 mm across.

Habitat: varied, including kwongan, banksia woodland and Jarrah forest in sand, gravel and clay loam.

Dist: 17, 18, 19, 20, 21.

H. chorizemifolia de Candolle (not illustrated) is similar in size and habit but has prickly toothed leaves; it is often found in association with *H. trisperma* in Jarrah forest and with *H. elliptica* in Karri forest.

Isotropis is a small endemic genus with ten species in WA. The flowers have a standard larger than the other petals and distinctively marked with dark red stripes, particularly prominent on the reverse side; the pod is almost flat and densely hairy. Several species are poisonous to stock.

168 *Isotropis cuneifolia* (Smith) Heynhold

Granny Bonnets

Dwarf or prostrate perennial herb to 50 cm high; leaves linear to wedge-shaped, 1.5–5.0 cm long, very variable, several leaf shapes may occur on the one plant; flowers c. 1–1.5 cm across, reverse side of standard with very dark red lines. Several forms of this species have been recognised and some are believed to be highly toxic to stock.

Habitat: sandy soil or lateritic gravel in Jarrah forest, banksia woodland and kwongan.

Dist: 16, 17, 18, 19, 20, 21, 22, 23.

165 *Hovea pungens*

166 *Hovea stricta*

167 *Hovea trisperma*

168 *Isotropis cuneifolia*

169 *Jacksonia cupulifera*

171 *Kennedia nigricans*

172 *Kennedia coccinea*

170 *Jacksonia sternbergiana*

175 *Leptosema tomentosum*

Jacksonia is an endemic genus with 38 described species in WA and a large number yet to be named. They are usually very floriferous shrubs or small trees, often leafless, greyish in appearance and with ridged, flattened or spiny stems. Pods are grey to brown, shortly hairy and flat or turgid.

169 ***Jacksonia cupulifera*** Meisner
Shrub or tree to 6 m high; old plants often gnarled or sculptured; branchlets spreading or pendulous, grey-green, leafless; juvenile leaves oval, to 4.5 cm long; flowers c. 8 mm across.
Habitat: sandy soil in heath or shrubland.
Dist: 16.

170 ***Jacksonia sternbergiana*** Huegel
Stinkwood
Shrub to 4 m high, leafless; branchlets usually pendulous, with pungent tips; flowers 10–12 mm across.
Habitat: sandy soil, usually in banksia woodland.
Dist: 16, 17, 18, 19, 21, 23.

Kennedia is an endemic genus of about 15 species with 11 in WA. They are mainly climbers or trailers with trifoliate leaves; the pods are straight and longer than broad; several species are vigorous, hardy climbers, well known in cultivation.

171 ***Kennedia nigricans*** Lindley
Black Coral Pea
Large, vigorous climber; leaves 1–3-foliate, leaflets 3–10 x 2–7 cm; flowers to c. 4 cm long.
Habitat: woodland or shrubland in sandy soil, usually near-coastal.
Dist: 21.

172 ***Kennedia coccinea*** Ventenat
Coral Vine
Twining or trailing shrub with rusty hairs particularly on stems and calyces; leaves trifoliate; leaflets usually ovate, up to 8 cm long; inflorescence a loose cluster of 4–20 flowers, each c. 15 mm wide; the standard is usually orange or orange-red as pictured but keel and wing petals may be combinations of orange, mauve or pink.
Habitat: common and very showy in Jarrah and Karri forest and mallee kwongan, particularly after fire and often festooning trees and shrubs; extends from about Eneabba to the Stirling Range and Cape Arid.
Dist: 16, 17, 18, 19, 20, 21.

173 **Leptosema daviesioides** (Turczaninow) Crisp
Upside-down Pea
Dense, prickly shrub forming a mound to 50 cm
high; flowers 2–3 cm long in dense racemes at base
of plant; colour varies from dull yellow or greenish
with red shadings to clear, bright red.
Habitat: sand or gravelly sand in mallee shrubland.
Dist: 10, 15, 16, 22, 23, 24.

174 **Leptosema aphyllum** (W.J.Hooker) Crisp
[syn. *Brachysema aphyllum* W.J.Hooker]
Ribbon Pea
Leafless shrub to 0.3 m high and 2 m wide, often
with most stems prostrate; flowers to 5 cm long. The
long, curved keel petals enclose the stamens and
style which are released by the pollinator.
Habitat: sand in shrubland.
Dist: 15, 16, 23, 24.

175 **Leptosema tomentosum** (Bentham) Crisp
[syn. *Brachysema tomentosum* Bentham]
Tufted, leafless shrub to 60 cm high; flowers to
4 cm long. One of the 'upside-down peas' with all
flowers at the base of the plant.
Habitat: sand in acacia or mallee shrubland.
Dist: 16, 23.

Mirbelia is an endemic genus of about 25 species with
16 in WA. They are very diverse shrubs, spiny and with
small leaves, leafless or with quite large toothed leaves.
Flowers vary in size and colour from shades of blue and
mauve to pink and yellow, with dark red or brown markings. All species have a distinctive ovoid or ellipsoidal
pod which is divided longitudinally by a false septum
into two cells.

176 **Mirbelia dilatata** R.Brown
Holly-leaved Mirbelia
Shrub to 3.5 m high; leaves very variable, 1–3.5 cm
long with three to seven pungent-tipped lobes and
prominent reticulate venation; flowers c. 1.5 cm
across; a very floriferous and showy shrub.
Habitat: diverse; forest, woodland and kwongan in
sand or gravel, often in areas subject to long wet
periods.
Dist: 18, 19, 20, 21, 22, 23.

See also *Mirbelia floribunda* p.64

173 *Leptosema daviesioides*

174 *Leptosema aphyllum*

176 *Mirbelia dilatata*

177 *Mirbelia spinosa*

179 *Gastrolobium leakianum*

178 *Gastrolobium ilicifolium*

180 *Gastrolobium retusum*

181 *Pultenaea barbata*

177 **Mirbelia spinosa** Bentham

Low, spreading shrub to 1 m high; branchlets reduced to slender spines with linear leaves 6–11 mm long clustered at the base of the spines; flowers c. 9 mm across. This shrub occurs on the heavier soils of the Darling Range and extends northwards to heathlands around Kalbarri. The distinctions between this and the closely related inland species *M. trichocalyx* Domin. (with smaller leaves and more densely hairy calyx) are unclear.

Habitat: sandy heathland and clay-loam soils in Jarrah forest.

Dist: 16, 17, 21, 22, 23, 24.

178 **Gastrolobium ilicifolium** Meisner [syn. *Nemcia ilicifolia* (Meisner) Crisp]

Erect shrub to 2 m high; leaves 3.5–6.5 x 1.5–2.5 cm; flowers c. 6 mm across.

Habitat: stony hillsides.

Dist: 16, 17, 18, 23.

179 **Gastrolobium leakianum** J.Drummond [syn. *Nemcia leakiana* (Drummond) Crisp]

Mountain Pea

Erect, spindly few branched shrub to 1.5 m high: leaves 3–7 cm long; flowers 2–3 cm long.

Habitat: endemic on the upper rocky quartzite slopes of the Stirling Range.

Dist: 21.

180 **Gastrolobium retusum** Lindley [syn. *Nemcia retusa* (Lindley) Domin]

Spreading shrub to 1 m high; leaves 10–33 x 4–9 mm, faintly and finely reticulate; flowers c. 10 mm across.

Habitat: sand or gravel in kwongan and Jarrah forest.

Dist: 17, 18, 19, 21, 23.

Pultenaea is a large endemic genus of shrubs with over 100 species, widespread in all states except the NT. About 29 species occur in south-western WA. The leaves are usually stipulate and alternate; two bracteoles are present on, or below, the calyx.

181 *Pultenaea barbata* C.R.P.Andrews
Shrub to 1 m high; leaves c. 15 mm long, without stipules; flowers 8–10 mm across; tip of style bearded. The absence of stipules and the bearded style are characters not usually found in *Pultenaea*.
Habitat: heath swamp on sandy soil.
Dist: 19.

182 *Pultenaea ericifolia* Bentham var. ***ericifolia***
Erect or straggling shrub to 1 m high; leaves almost terete, channelled above, 6–12 mm long, flowers in dense heads c. 2 cm across.
Habitat: winter-wet depressions in kwongan and Jarrah forest.
Dist: 17, 18, 19, 20.

182 *Pultenaea ericifolia* var. *ericifolia*

Sphaerolobium is a small genus of about 14 species, all but two endemic in south-west WA. They are mostly slender, almost leafless shrubs with elongated racemes of small flowers. The small, globular pods are distinctive.

183 *Sphaerolobium drummondii* Turczaninov
Sparsely stemmed shrub 0.2–1 m high; usually leafless at flowering; calyx, and leaves when present, with distinct black spots; flowers 7–14 mm across in colours varying from reds and pinks to pale yellow or cream.
Habitat: very diverse, including dry sands, swamp margins and woodland.
Dist: 16, 17, 18, 22, 23, 24.

184 *Sphaerolobium alatum* Bentham
Slender, open shrub to 1 m high; stems flattened and winged, usually leafless; flowers 5–7 mm across.
Habitat: heath swamp and Jarrah forest.
Dist: 19, 20, 21, 22, 23.

183 *Sphaerolobium drummondii*

Swainsona is a genus of 84 endemic species plus one in New Zealand; leaves are pinnate and most species have rather small purple, bluish or occasionally orange or red flowers in leafless axillary racemes. In WA the genus is uncommon in the higher rainfall areas of the south-west, but after good rains colourful displays can be seen on roadsides through semi-arid and arid areas. In the spring, travellers can usually see *S. formosa* and one or two of the smaller purple-flowered species on road verges in the eastern goldfields and along the Eyre Highway.

184 *Sphaerolobium alatum*

186 *Templetonia retusa*

185 *Swainsona formosa*

185 **Swainsona formosa** (G.Don) J.Thompson [syn. *Clianthus formosus* (G.Don) Ford and Vickery] Sturt's Desert Pea
Prostrate annual or short-lived perennial; leaves 10–15 cm long, leaflets about 15; flowers 5–6 cm long in racemes of 2–6 flowers. This plant is one of the state's most spectacular flowers and was first collected on a north-west island by William Dampier in 1699. It flowers profusely in inland areas after rain, often covering large areas.
Habitat: red sandy or loamy soils in open sites or Mulga woodland.
Dist: 5,10, 11, 12, 13, 14, 15, 23, 24; also NT, SA, Qld, NSW. Transfer of this species to a new genus *Willdampia* has been proposed.

Templetonia is an endemic genus of c. 12 species, 9 of which occur in WA. The large red or salmon flowers of *T. retusa* are unique; the remaining species have smaller, inconspicuous yellow and brown or purplish flowers. Pods are more than twice as long as broad and leathery in appearance.

186 **Templetonia retusa** (Ventenat) R.Brown
Cockies' Tongues
A much-branched, usually dense shrub 0.3–4 m high; leaves 15–52 mm long; flowers 2–3 cm long. A very showy plant when in flower.
Habitat: coastal sand and limestone in shrubland, occasionally in laterite in woodland.
Dist: 11, 16, 17, 19, 20, 21, 24; also SA.

Urodon contains two species endemic in WA; they were previously included in *Pultenaea* but lack the stipules typical of most *Pultenaea* species.

187 **Urodon dasyphyllus** Turczaninow
Spreading usually prostrate shrub; leaves 5–8 mm long, very hairy to almost glabrous, occasionally recurved from stem; flowers c. 10 mm across in tight heads 3–4 cm across.
Habitat: shrubland or mallee in sandy or gravelly soil.
Dist: 16, 22, 23, 24.

GERANIACEAE

The Geraniaceae is a world-wide family of herbs and shrubs with species occurring throughout temperate Australia. The long beaked fruits are distinctive and split on maturity, often elastically, to forcefully release the seeds. The geraniums of horticulture are various species or hybrids of *Pelargonium*. *Pelargonium asper* is cultivated as a source of oil for perfumes. Australian species of *Geranium* are generally inconspicuous with small pale pink or pale mauve flowers; three native species occur in Western Australia. Four native species of *Pelargonium* occur in Western Australia but only *P. littorale* is widespread.

188 ***Pelargonium littorale*** Huegel
Erect or semi-prostrate herb, usually softly hairy; leaves broadly ovate, 1.5–5.5 x 2–8 cm, margins slightly lobed and crenate; flowers 12–15 mm across in umbels.
Habitat: sand, lateritic gravel or sandy loam in coastal woodland and Jarrah forest.
Dist: 17, 18, 19, 20, 21, 24; also SA, Vic.

GOODENIACEAE

The Goodeniaceae is a family of c. 410 species of mainly shrubs and herbs and is almost entirely Australian with a few species extending to New Guinea, Java, southern Asia, New Zealand and Chile; a few littoral species occur in South Africa and the Carribean. In Australia members of the family are found in most habitats except rainforest. The flowers are easily distinguished by the cup at the top of the style into which the pollen is deposited before the flower opens. Some species have been brought into cultivation in Australia, particularly *Lechenaultia* and *Dampiera*. Several species of *Goodenia* contain bitter principles and *Goodenia ovata* is recorded as having been used by the Aborigines as a soporific for children but apparently no investigation of possible medicinal properties has been made. The fruits of *Scaevola spinescens* were prized as food by the Aborigines of the Flinders Ranges.

Anthotium R.Brown, from the Greek *anthos* (flower) and *otus* (ear), referring to the auriculate shape of the wings of the inner petals, is a genus of three species of small herbs endemic in south-western WA.

189 ***Anthotium rubriflorum*** F.Mueller ex Bentham
Red Anthotium
Tufted perennial herb to 15 cm high; leaves fleshy, lanceolate to spathulate, 4.5–8 x 3–6 mm; flowers 8–10 mm long in heads 2–3.5 cm across.
Habitat: sand or gravelly soil in kwongan.
Dist: 21, 22, 23.

Coopernookia, named after the Coopernook State Forest in NSW. where one species is common; a small genus of six species all endemic in Australia with three confined to WA formerly included in *Goodenia*. The genus differs from *Goodenia* in having obloid, wingless seeds with a distinct caruncle which is rich in oil and attractive to ants, hence assisting in seed dispersal. The corolla is white, pink or mauve.

187 *Urodon dasyphyllus*

188 *Pelargonium littorale*

189 *Anthotium rubriflorum*

190 *Coopernookia polygalacea*

191 *Coopernookia strophiolata*

192 *Dampiera altissima*

190 ***Coopernookia polygalacea*** (de Vriese) Carolin
Small shrub 40–80 cm high; leaves 12–30 mm long,
underside densely covered with stellate hairs; flow-
ers up to 15 mm long.
Habitat: sandy kwongan.
Dist: 21.

191 ***Coopernookia strophiolata*** (F.Mueller) Carolin
Spreading viscid shrub to 1 m tall, leaves dentate,
10–35 mm long and with a few stellate hairs; co-
rolla 10–12 cm across.
Habitat: in sand or clay, in kwongan or shrubland.
Dist: 21, 22, 24; also SA.

Dampiera R.Brown, named for William Dampier
(1652–1715), English navigator, buccaneer and naturalist,
who collected plants in north-western Australia; a genus
of about 90 species of sub-shrubs and perennial herbs
endemic in Australia, about 60 of which are confined to
south-western WA. Almost all species have distinctive
branched hairs.

192 ***Dampiera altissima*** F.Mueller ex Bentham
Soft, multi-stemmed shrub to 1 m high; leaves to
5 cm long, undersurface grey-tomentose; flowers c.
1.5 cm wide.
Habitat: gravelly lateritic or calcareous sand.
Dist: 16, 17.

193 ***Dampiera eriocephala*** de Vriese
Woolly-headed Dampiera
Erect perennial herb to 40 cm tall; leaves to 15 cm
long, densely grey-white woolly below and forming a basal rosette; flowers to 1.5 cm wide borne in
dense terminal heads; very similar to *D. wellsiana*
which has glabrous leaves.
Habitat: sandy soil in kwongan and mallee
shrubland.
Dist: 21, 22, 23, 24.

193 *Dampiera eriocephala*

194 *Dampiera hederacea*

194 *Dampiera hederacea* R.Brown
Karri Dampiera
Spreading to decumbent or scrambling perennial;
stems to 40 cm long; leaves 9–40 x 3–30 mm; co-
rolla 7–10 mm long.
Habitat: sand or clay loam in moist forest, particu-
larly Karri.
Dist: 17, 18, 19, 20.

195 *Dampiera lindleyi* de Vriese
Perennial herb 0.3–0.6 m high with many stems
arising from the base; leaves narrowly linear, to c.
15 mm long but often absent; flowers c. 1 cm across.
Habitat: gravelly sand and often on rocky hillsides.
Dist: 16, 17, 21, 22, 23.

195 *Dampiera lindleyi*

196 *Dampiera wellsiana* F.Mueller
Wells' Dampiera
Suckering herb 10–20 cm high, often forming large
floriferous patches 1–2 m across; flowers 7–9 mm
long, clustered in dense terminal heads.
Habitat: gravel, sandy loam and lateritic soil in
kwongan and woodland.
Dist: 15, 22, 23, 24.

Diaspasis is a monotypic genus similar to *Dampiera*
but differing in having simple hairs and a corolla without auricles.

196 *Dampiera wellsiana*

197 *Diaspasis filifolia* R.Brown
Many-stemmed perennial to 30 cm tall; leaves linear, sometimes dentate, to 4 cm x 2 mm; flowers
white, pink or, rarely, pale yellowish, petals to
c. 14 mm long.
Habitat: bogs and seasonally wet areas, mainly between Busselton and Cape Riche and near
Esperance.
Dist: 19, 20, 21.

Goodenia Smith, named after Samuel Goodenough
(1743-1827), Archbishop of Carlisle and a well-known
member of the Linnean Society; a large genus of herbs
and low shrubs, mostly endemic; corolla blue, white, pink
or yellow; ovary, with one exception, inferior; fruit usually
capsular with flattened, winged seeds.

197 *Diaspasis filifolia*

198 *Goodenia affinis* de Vriese
Silver Goodenia
Perennial herb, decumbent or ascending, stems to 50
cm long, often spreading to form mats; leaves 2–4 cm
long, both surfaces hairy; flowers 12–18 mm across.
Habitat: mallee woodland in sand or gravelly sand.
Dist: 11, 16, 21, 22, 23, 24; also SA.

198 *Goodenia affinis*

199 *Goodenia berardiana*

200 *Goodenia coerulea*

199 ***Goodenia berardiana*** (Gaudichaud) Carolin
Annual herb with stems to 40 cm long, size and habit variable, may be erect or prostrate with size dependent on seasonal conditions; leaves 2–16 cm long, variable in shape from linear to obovate, pinnatifid to dentate; flowers 6–15 mm long.
Habitat: sandy soil in inland kwongan or coastal among sandstone.
Dist: 4, 14, 15, 16, 22, 23, 24; also NT, SA, Qld.

200 ***Goodenia coerulea*** R.Brown
A rather rigid perennial herb forming a tangled, usually erect clump; leaves mainly basal, 3–7 cm long; flowers 15–25 mm long.
Habitat: various, in sand and clay loam soil.
Dist: 16, 17, 18, 19, 20, 21, 22, 23.

201 ***Goodenia dyeri*** K.Krause
Herb to 20 cm tall; leaves 3–5 cm long, crowded in a basal rosette; flowers 12–14 mm long.
Habitat: acacia or mallee woodland in red clay loam.
Dist: 15, 23, 24.

202 ***Goodenia pterygosperma*** R.Brown
Erect perennial to 40 cm tall; basal leaves 2–5 cm x 3–8 mm but leaves often withered at flowering time; flowers 12–14 mm long.
Habitat: sandy soil in kwongan and open woodland, between Jerramungup and Israelite Bay.
Dist: 21, 22.

203 ***Goodenia pterigosperma*** R.Brown
White Goodenia
Erect perennial to 1 m tall, leaves variable, entire or serrate, 4–6 cm x 2–10 mm; flowers 8–18 mm long.
Habitat: woodland or kwongan in sandy loam.
Dist: 17, 19, 21, 22, 23.

201 *Goodenia dyeri*

202 *Goodenia pterigosperma*

204 *Goodenia varia* R.Brown

Prostrate, spreading shrub to 20 cm high and 1.5m wide; leaves 2–4 x 2–4.5 cm, often held erect relative to the prostrate stem.

Habitat: coastal cliffs and dunes in alkaline sand or among limestone rocks.

Dist: 24; also NSW, SA, Vic.

This is a very variable species whose distribution extends from the far east of southern WA through SA to western Victoria; it is often upright with narrow toothed leaves up to 4 cm long.

Lechenaultia R.Brown, named after Jean-Baptiste Leschenault de la Tour, botanist with Nicholas Baudin's expedition to Australia (1800–1804); a genus of 26 species of perennial herbs or small shrubs all occurring in Australia with one extending to New Guinea; 20 species endemic in south-western WA.

205 *Lechenaultia formosa* R.Brown

Red Leschenaultia

Perennial herb; prostrate and mat-forming or erect to about 50 cm high; leaves terete, 2–10 mm long; flowers 15–21 mm long, colour varies from pink to orange or bright red.

Habitat: kwongan, scrub, mallee and woodland in a wide variety of soils.

Dist: 11, 16, 21, 22, 23, 24.

206 *Lechenaultia hirsuta* F.Mueller

Hairy Leschenaultia

Perennial hirsute herb with trailing, semi-prostrate branches; leaves linear, 1–3 cm long; flowers 29–36 mm long.

Habitat: kwongan.

Dist: 16.

203 *Goodenia scapigera*

204 *Goodenia varia*

205 *Lechenaultia formosa*

206 *Lechenaultia hirsuta*

207 *Lechenaultia linarioides*

209 *Lechenaultia superba*

210 *Lechenaultia tubiflora*

207 *Lechenaultia linarioides* A.P.de Candolle
Yellow Leschenaultia
A rather tangled, sprawling shrub to 1m high.
Habitat: widespread in sand, sometimes over limestone, in coastal areas and inland.
Dist: 14, 16, 17, 18.

208 *Lechenaultia macrantha* K.Krause
Wreath Leschenaultia
Prostrate shrub with spreading branches usually forming a wreath-like mat; leaves linear, 2–4 cm long; flowers to c. 3.5 cm across, pale yellow with pink or red shading, deepening with age.
Habitat: gravelly soil in open shrubland.
Dist: 15, 16, 23.

209 *Lechenaultia superba* F.Mueller
Barrens Leschenaultia
Erect shrub to c. 70 cm high; leaves 11–22.5 mm long, crowded, fleshy; flowers 17–23 mm long, yellow suffused with orange or red, sometimes completely red.
Habitat: open scrub on rocky quartzite hillsides.
Dist: 21.

208 *Lechenaultia macrantha*

210 **Lechenaultia tubiflora** R.Brown
Heath Leschenaultia
Usually a spreading cushion-like plant, also erect
to 70 cm high; flowers 13–17 mm long, colour can
be pure white or red, or various combinations of
both.
Habitat: sandy kwongan.
Dist: 16, 17, 18, 19, 21, 23.

Pentaptilon E.Pritzel, from Greek *penta* (five) and *ptilon*
(wing), referring to the five-winged fruit, is a monotypic
genus restricted to WA. The flowers are superficially similar to *Goodenia* but the species is easily distinguished by
the swollen wings on the ovary and fruit.

211 *Pentaptilon careyi*   212 *Scaevola calliptera*

211 **Pentaptilon careyi** (F.Mueller) E.Pritzel
Herb to 45 cm tall with a basal rosette of silvery-
hairy leaves 3–7 cm long; flowers with petals
7–9 mm long with glandular hairs on the outside
and a dense tuft of white hairs in the throat.
Habitat: sandy kwongan.
Dist: 16.

Scaevola Linnaeus, from Latin *scaevola* (left-handed),
scaevus (left), referring to the five corolla lobes all on one
side of the axis, or alternatively possibly referring to the
dried flower's appearance like a withered hand. The genus contains about 96 species in Australia and tropical
areas of the Indo-Pacific region; 71 species occur in Australia, 70 of which are endemic.

212 **Scaevola calliptera** Bentham
Royal Robe
Erect herb to 40 cm tall with glandular hairs and
long or short simple hairs; leaves 2–6 cm long; flow-
ers 17–30 mm long.
Habitat: forest, woodland and kwongan from
Bullsbrook to the south coast.
Dist: 17, 19, 20.

213 **Scaevola crassifolia** Labillardière
Thick-leaved Fanflower
Spreading shrub to 1.5 m high; young growth vis-
cid; leaves ovate to orbicular, up to 8 cm long; flow-
ers 8–11 mm across in spikes up to 6 cm long.
Habitat: coastal sand dunes and limestone.
Dist: 11, 14, 16, 17, 19, 21, 24; also SA.

213 *Scaevola crassifolia*

215 *Scaevola phlebopetala*

217 *Scaevola porocarya*

214 *Scaevola lanceolata*

214 **Scaevola lanceolata** Bentham
Erect or decumbent many-stemmed perennial to 50 cm tall; leaves 6–10 cm long, mostly at base of stems; flowers in spikes to 10 cm long; corolla c. 3 cm across.
Habitat: sand and gravelly sand in kwongan and shrubland.
Dist: 16, 17, 18, 23.

215 **Scaevola phlebopetala** F.Mueller
Velvet Fanflower
Prostrate, spreading herb with stems to 50 cm long; leaves to 10 cm long, cuneate to linear, usually toothed; flowers 3–4 cm across, blue to deep violet, very showy.
Habitat: sandy kwongan.
Dist: 16, 17, 18, 19, 21, 22.

216 **Scaevola pilosa** Bentham
Hairy Fanflower
Ascending to decumbent herb to 70 cm high; lower leaves to 7.5 cm long; upper leaves smaller; flowers to 4 cm across.
Habitat: sandy soil in kwongan, shrubland and Jarrah forest.
Dist: 17, 18, 19, 20.

217 **Scaevola porocarya** F.Mueller
Weak, ascending, often tangled shrub to 1.8 m tall; leaves to 12 cm long, linear or oblanceolate; flowers to 2.5 cm across in loose spikes.
Habitat: red sandy clay or rocky soil in shrubland.
Dist: 14, 16.

216 Scaevola pilosa

218 *Scaevola pulvinaris* (E.Pritzel) K.Krause
Cushion Fanflower
Prostrate, mat-forming shrub; leaves linear, thick,
to 4 cm long; flowers to 11 mm across.
Habitat: sandy soil in kwongan or mallee wood-
land.
Dist: 21, 22, 23.

219 *Scaevola sericophylla* F.Mueller ex Bentham
Spreading shrub to 1.5 m tall; leaves 12–45 mm
long, silky hairy; flowers 10–19 mm long, silky hairy
outside, bearded inside.
Habitat: sandy kwongan and sand dunes, usually
coastal.
Dist: 12, 13, 14, 16.

218 *Scaevola pulvinaris*

220 *Scaevola striata* R.Brown var. *arenaria*
E. Pritzel
Ascending to prostrate herb to 20 cm high; stems
with a mixture of long stiff hairs, minute simple
hairs and some glandular hairs; leaves 1–4 cm
long; flowers 13–27 mm long.
Habitat: kwongan or shrubland in sandy soil approximately between the Stirling Range and Lake
Grace area.
Dist: 21, 22, 23.
The var. *striata* (Royal Robe) differs in having appressed hairs and occurs along the southern coast
between West Mt Barren and Denmark in moister
more sheltered habitats.

219 *Scaevola sericophylla*

Velleia Smith, named after Thomas Velley, an algologist
and friend of James Smith. The genus contains 21 species of which 20 are endemic in Australia with 12 in
WA. The flowers are similar to some species of *Goodenia*
but have a superior ovary.

221 *Velleia macrophylla* (Lindley) Bentham
Large-leaved Velleia
Glabrous perennial; stems to 1.1 m high; leaves
cauline 5–20 x 0.5–8 cm, mainly clustered towards
base of stems; flowers to 2 cm long.
Habitat: moist loam in Jarrah or Karri forest.
Dist: 20.

220 *Scaevola striata* var. *arenaria*

221 *Velleia macrophylla*

222(a) *Velleia rosea*

222 *Velleia rosea* S.Moore
Pink Velleia
Annual herb; leaves basal, coarsely toothed, 3–7 x
0.5–2 cm; flowering stems erect or prostrate 10–30
cm long; flowers to 15 mm long, pink, mauve or
white. Often seen carpeting large areas after seasonal rain.
Habitat: sandy or loamy soil in open woodland or
shrubland.
Dist: 13, 15, 16, 23, 24.

223 *Verreauxia reinwardtii*

Verreauxia Bentham, named for the French naturalist Jules
Verreaux who collected plants in Australia during the late
1840s. Herbs or shrubs with one to a few erect stems and a
loose, spike-like inflorescence; a genus of three species endemic in south-western WA, related to *Pentaptilon* but
having a hairy indehiscent nut-like fruit.

223 *Verreauxia reinwardtii* (de Vriese) Bentham
Common Verreauxia
Erect, few-stemmed shrub to 1 m tall; leaves
5–7 cm long, cauline but with several close together
at the base of stem; flowers 8–10 mm long in an
interrupted spike.
Habitat: sandy soil in kwongan and open woodland.
Dist: 16, 17, 18, 22, 23, 24.

222(b) *Velleia rosea*

GYROSTEMONACEAE

An endemic Australian family of four genera and about 17 species, either dioecious or monoecious and with flowers lacking a conspicuous corolla. Most species are fire-opportunists or plants of disturbed areas in dry habitats of the coast or inland.

224 *Gyrostemon racemiger* H.Walter

Pyramidal dioecious shrub or small, single-stemmed tree; makes rapid growth following fire. Flowering spikes from separate plants are depicted here, female flowers on the right in plate 224(b).
Habitat: in sand or gravel in shrubland.
Dist: 16, 17, 22, 23, 24.

224(a) and (b) *Gyrostemon racemiger*

225 *Gyrostemon ramulosus* Desfontaines

Camel Poison

Shrub, or small tree to 5 m; trunk stout with corky bark, leaves terete, 2–9 cm long, usually forming a bushy crown. Male and female flowers are borne on separate plants. Depicted here is the female plant with semi-mature fruits. The apparent flower is formed by a ring of styles which whither and fall as the fruit matures. The genus is endemic in Australia with 11 of the 12 species occurring in WA.
Habitat: coastal dunes, sandy rises and desert dunes in shrubland and low woodland.
Dist: 6, 8, 9, 10, 13, 14, 15, 16, 17, 18, 23, 24; also NT and SA.

225 *Gyrostemon ramulosus*

226 *Tersonia cyathiflora* (Fenzl) A.S.George

Button Creeper

Prostrate, dioecious herb with stems to 2m long; flowers of the female plant consist of a cluster of stigmas surrounded by a small calyx. The hard, rough fruit [plate 226(b)] is at first orange-brown, c. 1–1.5 cm across. Plate 226(a) shows male flowers.
Habitat: sand, often over limestone, in kwongan and low, open woodland.
Dist: 16, 17.

226(b) *Tersonia cyathiflora*

226(a) *Tersonia cyathiflora*

227 *Anigozanthos bicolor* subsp. *bicolor*

HAEMODORACEAE

This is a family of perennial rhizomatous herbs which, although not endemic in Australia, reaches its peak of diversity in south-western Western Australia where seven genera with about 70 species occur. Of these, the best known are probably the Kangaroo Paws (*Anigozanthos*), many of which are widely cultivated and valued as bird-pollinated ornamentals.

227 **_Anigozanthos bicolor_** Endlicher subsp. **_bicolor_**

Perennial plant forming clumps, flowering stems 20–60 cm tall; leaves 10–35 cm long; perianth 45–65 mm long and slightly constricted above the middle; hybridises freely with *A. manglesii* and *A. viridis*, occasionally with *A. humilis* and rarely with *A. flavidus*.

Habitat: in winter-wet clay of the Darling Range north and south of Perth, in open areas among woodland.

Dist: 17, 18, 23.

Subsp. *extans* Hopper with shorter stems and elongated perianths is found in the Meckering–Pingelly area.

Subsp. *decrescens* Hopper has red-purple hairs on stems and flowers and extends from Williams to Nannup.

Subsp. *minor* Hopper is a rare dwarf plant up to 20 cm tall confined to the Ravensthorpe–Hopetoun area.

A. bicolor and its subspecies constitute the most variable group in the genus.

228 **_Anigozanthos humilis_** Lindley

Common Catspaw

This is the most widespread species of *Anigozanthos*. Flowering stems rarely exceed 30 cm high and the yellow flowers are variously suffused with red or orange. It flowers profusely in the first spring after fire, often making a spectacular display, together with various terrestrial orchids.

Habitat: well-drained sand over laterite or limestone in kwongan, mallee, low woodland, and occasionally forest.

Dist: 16, 17, 18, 19, 20, 21, 22, 23.

229 **_Anigozanthos kalbarriensis_** Hopper

A perennial herb 10–20 cm, usually in clumps; similar in habit to *A. humilis*, but differs in having a distinctly two-coloured perianth with reflexed lobes; flowers abundantly after fire.

Habitat: sandy depressions and winter-wet slopes, in kwongan.

Dist: 16.

228 *Anigozanthos humilis*

229 *Anigozanthos kalbarriensis*

230 **Anigozanthos manglesii** D.Don subsp. **manglesii**
Mangles' Kangaroo Paw
Perennial plant with short underground stem and
strap-like leaves 10–40 cm long; flowering stem usually unbranched and overtopping the leaves; flowers 6–l0 cm long. This is WA's floral emblem and is
very common throughout its range, which extends
from Gingin south to Scott River and Mt Barker.
Habitat: very diverse, including sand and gravel soil
on plains, coastal limestone hills and Darling Plateau; in kwongan, woodland and forest.
Dist: 16, 17, 18, 19, 20.

233 *Anigozanthos rufus*

231 **Anigozanthos manglesii** D.Don subsp. **quadrans**
Hopper
This subspecies is distinguished by having a greater
proportion of the flower covered by orange-red hairs.
Habitat: kwongan, from Jurien Bay north to
Kalbarri and Shark Bay.
Dist: 16.

232 **Anigozanthos preissii** Endlicher
Albany Catspaw
Perennial herb; leaves 10–25 cm long; flowering
stem to 70 cm high, covered with reddish hairs; flow-
ers 5–6 cm long, more deeply lobed than any other
species. Restricted to about a 50 km radius of Albany
and near Walpole.
Habitat: low open woodland of *Eucalyptus staeri*
(Albany Blackbutt).
Dist: 19, 20.

230 *Anigozanthos manglesii* subsp. *manglesii*   232 *Anigozanthos preissii*

233 **Anigozanthos rufus** Labillardière
Red Kangaroo Paw
Perennial plant forming a clump of several branch-
ing stems 50–l00 cm tall; leaves flat, strap-like,
mainly basal; flowers 2–3 cm long.
Habitat: in deep sand in kwongan.
Dist: 19, 21, 24.

231 *Anigozanthos manglesii* subsp. *quadrans*

234 **Blancoa canescens** Lindley
Winter Bell
Dwarf, clump-forming rhizomatous herb; leaves
25 x 0.5 cm, covered with short silky hairs when
young, and having conspicuous parallel veins; flowers 25–35 mm long, adapted for bird pollination
and varying in colour from pink to brick red.
Habitat: deep sand in banksia woodland and
kwongan.
Dist: 16, 17.

234 *Blancoa canescens*

235 *Conostylis aculeata*

236 *Conostylis argentea*

237 *Conostylis aurea*

238 *Conostylis candicans*

235 **Conostylis aculeata** R.Brown subsp. **septentrionora** Hopper

A variable species with ten recognised subspecies, the one here depicted occurring within about 10 km of the coast between Kalbarri and Tamala. All subspecies are tufted or proliferous plants with flat leaves with rigid, ascending sharp bristles along the margin. Subspecies *septentrionora* has leaves 6–30 cm long and 2–4 mm wide; flowers are 6–10 mm long on stems usually longer than the leaves.
Habitat: sand over limestone.
Dist: 16.

236 **Conostylis argentea** (J.Green) Hopper

Plants forming clumps; leaves 7–25 cm long, flat with silvery hairs; perianth tube 2–3 cm long, lobes 12–20 mm long. This species is superficially similar to *C. androstemma* which has terete, glabrous leaves; together they form a distinctive group unusual for the long tubular perianth and elongated stamens. *C. argentea* ranges from near Ravensthorpe to about 100 km north-east of Southern Cross, the furthest inland of any *Conostylis*.
Habitat: sandy loam in mallee kwongan and (at inland localities) on rocky hills under scrub.
Dist: 15, 21, 22, 23, 24.

237 **Conostylis aurea** Lindley

Golden Conostylis

Tufted perennial to 40 cm high; leaves striate, usually with a row of small, appressed hairs along the margin; flowers 10–15 mm long, often ageing to dull red.
Habitat: sand or gravelly loam in kwongan, woodland and forest.
Dist: 16, 17, 18, 23.

238 **Conostylis candicans** Endlicher

Grey Cottonheads

Tufting perennial up to 25 cm high; leaves usually 20–40 cm long covered with dense, grey hairs; flowers 9–13 mm long. A variable species with several subspecies.
Habitat: sand, and sand over limestone in woodland and coastal heath.
Dist: 16, 17, 18, 23.

239 *Conostylis neocymosa* Hopper

Stilt-rooted perennial plant; leaves 10–25 cm long with closely spaced marginal bristles; flowering stem 5–15 cm long, shorter than the leaves; perianth tube 8–15 mm long, lobes 6–10 mm long.
Habitat: deep sand in kwongan and mallee.
Dist: 16, 23.

240 *Conostylis prolifera* Bentham

Mat Cottonheads

Low perennial often forming swards that consist of numerous small tufts connected by a network of wiry stolons; leaves 1–10 cm long, usually glabrous or with minutely hairy margins; flowers 7–13 mm long on stems equal to or exceeding the leaves. The flowers darken with age to green and golden brown.
Habitat: clay loam, often over laterite in kwongan, and on winter-damp flats in open woodland and scrub.
Dist: 16, 17, 23.

241 *Conostylis setigera* Lindley subsp. *setigera*

Bristly Cottonheads

Plants forming distinct tufts; leaves 6–30 cm long with soft, marginal spines; perianth tube 10–17 mm long; lobes 5–9 mm long; a widespread, very variable plant.
Habitat: very diverse from rich gravelly loam in forest to sand in woodland and kwongan.
Dist: 17, 18, 19, 20, 21, 22, 23.

Subsp. *dasys* differs in having long shaggy hairs on the leaf blade which age to black, it is uncommon and confined to the Kojunup area in Jarrah and Wandoo open woodland.

242 *Conostylis setosa* Lindley

White Cottonheads

Slender, tufted plant; flowering stems rarely more than 4; leaves 15–30 cm long with 2 or more ranks of long white hairs on each margin; flowers 12–20 mm long, white or pinkish maroon to purple.
Habitat: lateritic soil in Jarrah–Marri forest, restricted to the Darling Range between Bindoon and Dwellingup.
Dist: 17, 18.

239 *Conostylis neocymosa*

240 *Conostylis prolifera*

241 *Conostylis setigera* subsp. *setigera*

242 *Conostylis setosa*

243 *Haemodorum simplex*

244 *Macropidia fuliginosa*

245 *Phlebocarya ciliata*

246 *Tribonanthes australis*

243 ***Haemodorum simplex*** Lindley
Bloodroot
Bulbous-rooted rush-like plant to 65 cm high with one or two lax, grass-like basal leaves and up to four stem leaves diminishing in length upwards and grading into blackish bracts; inflorescence a dense head-like cluster of black or partly greenish, strongly fragrant flowers with narrow petals. The bulging tops of the three-celled ovary are a prominent part of the flower.
Habitat: winter wet clay or sand over clay.
Dist: 17, 18, 19, 20, 21, 23.

244 ***Macropidia fuliginosa*** (W. J. Hooker) Druce
Black Kangaroo Paw
Rhizomatous perennial, leaves in basal fans 20–50 cm long; flowering stem to 1.5m tall; flowers 5–6 cm long.
Habitat: in kwongan and woodland in lateritic soil.
Dist: 16, 17, 18.

245 ***Phlebocarya ciliata*** R.Brown
Tufted perennial herb forming large clumps superficially similar to some species of *Lomandra*; leaves flat, 25–65 cm long; inflorescence a panicle about one quarter as long to slightly longer than leaves, individual flowers c. 5 mm across.
Habitat: sandy soil in seasonally wet depressions or dry banksia woodland, occasionally in Jarrah forest.
Dist: 16, 17, 18, 19, 20, 21.

246 ***Tribonanthes australis*** Endlicher
Tuberous perennial; flowering stem 17–39 cm tall with two or three stem leaves; flowers to 2 cm across, covered with dense, felty hairs, sometimes sweetly scented.
Habitat: seasonally wet soil, especially round swamps.
Dist: 16, 17, 18, 19, 20, 22, 23.

HALORAGACEAE

The Haloragaceae is a large world wide family of herbs and shrubs, including a large number of aquatic species. In Australia the genus *Myriophyllum* is widespread in swamps and streams and *Haloragis* and *Haloragodendron* occur in dry habitats; all these genera have small, usually inconspicuous greenish or red flowers. Only the genus *Glischrocaryon*, of which there are three species in Western Australia, has colourful flowers. They are early colonisers of burnt or disturbed areas and often make extensive spectacularly colourful displays.

247 *Glischrocaryon flavescens*

247 ***Glischrocaryon flavescens*** (Drummond) Orchard
Robust herb with woody rootstock and annual stems
to 90 cm tall; leaves linear to narrowly lanceolate,
2–3 cm long; flowers 8–10 mm across, surmounting a narrowly winged ovary similar in colour. The
ovary enlarges and remains colourful long after the
flowers wither.
Habitat: diverse including gravel, clay-loam, sand
and near-coastal limestone areas.
Dist: 11, 14, 16, 17, 18, 21, 22, 23, 24; also SA.

248 ***Haloragodendron glandulosum*** Orchard
Glandular Raspwort
Erect, compact shrub to 1.5m high; stems four-angled with scattered red glands along margins of
wings; leaves to c. 1.5 cm long, the margins toothed
and with red glands; flowers c. 1 cm across surmounting four-winged, reddish fruits.
Habitat: southern shrublands in sandy or clay soil.
Dist: 21, 22, 24.

248 *Haloragodendron glandulosum*

249 *Orthrosanthus laxus*

250 *Orthrosanthus multiflorus*

251 *Patersonia occidentalis*

252 *Patersonia umbrosa* var. *xanthina*

IRIDACEAE

The Iridaceae is a large world-wide family of c. 1800 species of which 74 species occur in Australia. In many respects the family is similar to the Liliaceae but can be distinguished by the combination of three stamens and a usually inferior ovary. Many members of the family are widely used in horticulture. Fifteen native species occur in Western Australia with an additional 44 introduced species naturalised. Many of these latter have become troublesome weeds, particularly species of *Watsonia* and *Gladiolus*. The pink flowers of *G. caryophyllaceus* are a dominant feature in spring in disturbed or frequently burnt bushland between Yanchep and Fremantle. The species is native to, but now very rare, in south-western Cape Province of South Africa.

249 ***Orthrosanthus laxus*** (Endlicher) Bentham
Morning Iris
Plants forming dense, many-stemmed clumps; leaves grass-like 10–40 cm x 1–6 mm; flowers 2–3 cm across in spathes containing 1–4 pedunculate flowers; anther filaments free.
Habitat: a widespread species found on a variety of soils in kwongan, forest and woodland.
Dist: 16, 18, 19, 21, 23.

250 ***Orthrosanthus multiflorus*** Sweet
Many-flowered Orthrosanthus
Herb 30–60 cm tall; leaves 15–50 cm long; flowers 2–3 cm across; filaments of stamens united in the lower part; differs from *O. laxus* in having anther filaments partly united and spathes containing up to seven usually sessile flowers.
Habitat: shrubland in sandy soil from Stirling Range eastward.
Dist: 21; also SA.

Patersonia contains about 19 species of which 17 are endemic in Australia and all but five of these are endemic in WA; all are perennial herbs, usually forming rush-like clumps with linear leaves. The flowers are blue-violet or, rarely, white or yellow. The flower has three conspicuous spreading sepals with three very small, erect linear petals; the flowers live for only one day and tend to remain closed in overcast and cold weather.

251 ***Patersonia occidentalis*** R.Brown
Purple Flag
Tufted rush-like herb; leaves 8–55 cm long; flowers 3–4 cm across. A very widespread, variable species.
Habitat: shrubland and woodland, usually in poorly drained situations.
Dist: 16, 17, 18, 19, 20, 23; also SA, Vic and Tas.

252 **Patersonia umbrosa** Endlicher var. **xanthina** (Oldfield and F.Mueller ex F.Mueller) Domin
Yellow Flags
Tufted plant with linear leaves 30–90 cm long; flowers 4–5 cm across.
Habitat: lateritic soil in woodland and Jarrah forest from southern Darling Range to Deep River north of Walpole.
Dist: 17, 18, 19, 20.
Var. *umbrosa* has blue-violet flowers and a more easterly distribution from Deep River to the Stirling Range and Fitzgerald River.

253 *Hemiandra glabra*

LAMIACEAE

The Lamiaceae is a large, easily recognised family whose members often have square stems, opposite, aromatic leaves and two-lipped corollas. The family occurs throughout the world but is uncommon in rainforest. Many species are important culinary herbs including *Thymus* (thyme), *Mentha* (mint), *Rosmarinus* (rosemary), *Salvia* (sage), *Origanum* (marjoram). These and other genera are also widely grown as ornamental plants including *Phlomis*, *Nepeta*, *Stachys*, *Coleus*, *Plectranthus* and *Leonotis*. *Lavandula* (lavender) is widely cultivated for the perfume industry.

In Australia many species of *Prostanthera* and *Westringia* have been brought into cultivation.

253 **Hemiandra glabra** Bentham
Dense, rounded much-branched shrub 30–50 cm high; leaves 1–3 cm long; flowers 2–2.5 cm across. The plant illustrated is an undescribed subspecies; photographed between Eneabba and Three Springs.
Habitat: heathy woodland on sandy soil.
Dist: 16.

254 **Hemigenia brachyphylla** F.Mueller
Erect shrub 30–60 cm high; leaves terete, 6–10 mm long; flowers 10–12 mm long.
Habitat: sandy soil in shrubland.
Dist: 22.

254 *Hemigenia brachyphylla*

255 **Hemigenia diplanthera** F.Mueller
Shrub to 1 m high; leaves linear, to c. 1 cm long; flowers glabrous, c. 8–10 mm across; colour varies from purple to mauve.
Habitat: sand or gravel in shrubland.
Dist: 15, 16, 17, 23.

255 *Hemigenia diplanthera*

256 *Hemigenia macrantha*

258 *Microcorys eremophiloides*

257 *Hemigenia sericea*

259 *Microcorys obovata*

260 *Prostanthera eckersleyana*

261 *Prostanthera laricoides*

256 ***Hemigenia macrantha*** F.Mueller
Erect, bushy shrub to 1 m high; leaves and calyx densely covered with stellate hairs; leaves 1.5–3 cm long; flowers 3–4 cm long; colour varies from pink to red.
Habitat: in sand in kwongan.
Dist: 16.

257 ***Hemigenia sericea*** Bentham
Silky Hemigenia
Spreading to semi-prostrate shrub to 1 m high. A widespread and extremely variable species; leaves 2–4 cm long; flowers to 1.5 cm long.
Habitat: sand and lateritic gravel, common in Jarrah forest.
Dist: 17, 18, 19, 20, 21, 23.

258 ***Microcorys eremophiloides*** K.Kenneally
Shrub 0.5–2 m high with long willowy branches; leaves to 7 cm long; flowers 3–4 cm long. It is the largest-flowered species of the genus, with flowers twice as large as its closest relative *M. longifolia*, which occurs on the Darling Scarp.
Habitat: shallow soil over laterite, and restricted to the Wongan Hills area.
Dist: 23.

259 ***Microcorys obovata*** Bentham
Erect shrub 1–2 m high; leaves obovate, 6–9 mm long, glabrous when mature; flowers 15 mm long.
Habitat: mallee shrubland.
Dist: 23, 24.

260 ***Prostanthera eckersleyana*** F.Mueller
Crinkly Mintbush
Compact shrub to 1 m high; leaves 8–12 mm long, strongly aromatic; flowers c. 2.5 cm long.
Habitat: shrubland in red sand.
Dist: 23, 24.

261 ***Prostanthera laricoides*** Conn
Erect shrub to 1.5 m high; leaves narrow, linear, 1–2 cm long; flowers c. 2.5 cm long.
Habitat: sandy soil in open mallee or acacia woodland, often near granite outcrops.
Dist: 10, 14.

262 **Prostanthera serpyllifolia** (R.Brown) Briquet subsp. **microphylla** (R.Brown) Conn
Small-leaf Mintbush
Rigid, usually compact bushy shrub to 1 m high; leaves ovate, to 3 mm long; flowers 12–17 mm long; colour varies from bright pink to mid-red, often white basally or with a yellow tinge, or light metallic blue-green.
Habitat: associated with mallees, in sandy soil over limestone.
Dist: 11, 18, 21, 22, 23, 24.
Subsp. *serpyllifolia* has slightly larger leaves and is not known to occur in WA.

263 **Westringia rigida** R.Brown
Stiff Westringia
Rigid, low, divaricate shrub to 60 cm high; leaves 2–7 mm long; flowers 6–7 mm long; a highly variable species and difficult to distinguish from *W. dampieri* which occurs on coastal limestone and dunes and usually has longer leaves and flowers.
Habitat: mallee shrubland or eucalypt woodland in sandy loam and clay soil.
Dist: 10, 11, 15, 18, 22; also SA, Qld, NSW, Vic, Tas.

LENTIBULARIACEAE bladderworts

The Lentibulariaceae is a cosmopolitan family of carnivorous herbs all adapted to obtaining nutrition by trapping small organisms. World-wide the family contains c. 280 species in three genera and all grow in wet habitats.

Utricularia, from Latin *utriculus* (a little bladder), is the only genus represented in Australia, with 28 species in WA; plants are either rooted in mud or free-floating with tiny bladders attached along the submerged or basal stems. The bladders are equipped with an intricate combination of valves and bristles that enable the trapping and ingestion of small organisms.

264 **Utricularia menziesii** R.Brown
Redcoats
Perennial herb; leaves 2–4 mm long; flowering stems 20–70 mm high; flowers 15–20 mm long.
Habitat: winter-wet depressions and swamps.
Dist: 16, 17, 18, 19, 20, 21.

262 *Prostanthera serpyllifolia* subsp. *microphylla*

263 *Westringia rigida*

264 *Utricularia menziesii*

265 *Utricularia multifida*

265 ***Utricularia multifida*** R.Brown [syn. *Polypompholyx multifida* (R.Brown) F.Mueller]
Pink Petticoats
Slender herb 8–23 cm high; leaves basal, narrowly spathulate, 6–11 mm long; lower lip of corolla 8–13 mm long.
Habitat: sandy soil in winter wet depressions between Mt Lesueur and the Porongurup Range.
Dist: 16, 17, 18, 19, 20, 21, 22.

LILIACEAE lilies

In a broad sense, the Liliaceae is a large, complex family of perennial herbs with corms, bulbs, tubers or rhizomes. World-wide the family contains c. 4000 species with c. 266 species in Australia, of which 202 are endemic. The family contains many species highly prized in horticulture, although very few Australian species are cultivated. The roots of many species were a valuable food source for the Aborigines.

266 ***Agrostocrinum scabrum*** (R.Brown) Baillon
Blue Grass Lily
Tufted herbaceous perennial to 1 m high; leaves 2–35 cm x 1.5–11 mm; flowers 2.5–4 cm across; perianth segments five-nerved.
Habitat: forest and swampy heath in laterite, sand and peaty sand.
Dist: 17, 18, 19, 20, 21, 22, 23.

267 ***Dichopodium preissii*** (Endlicher) Brittan [syn. *Arthropodium preissii* Endlicher]
Nodding Chocolate Lily
Slender plant to 50 cm tall with a few basal leaves to 25 cm long; inflorescence an open, branched panicle, with a single pendulous flower up to 2 cm across in the axil of each bract..
Habitat: sand or lateritic gravelly soil in woodland.
Dist: 15, 23, 24.

267 *Dichopodium preissii*

266 *Agrostocrinum scabrum*

268 *Borya constricta* Churchill

Dwarf, perennial tussock-forming plant to 25 mm high; leaves pungent, 8–20 x 0.6–1.2 mm; flower heads 4–l0 mm wide with 6–12 flowers. This species is widespread in south-western WA, east of a line from Wubin to Cape Riche and with a few populations near Perth.

Habitat: locally common around granite outcrops, sometimes with other *Borya* spp.

Dist: 15, 21, 22, 23, 24.

Plate 268(b) shows *Borya constricta* and *Cladia ferdinandii* (a coral lichen), growing under extremely harsh conditions on a granite outcrop in the semi-arid Norseman region; both are members of a diverse group known as 'resurrection plants' which become dessicated and appear to die in dry seasons but return to life after rain. Several mosses, liverworts and grasses also have this ability. Plants forming large circles [plate 268(c)] are occasionally found on granite outcrops.

268(a) *Borya constricta*

268(b) *Borya constricta*

268(c) *Borya constricta*

269 Borya laciniata

272 Laxmannia grandiflora subsp. grandiflora

270 Burchardia rosea

271 Johnsonia pubescens

269 *Borya laciniata* Churchill

Summer-deciduous herb forming prostrate mats to 3 cm high; leaves flexible, 6–20 mm long; flower heads 2.5–5.5 mm wide containing three to six flowers. Flowering stems and leaves are shed in late spring or early summer. Although the leaves are pungent, the plant is less harsh and prickly than the drought-tolerant species that retain their leaves through summer.

Habitat: acid soil in areas subject to flooding and tending to be brackish.

Dist: 16, 18, 22, 23.

270 *Burchardia rosea* Keighery

Perennial herb 20–50 cm high with fibrous roots; stem simple or with up to three branches; basal leaves four or five and also two or three leaf-like bracts up the stem; flowers 2–3 cm across. A species confined to the Kalbarri area and distinctive for its pink tepals.

Habitat: shallow soil over rock in seasonally wet depressions or along seepage lines.

Dist: 16.

271 *Johnsonia pubescens* Lindley

Pipe Lily

Tufted, finely hairy perennial herb; leaves 6–28 cm long; flowering stem shorter than leaves; flower spike to 5 cm long, erect, with many overlapping bracts, each enclosing a single white flower c. 5 mm long.

Habitat: sandy soil in kwongan or banksia woodland.

Dist: 16, 17.

272 *Laxmannia grandiflora* Lindley subsp. *grandiflora*

Tufted perennial; stems short, stout, covered with leaf sheaths or remains of old ones; flower heads 10–26 mm across surrounded by brown bracts and held erect on naked peduncles 7–14 cm long; individual flowers 6.5–9 mm long.

Habitat: lateritic sand or clay soil in woodland.

Dist: 18, 23.

Subsp. *stirlingensis* G.Keighery differs in having stilt roots and peduncles 12–22 cm long. It occurs in a small area south-east of the Stirling Range in winter wet depressions.

273 *Sowerbaea laxiflora* Lindley

Purple Tassels

Tufted, herbaceous, perennial; leaves linear 10–30 cm long, flowering stem 10–70 cm long; flower clusters 1.5–4.0 cm wide containing more than 30 flowers.

Habitat: in sand in near-coastal woodland and shrubland or in clay soil in woodland of the Darling Plateau.

Dist: 16, 17, 18, 19.

274 **Stypandra glauca** R.Brown
Blind Grass
Tufted grass-like plant in clumps of a few stems or up to 1 m across at base and up to 1.5 m high; leaves distributed along stems with sheathing bases and blades 4–20 cm long; flowers 2–3 cm across, pale to deep blue or occasionally white. A highly variable, widespread species. In WA many forms are toxic to livestock and can cause blindness in sheep.
Habitat: lateritic or clay soil in woodland, on granite rocks and coastal limestone.
Dist: 15, 16, 17, 18, 19, 20, 21, 22, 23, 24; also SA, Qld, NSW and Vic.

Thysanotus (fringed lilies), a genus of perennial herbs with fibrous or tuberous roots. The lax, linear leaves are annual and in some species are withered at flowering time. The flowers have narrow, linear sepals and much broader elliptic petals with fringed margins. The genus contains 49 species of which all but three are confined to Australia, with the south-west of WA being particularly rich in species. Each flower lasts only one day and is usually closed by early afternoon.

275 **Thysanotus dichotomus** (Labillardière) R.Brown
Branching Fringe Lily
Plant with several dichotomously branching stems to 40 cm long, often forming a loose mound; leaves basal, linear 8–14 cm long, 5–10 per plant, usually withered before flowering time; flowers 2–3 cm across, in small umbels at tips of branches.
Habitat: sand or lateritic gravel, very widespread.
Dist: 16, 17, 18, 19, 20, 21, 22, 23, 24.

273 *Sowerbaea laxiflora*

275 *Thysanotus dichotomus*

274 *Stypandra glauca*

276 Thysanotus multiflorus

278 Thysanotus pyramidalis

277 Thysanotus patersonii

279 Thysanotus sparteus

280 Tricoryne elatior

276 **Thysanotus multiflorus** R.Brown
Many-flowered Fringe Lily
Tufted perennial herb with a fibrous rootstock; leaves basal, glabrous, usually 20–30 cm long; inflorescence a terminal umbel of up to 60 flowers, each 10–30 mm across; only one or two flowers in each umbel are open at the same time.
Habitat: in sand in coastal banksia forest and lateritic soil in Jarrah forest.
Dist: 17, 18, 19, 20, 21.

277 **Thysanotus patersonii** R.Brown
Twining Fringe Lily
Twining perennial, usually single-stemmed plant with tubers; stem to 1 m long, usually much-branched, prostrate or twining through adjacent shrubs; flowers c. 2 cm across.
Habitat: very diverse; the commonest and most widespread species in the genus.
Dist: 10, 13, 14, 15, 16, 17, 18, 19, 20, 21, 22, 23, 24; also all states.

278 **Thysanotus pyramidalis** Brittan
Tuberous perennial;, leaves linear, flat, 12–16 cm long, withering near flowering time; inflorescence a distinctively shaped pyramidal panicle 18–30 cm long; flowers c. 2 cm across.
Habitat: kwongan.
Dist: 16.

279 **Thysanotus sparteus** R.Brown
Rhizomatous perennial to 1 m tall without leaves; flowers 2–3.5 cm across; a wide-ranging species from Kalbarri to Israelite Bay including the Wheatbelt.
Habitat: Jarrah–Marri woodland in lateritic or loamy soil, also in sand in banksia woodland and in mallee sandplain areas.
Dist: 16, 17, 18, 19, 20, 21, 22, 23.

280 **Tricoryne elatior** R.Brown
Yellow Autumn Lily
Rhizomatous perennial, usually tall and twiggy; stems to 50 cm long with long internodes; leaves to 90 mm long but stem leaves shorter and often reduced to small brown scales; outer umbel bracts 3–10 mm long, usually much shorter than the flowers.
Habitat: common in sandy soil of the coastal plain, also in lateritic soil of the Darling Range.
Dist: 1, 10, 16, 17, 18, 19, 20, 21, 23; also NT, SA, Qld, NSW, Vic and Tas.

281 *Tricoryne humilis* Endlicher

Rhizomatous perennial; stems 4.5–26 cm long; leaves 35–130 x 4–5 mm, conspicuous and green; inflorescence an umbel subtended by leafy green bracts 12–35 mm long and usually longer than the flowers; perianth 10–20 mm across.

Habitat: lateritic gravel and sand, often swampy; from Perth to the Stirling Range and south coast. Dist: 17, 18, 19, 20, 21.

LOGANIACEAE

The Loganiaceae is a diverse family occurring mainly in the tropics with a few genera in warm temperate areas of the world. A number of genera including *Buddleja* and *Gelsemium* are cultivated as ornamentals, and two species of *Strychnos* are cultivated for their seeds from which are obtained the alkaloids strychnine and brucine.

In Australia most species belong to the genera *Logania* and *Mitrasacme*. Members of the family have simple, opposite leaves that are distinctive in being joined at the base by a sheath or stipule that is occasionally reduced to a stipular membrane.

282 *Logania callosa* F.Mueller

Dwarf shrub 15–20 cm high; stems usually ascending but often becoming prostrate when flowering; leaves 6–20 x 1–2 mm; flowers 7–10 mm across, usually white or occasionally pale yellow.

Habitat: sandy soil in kwongan or shrubland. Dist: 21.

283 *Logania flaviflora* F.Mueller

Yellow Logania

Dwarf shrub to 20 cm high, occasionally prostrate; leaves hairy, 5–10 mm long; flowers 10–15 mm across; a very showy species often forming large colonies.

Habitat: shrubland or kwongan in sandy soil. Dist: 16, 17, 23, 24.

284 *Logania tortuosa* D.A.Herbert

Dwarf shrub to 30 cm high; stems rush-like, twisted and curled; leaves reduced to small scales; flowers c. 8–15 mm across.

Habitat: kwongan or shrubland in sandy soil. Dist: 22, 23, 24.

281 *Tricoryne humilis*

282 *Logania callosa*

283 *Logania flaviflora*

284 *Logania tortuosa*

285 *Amyema melaleucae*

286 *Nuytsia floribunda*

LORANTHACEAE   mistletoes

The Loranthaceae is a family of parasitic shrubs or, rarely, trees that grow attached to the branches of trees and shrubs, or in some cases such as *Nuytsia*, to roots. The family is widely distributed but most species are tropical. World-wide there are c. 900 species with c. 65 in Australia.

The leaves of most Australian mistletoes resemble those of their host making them inconspicuous when not in flower. The sticky layer around the seed is rich in glucose and is a major source of food for birds. The Mistletoe Bird is the main dispersal agent for the seed; it has a very short gut through which the seed passes rapidly with the sticky layer intact. When defecating, the bird's tail gives a characteristic twist which deposits the seed onto the branch on which it is perched. The seed's sticky layer cements it to the branch, where it germinates spontaneously. The traditional European mistletoe is *Viscum album* of the related family Viscaceae.

285 ***Amyema melaleucae*** (Miquel) Tieghem
Pendulous, glabrous parasite; leaf blade 6–25 x 1–2.5 cm, narrowing into a long petiole; flowers 3–5 cm long.
Habitat: parasitic on *Melaleuca* and *Eucalyptus*.
Dist: 1, 2, 4, 5, 6, 7, 8, 9, 12, 14, 15, 16; also NT, SA and Qld.

286 ***Nuytsia floribunda*** (Labillardière) R.Brown ex Fenzl
Christmas Tree
Spreading tree or shrub to 7 m high; leaves 2.5–10 cm long; flowers in terminal fascicles up to 25 cm long. Parasitic on the roots of many species including annuals and often connected by runners to hosts some distance away; can be seen as solitary trees in paddocks and suburban house blocks; spectacular when in full flower, particularly in the first season after fire.
Habitat: sand or granitic soil in open forest, woodland and kwongan.
Dist: 16, 17, 18, 19, 20, 21, 22, 23.

287 *Alyogyne hakeifolia*

288 *Alyogyne huegelii*

MALVACEAE mallow, hibiscus

The Malvaceae is a large cosmopolitan family of trees, shrubs and herbs; widely distributed in warm and temperate regions but absent from rainforest and very cold areas. Many species are horticulturally important and can often be recognised by their large, hibiscus-like flowers. *Alcea rosea* is the common ornamental hollyhock, *Abutilon striatum* Chinese lantern, and *Hibiscus rosa-sinensis* with its cultivars is a striking shrub. The family also contains a number of weedy species that are troublesome in pastures, crops and gardens. Economically the most important species is *Gossypium hirsutum* cultivated world-wide in warm areas as the source of cotton.

Many Australian species were used by the Aborigines for food, fibre and timber and many are now important range land stock foods. Some native species of *Hibiscus*, *Alyogyne* and *Radyera* have been introduced successfully into horticulture.

287 ***Alyogyne hakeifolia*** (Giordano) Alefeld
Red-centred Hibiscus
Open shrub 1–3m high with long willowy stems and well-spaced leaves one to three time divided into segments 5–10 cm long; flowers 5–6 cm long, not opening widely.
Habitat: dry situations, usually in open woodland.
Dist: 11, 16, 17, 21, 22, 23, 24, also SA.

288 ***Alyogyne huegelii*** (Endlicher) Fryxell
Lilac Hibiscus
Spreading shrub to 3 m high; leaves 2–7 cm long, deeply lobed into three to five segments; flowers 7–10 cm across in shades of mauve, purple and occasionally white or cream.
Habitat: sandy, rocky soil in woodland, common along creek banks.
Dist: 15, 16, 17, 21, 22, 23, 24; also SA.

289 *Alyogyne pinoniana*

290 *Lawrencia berthae*

291 *Lawrencia helmsii*

292 *Villarsia albiflora*

289 ***Alyogyne pinoniana*** (Gaudichaud) Fryxell
Sand Hibiscus
Sprawling shrub up to 3 m high; leaves 2–6 cm long, divided into three to five segments with curled or crinkled margins; flowers 7–9 cm across.
Habitat: dry areas, both coastal and inland.
Dist: 13, 14, 15, 16, 21, 23, also SA and NT.

290 ***Lawrencia berthae*** (F.Mueller) Melville
Showy Lawrencia
Small dioecious multi-stemmed shrub up to 1m high; leaves long-petiolate, blade 5–20 mm long, coarsely toothed; male flowers (pictured) 2–2.5 cm across, female flowers smaller.
Habitat: sandy loam and gypsum loam, plentiful following fire.
Distr: 21, 22, 23, 24; also SA, Vic.

291 ***Lawrencia helmsii*** (F.Mueller and Tate) N.S.Lander
Dunna-dunna
Erect, dioecious shrub; lateral branches contracted to form cactus-like stems, leaves 1.5–7 mm long in dense fascicles; flowers unisexual, 2–5 mm long. This curious atypical member of the Malvaceae family exhibits an interesting adaptation to its highly saline habitat. It is host to a beautifully camouflaged caterpillar (see plate 291, inset).
Habitat: saline sand or gypseous clay soil on margins of inland lakes.
Dist: 15, 24.

MENYANTHACEAE marshworts

The Menyanthaceae is a small family of chiefly aquatic or semi-aquatic emergent fresh-water herbs. Of c. 50 species world-wide 30–35 occur in Australia. *Villarsia* is widespread in the warmer, wetter parts of south-eastern and south-western Australia; flower colour is yellow or more rarely white.

292 ***Villarsia albiflora*** F.Mueller
Perennial aquatic herb; flowering stems erect up to 1.2 m high; leaves floating or emergent; petiole up to 28 cm long, blade reniform to almost circular, 10–70 x 10–80 mm; flowers 2–3 cm across.
Habitat: swamps, lake margins and streams from about 130 km north of Perth, south to Cape Leeuwin area and also in the Porongurup Range.
Dist: 17, 18, 19, 20.

MIMOSACEAE wattles

The Mimosaceae is a very large, cosmopolitan family with about 60 genera. In Australia it is best known for the genus *Acacia* which is widespread throughout the continent and contains about 900 species varying from large trees to small shrubs.

As a legume the genus is an important contributor to soil nutrition and is an early coloniser of disturbed sites and in post-fire regeneration. Many species are important in agriculture for shelter belts and stock fodder. Acacias are also widely planted as ornamentals and many produce valuable timber. *A. mearnsii* and *A. dealbata* have been grown for over 100 years, both in Australia and overseas, as a source of bark for tanning.

Many acacias were an important Aboriginal food source throughout the continent; seeds, seed pods and roots were eaten; the sticky sap was gathered into balls and chewed or used to make a sweet drink, and the roots of some species are hosts to such delicacies as witchetty grubs and honey ants. Bark strips were also used in making fishing nets and bags and the bark of *A. salicina* was observed by explorers Hume and Hovell in use as a fish poison. The wood of many species was highly valued in the manufacture of spears, boomerangs and handles for stone tools.

Most Australian acacias, particularly in arid areas, have phyllodes instead of true leaves, a character thought to be an adaptation to the dry environment. True bi-pinnate leaves are seen on seedlings of phyllodinous species.

293 ***Acacia acanthoclada*** F.Mueller
Harrow Wattle
Rigid, divaricate shrub to 2 m high; branchlets spine-tipped; phyllodes 2–10 x 0.5–4 mm, asymmetrical with obliquely hooked tips.
Habitat: sandy soil in open low woodland or shrubland.
Dist: 15, 21, 22, 23, 24; also SA and Vic.

294 ***Acacia acuminata*** Bentham
Raspberry Jam
Tall shrub or small tree 2–7 m, occasionally to 12 m high; phyllodes narrow, 7–20 cm long with a slender recurved but not pungent tip. The wood is hard and durable with a strong smell of raspberry jam when cut. It is often used for fence posts, and was used by the Aborigines for making weapons.
Habitat: diverse, including sand and loam, common throughout the wheatbelt.
Dist: 14, 15, 16, 17, 18, 19, 21, 22, 23, 24.

293 *Acacia acanthoclada*

294 *Acacia acuminata*

296 *Acacia colletiodes*

297 *Acacia denticulosa*

295 ***Acacia alata*** R.Brown
Winged Wattle
Upright to spreading shrub 1–2 m high; phyllodes
continuous with the winged stem.
Habitat: various, often in moist sites by streams, also
recorded on rocky slopes and granitic sand near the
coast.
Dist: 16, 17, 18, 19, 20, 23.

296 ***Acacia colletioides*** Bentham
Wait-a-while
Widely spreading, rounded shrub, sometimes pros-
trate, usually densely branched; phyllodes 1.5–2.5
cm long, growing at right-angles to the stem.
Habitat: sandy soil in open mallee woodland.
Dist: 10, 15, 16, 23, 24; also SA, NSW, Vic.

297 ***Acacia denticulosa*** F.Mueller
Sandpaper Wattle
Upright, open shrub 2–4 m high; a rare species re-
stricted to the north-eastern wheatbelt.
Habitat: granite outcrops.
Dist: 23.

295 *Acacia alata*

298 *Acacia drummondii* Lindley subsp. ***elegans*** Maslin
Drummond's Wattle
Shrub to 2 m tall; branches hairy, without spines; leaves bipinnate; flowers in spikes up to 5 cm long; a particularly attractive plant.
Habitat: loam or sandy soil in moist, often swampy situations, particularly in the Stirling Range and Albany area.
Dist: 17, 19, 20, 21.
A. drummondii and *A. varia* are two similar, highly variable species in both of which several subspecies are recognised. Together they range from just north of New Norcia through coastal southern wheatbelt areas to just beyond Esperance.

299 *Acacia botrydion* Maslin
Spreading, densely branched spiny shrub, prostrate or ascending, to 2 m high; phyllodes 3-6 mm long, occasionally almost leafless; young growth red.
Habitat: confined to lateritic hills in the Wongan Hills area.
Dist: 23.

300 *Acacia glaucoptera* Bentham
Clay Wattle
Widely spreading shrub to 2.5 m high; phyllodes triangular, to 5 cm long forming continuous lobes along the stems; young growth may be purple-red.
Habitat: kwongan or shrubland in sandy or lateritic clay soil, common in winter-moist areas.
Dist: 21, 22.

299 *Acacia botrydion*

300 *Acacia glaucoptera*

298 *Acacia drummondii* subsp. *elegans*

301 *Acacia heterochroa*

305 *Acacia rostellifera*

301 **Acacia heterochroa** Maslin
Shrub to 1 m high; branches long and arched; phyllodes 1–2.5 cm long.
Habitat: shrubland in rocky clay-loam on hillsides of the Ravensthorpe Range.
Dist: 21.

302 **Acacia lasiocalyx** C.Andrews
Wilyurwur
Single-trunked spreading shrub or small tree 3–5 m high; phyllodes gently curving, up to 25 cm long.
Habitat: found in thickets around the base of granite outcrops.
Dist: 17, 18, 21, 22, 23, 24.

303 **Acacia celastrifolia** Bentham
Glowing Wattle
Erect, compact shrub or small tree to 3m high; phyllodes 2-4 cm x 5-15 mm with prominent central and marginal nerves.
Habitat: sandy or gravelly lateritic and granitic soil in woodland or kwongan.
Dist: 17, 18, 23.

304 **Acacia restiacea** Bentham
Wiry, small, rush-like shrub to 1 m high; phyllodes needle-like and slender but usually absent.
Habitat: shrubland in sandy soil.
Dist: 16, 23.

305 **Acacia rostellifera** Bentham
Shrub or small tree 2–5 m high with arching stems; phyllodes 5–15 cm long; flower heads c. 5 mm across; pods to 10 cm long, constricted between the seeds. In coastal situations it forms a dense, dome-shaped shrub.
Habitat: lateritic sand or gravel, common in coastal limestone and sand.
Dist: 14, 16, 17, 19, 20, 21, 23.

302 *Acacia lasiocalyx*

303 *Acacia celastrifolia*

304 *Acacia restiacea*

306 *Acacia scirpifolia*

307 *Acacia sericocarpa*

308 *Acacia stenoptera*

309 *Acacia stereophylla*
var. *cylindrata*

310 *Acacia unifissilis*

306 *Acacia scirpifolia* Meisner

Dense shrub to 5 m high; phyllodes to 15 cm long; flowers in racemes; pods long, narrow, convex over the seeds.

Habitat: shrubland in sand.

Dist: 16, 17, 23.

307 *Acacia sericocarpa* W.V.Fitzgerald

Rigid shrub c. 1 m high; branches and young foliage woolly tomentose; leaves 1–2.5 cm long. Very similar and closely related to *A. merrallii* which differs in being almost glabrous and having margins of phyllodes much thickened.

Habitat: mallee and wattle shrubland.

Dist: 23.

308 *Acacia stenoptera* Bentham

Narrow Winged Wattle

Rigid shrub 1–2 m high with ridged stems and curving spine-tipped phyllodes forming continuous wings along the stems; flowers globular, creamy yellow, borne singly in the axils of the phyllodes. The distinctive quadrangular pods depicted here are 3–7 cm long and prominently ridged.

Habitat: sand or gravelly loam, including granitic soil in heath, shrubland and banksia woodland.

Dist: 6, 7, 8, 9, 22, 23.

309 *Acacia stereophylla* Meisner var. ***cylindrata*** Cowan and Maslin

Medium shrub to small tree to 6 m high; phyllodes terete or sub-terete, 10–18 cm long, 1.3–2 mm across.

Habitat: sandstone cliffs and sand over sandstone in acacia shrubland, confined to Kalbarri area.

Dist: 16.

The typical variety is widespread from Nerren Nerren Station north of Kalbarri National Park south-east to Tammin and Boorabbin; it has flat phyllodes 3.5–6.5 mm wide.

310 *Acacia unifissilis* A.B.Court

Dwarf, compact shrub, branches with white hairs along the yellowish nerves and mealy between the nerves; phyllodes to 3 cm long; flower heads c. 8 mm across; pods to 5 cm long, irregularly coiled or twisted, surface dark brown and wrinkled.

Habitat: sandy soil in mallee and kwongan.

Dist: 21, 22, 23, 24.

311 *Eremophila alternifolia*

312 *Eremophila calorhabdos*

MYOPORACEAE emu bush, poverty bush

The Myoporaceae is a small family of viscid or resinous shrubs and small trees with its centre of diversity in Australia and extending to the south-west Pacific, Indian Ocean islands and the West Indies. *Eremophila* is the largest genus with c. 170 species of which c. 125 occur in Western Australia. It is widespread in the drier areas of the state. *Myoporum* is the only other genus in Australia and contains c. 18 species, with ten in Western Australia; they are shrubs or small trees with small white or purplish regular flowers.

311 ***Eremophila alternifolia*** R.Brown
Poverty Bush
Erect shrub 2–3 m high; leaves 1–5 cm long; flowers 2.5–3 cm long, colour varies from pink to white with darker spots.
Habitat: in shrubland or woodland, in skeletal soil, in rocky places, red loam and granitic sand.
Dist: 11, 15, 21, 24, also NT and SA.

312 ***Eremophila calorhabdos*** Diels
Red Rod or Spiked Eremophila
Erect, often few-stemmed shrub to 3 m high; leaves 1.5–2.5 cm long; flowers to 3 cm long, colour varies from pink to red or purplish.
Habitat: sand or loam in shrubland or woodland.
Dist: 22, 24.

313 *Eremophila clarkei*

314 *Eremophila decipiens*

315 *Eremophila dempsteri*

316 *Eremophila drummondii*

317 *Eremophila glabra*

313 ***Eremophila clarkei*** Oldfield and F.Mueller
Turpentine Bush
Shrub to 4 m high, very variable; leaves 15–30 mm long; flowers to 3 cm long. This specimen was photographed on a rocky outcrop above the Murchison River, and was a plant 2–3 m high. Further east and south it is usually a small, rounded shrub with broader leaves and calyx lobes. Flower colour also varies and may be white, pale pink or mauve.
Habitat: very diverse, sand, loam and rocky soils in shrublands and mulga woodland, and on hillsides.
Dist: 12, 13, 14, 15, 16, 24, also SA.

314 ***Eremophila decipiens*** Ostenfeld
Slender Fuchsia
Erect shrub 1–2 m high; young growth sticky; leaves 2–4 cm long; flowers to 2.5 cm long.
Habitat: shrubland or open woodland in a wide variety of soils.
Dist: 11, 13, 15, 16, 22, 23, 24, also S.A.

315 ***Eremophila dempsteri*** F.Mueller
Erect, broom-like shrub 2–4 m high; leaves linear 3–5 mm long, spreading and commonly recurved or hooked at the tip; flowers 5–6 mm long with a densely ciliate calyx.
Habitat: open woodland in a variety of soils.
Dist: 11, 22, 24.

316 ***Eremophila drummondii*** F.Mueller
Small bushy shrub 0.5–1.5 m high; leaves 2–6 cm long; flowers to 2 cm long.
Habitat: heath or woodland in sandy and lateritic soil.
Dist: 15, 22, 23, 24.

317 ***Eremophila glabra*** (R.Brown) Ostenfeld
Tar Bush
Shrub to 1 m high; leaves 1.5–5 cm long, young growth often sticky; flowers to 3 cm long, green, yellow, orange or red; a widespread and very variable species of which many forms are popular in cultivation.
Habitat: shrubland, mallee or open woodland in brown or red, commonly calcareous loam.
Dist: 11, 14, 16, 17, 19, 20, 21, 22, 23, 24; also NT, SA, Qld, NSW, Vic.

318 **Eremophila psilocalyx** F.Mueller
Shrub 1–3 m high; leaves to 2.5 cm long with apex pointed and hooked; flowers to 2 cm long; calyx segments widely spreading, at first pale violet like the flowers and later darkening to purple.
Habitat: clay soil in eucalypt woodland.
Dist: 15, 22, 24.

319 **Eremophila serpens** Chinnock
Snake Eremophila
Prostrate, creeping shrub; leaves to 5 cm long; flowers 3 cm long.
Habitat: sandy loam in mallee scrub.
Dist: 21, 22.

320 **Eremophila viscida** Endlicher
Varnish Bush
Sticky shrub 2–6 m high with shiny brown branches and leaves 5–10 cm long; flowers c. 2 cm long.
Habitat: granitic soil in shrubland, rare.
Dist: 23.

319(a) *Eremophila serpens*

319(b) *Eremophila serpens*

318 *Eremophila psilocalyx*

320 *Eremophila viscida*

MYRTACEAE gum trees, paperbarks, bottle brushes

The Myrtaceae is a large, very diverse family of trees and shrubs comprising about 155 genera and about 3500 species, mainly in the southern hemisphere and tropics, with a few species in the northern hemisphere.

Australia has about 75 genera, of which 55 are endemic, and over 1500 species, of which well over half are in Western Australia.

Many species are economically important for timber, paper pulp, honey, medicinal and aromatic oils, and in horticulture. A few exotic species provide commercial edible products such as *Syzygium aromaticum* (cloves), *Pimenta dioica* (allspice) and *Psidium guajava* (guava).

In Australia, the Aborigines made use of a wide variety of the Myrtaceae; species of *Acmena* and *Syzygium* yield edible fruits, the flowers of many *Eucalyptus* and *Leptospermum* species are a rich source of nectar, and the oils have various medicinal uses as infusions and poultices. Timber from eucalypts is used in the manufacture of various artefacts and the bark may be used for making dishes, canoes and shelters. The roots of several arid area eucalypts are a reliable source of drinking water.

Western Australia is particularly rich in showy-flowered species, many of which have been brought into cultivation successfully, and some are extensively exploited by the fresh and dried flower industries.

Most Australian Myrtaceae species belong to the sub-family Leptospermoideae. Many genera are superficially very similar, and a detailed description of differences is beyond the scope of this book. Interested readers are referred to specialised publications, some of which are listed in the reference section of this book.

321 *Actinodium* sp.

321 **Actinodium** sp.
Albany Daisy
Sparsely branched, erect shrub to 1 m high; leaves
c. 5–6 mm long; flower heads daisy-like, 4–5 cm
across.
Habitat: moist situations in sand in kwongan or
open forest.
Dist: 17, 19, 20, 21.
This species has been incorrectly known for many
years as *A. cunninghamii* but differs in being a larger
plant, with larger, paler flowers. It is much more
common.

322 **Actinodium cunninghamii** Schauer
Swamp Daisy
Compact shrub to 30 cm high; leaves c. 4 x 1–2 mm;
flower heads 2–3 cm across.
Habitat: sandy soil, usually in seasonally wet de-
pressions, uncommon.
Dist: 19, 20. 22.

322 *Actinodium cunninghamii*

323 **Agonis baxteri** (Bentham) J.R Wheeler &
N.G.Marchant [syn. *Agonis obtusissima* F.Mueller]
Shrub 2–3 m high, usually spreading and dense;
leaves 2.5–4 cm long, new growth often pinkish;
flowers in tight, axillary clusters c. 2–3 cm across.
Stamens up to 30 in clusters of 3–6 opposite each
sepal.
Habitat: near-coastal shrubland and mallee
kwongan in sand or among rocks.
Dist: 21.

324 **Taxandria spathulata** (Schauer) J.R. Wheeler &
N. G. Marchant [syn. *Agonis spathulata* Schauer]
Dense shrub to 2 m high; leaves 3–7 mm long;
flowers c. 1 cm across in dense clusters of up to 20
flowers. Stamens usually 10, one opposite each sepal
and petal.
Habitat: rocky hillsides in thick scrub.
Dist: 21.

324 *Taxandria spathulata*

325 **Baeckea grandiflora** Bentham
Large- flowered Baeckea
Shrub 1–2 m high; leaves 5–10 mm long, almost
terete and widely spaced on the flowering branches;
flowers 1–1.5 cm across.
Habitat: sandy kwongan.
Dist: 15, 16, 17, 23.

323 *Agonis baxteri*   325 *Baeckea grandiflora*

326 *Baeckea ovalifolia*

327 *Balaustion microphyllum*

328 *Balaustion pulcherrimum*

329 *Beaufortia decussata*

330 *Beaufortia elegans*

326 *Baeckea ovalifolia* (F.Mueller) F.Mueller
Erect shrub to 1 m high, leaves variable in shape, linear-oblong, broadly linear or ovate, 3–6 mm long; flowers c. 1.5 cm across.
Habitat: near coastal in sandy soil or among quartzite rocks.
Dist: 21.

327 *Balaustion microphyllum* C.A.Gardner
Bush Pomegranate
Dense, dwarf shrub 20–40 cm high; leaves 1–2 mm long; flowers to 1 cm long.
Habitat: sandy soil in shrubland and open woodland, becoming rare due to land clearance.
Dist: 23.

328 *Balaustion pulcherrimum* W.J.Hooker
Native Pomegranate
Prostrate shrub to 0.5 m across; leaves c. 1 cm long; flowers to 2.5 cm long.
Habitat: sandy kwongan.
Dist: 22, 23, 24.
Balaustion is a genus of two species endemic in south-western WA. The name was used by Dioscorides, 1st-century Greek physician, for wild pomegranate flowers.

329 *Beaufortia decussata* R.Brown
Gravel Bottlebrush
Shrub 2–3 m high, leaves c. 1 cm long; flowering spikes to 10 x 4 cm.
Habitat: tall shrubland in rocky or sandy soil.
Dist: 19, 20, 21.

330 *Beaufortia elegans* Schauer
Spreading shrub to 2.5 m high; leaves opposite with stem-clasping base and recurved apex, 2–5 mm long, crowded along stem; flower heads c. 2 cm wide, reddish-pink to purple.
Habitat: kwongan or shrubland in sandy soil.
Dist: 16, 17, 21, 23.

331 *Beaufortia cyrtodonta* (Turczaninow) Bentham.
[syn. *Beaufortia heterophylla* Turczaninow]
Stirling Range Bottlebrush
Low, compact shrub to 1 m high; leaves 5–10 mm long, often covered with fine hairs giving a greyish appearance; flower heads c. 2.5 cm across.
Habitat: gravelly soil in kwongan and woodland of the Stirling Range.
Dist: 21, 22

331 *Beaufortia cyrtodonta*

332 *Beaufortia incana* (Bentham) A.S.George
A rigidly branched, spreading shrub 1–2 m high;
leaves 5–12 mm long, densely clustered, often grey
hoary due to a dense indumentum of very fine hairs;
flower heads c. 2.5 cm across.
Habitat: sandy soil in kwongan or shrubland.
Dist: 18, 22, 23.

333 *Beaufortia micrantha* Schauer
Little Bottlebrush
A much-branched shrub 0.5–1.5 m high; leaves
1–2 mm long; flowers in dense heads to 1 cm diam-
eter.
Habitat: lateritic sand.
Dist: 17, 21, 22, 23, 24.

334 *Beaufortia schaueri* Preiss ex Schauer
Pink Bottlebrush
Dwarf, spreading shrub to 1 m high; leaves c. 5 mm
long; flower heads c. 2 cm across.
Habitat: in sandy or gravelly or rocky soil, in
kwongan.
Dist: 21, 22.

332 *Beaufortia incana*

333 *Beaufortia micrantha*

334 *Beaufortia schaueri*

335 *Beaufortia orbifolia*

336 *Beaufortia aestiva*

335 *Beaufortia orbifolia* F.Mueller
Ravensthorpe Bottlebrush
Erect shrub to 3 m high; leaves c. 6 mm long; flower spikes 6 x 4 cm.
Habitat: lateritic hills mainly in the Ravensthorpe district.
Dist: 21, 22, 24.

336 *Beaufortia aestiva* K.J.Brooks
Sand Bottlebrush
Open or dense shrub to 4 m high; leaves obovate, 4–11 mm long; flowers in heads 3.5–4.5 cm across; stamens bright red or yellow. Closely related to *B. squarrosa*, a smaller shrub of low-lying flats farther south, with more open flowers that are always red.
Habitat: Sandy kwongan, mainly from Eneabba to Kalbarri, rarely south to Tammin.
Dist: 16, 17, 18, 23.

337 *Callistemon glaucus* (Bonpland) Sweet [syn. *C. speciosus* (Sims) Sweet]
Albany Bottlebrush
Rigid, erect shrub to 3 m high; leaves to 15 cm long; flower spikes to 15 x 7.5 cm.
Habitat: swampy heathland, seasonally inundated.
Dist: 18, 19, 20.

Calothamnus (clawflower, one-sided bottlebrush, netbush), a genus of c. 40 species endemic in WA, mainly in the south-west. The common names refer to the claw-like appearance of the flowers, their apparent clustering on one side of the stem in some species and the fine tangled net-like foliage on others.

The flower is formed of a tubular calyx, very small brownish or green papery petals and large, usually scarlet stamens, united into four or five staminal claws. The genus is popular in cultivation, many species being adaptable to a wide variety of soils and climates, and valued as bird attractors.

338 *Calothamnus blepharospermus* F.Mueller
Spreading, bushy shrub 1–2 m high; leaves to 8 cm long; flowers with five equal staminal bundles about 3–4 cm long.
Habitat: sandy soil in kwongan.
Dist: 16, 17.

337 *Callistemon glaucus*

338 *Calothamnus blepharospermus*

339 ***Calothamnus homalophyllus*** F.Mueller
Murchison Clawflower
Much-branched glabrous shrub 2–4 m high; erect
or dense, low and spreading in exposed coastal situations; leaves oblanceolate, to 5 cm long; flowers 2–
3 cm long divided into four staminal claws; a very
showy species.
Habitat: sandy areas near Kalbarri.
Dist: 16.

340 ***Calothamnus longissimus*** F.Mueller
Shrub 0.3–1.5 m high with corky stems; leaves gently curving, to 30 cm long; flowers with four un-
equal staminal bundles, the upper two broader and
c. 3 cm long.
Habitat: sandy kwongan.
Dist: 16, 17, 23.

341 ***Calothamnus oldfieldii*** F.Mueller
Small, spreading shrub 0.5–1.5 m high; leaves to
5 cm long, terete or slightly flattened; flowers with
five staminal bundles c. 2.5 cm long.
Habitat: sandy kwongan.
Dist: 16.

339 *Calothamnus homalophyllus*

340 *Calothamnus longissimus*

341 *Calothamnus oldfieldii*

342 *Calothamnus pinifolius*

342 *Calothamnus pinifolius* F.Mueller
Dense Clawflower
Erect shrub to 1.5 m high; leaves pungent, 2–3 cm long; flowers 2–3 cm long in dense clusters, often partially hidden by the leaves.
Habitat: dense scrub on rocky lateritic or quartzite slopes.
Dist: 21.

343 *Calothamnus quadrifidus* R.Brown
Common Net-bush
Shrub, spreading or upright, 2–4 m high; leaves to 3 cm long, terete or flattened, hairy or glabrous; flowers c. 2.5 cm long with four staminal claws. This is a widespread, variable species.
Habitat: diverse, including kwongan and granite outcrops.
Dist: 16, 17, 18, 21, 22, 23, 24.

344 *Calothamnus torulosus* Schauer
Spreading, decumbent shrub 2–3 m high; leaves 2–4 cm long, terete, usually with a few spreading hairs. This species is distinguished from *C. sanguineus* by the long cobwebby hairs covering the anthers; in both species the two broad, upper staminal claws are united for part of their length and the lower three are narrow and free. Flower colour in *C. torulosus* varies from greenish with red tips to pure scarlet.
Habitat: usually on laterite.
Dist: 16, 17, 18.

345 *Calothamnus validus* S.Moore
Barrens Clawflower
Upright or rounded shrub to 3 m; leaves rigid, terete, incurved, to 4 cm long; flower clusters c. 5 cm long, each flower with four staminal bundles.
Habitat: kwongan on rocky quartzite hills of the Barren Range.
Dist: 21.

346 *Calytrix acutifolia* (Lindley) Craven
Shrub to 2 m tall; leaves 2.5–15 mm long; flowers 9–17 mm across, white or cream in an elongated spike; calyx segments to 2 mm long, obtuse or emarginate. Differs from most species of *Calytrix* in lacking the long setaceous calyx bristles.
Habitat: loam or sand, including granite in kwongan and Jarrah forest.
Dist: 16, 17, 18, 19, 20, 21.

344 *Calothamnus torulosus*

343 *Calothamnus quadrifidus*

345 *Calothamnus validus*

346 *Calytrix acutifolia*

347 **_Calytrix angulata_** Lindley
Yellow Starflower
Shrub to 1 m high; leaves 2–7 mm long; flowers c.
15 mm across.
Habitat: sandy soil in wet and dry kwongan, banksia
woodland and Jarrah forest.
Dist: 17, 18, 23.

347 _Calytrix angulata_

348 **_Calytrix brevifolia_** Bentham
Erect shrub to 1 m high; leaves thick, 2–4 mm long,
varying from trigonous to terete; flowers 15–20 mm
across, colour varies from pink to purple. The awns
on the calyx fall off as the flowers open.
Habitat: sandy kwongan, and banksia woodland
with heath understorey.
Dist: 15, 16.

348 _Calytrix brevifolia_

349 **_Calytrix decandra_** A.P.de Candolle
Pink Starflower
Shrub to 1 m high; leaves to 1 cm long; flowers c. 2
cm across; sepals with hair-like awns twice as long
as petals.
Habitat: sandy kwongan.
Dist: 21, 22.

349 _Calytrix decandra_

350 **_Calytrix depressa_** (Turczaninow) Bentham
Purple Starflower
Spreading shrub to 1 m high; leaves 3–16 mm long;
flowers to 2 cm across, varying from cream as depicted here to mauve or violet; some cream forms
become reddish purple as the flowers age.
Habitat: very diverse including sand, gravelly sand
and granite outcrops in swamps, near-coastal
heathland and Jarrah forest.
Dist: 16, 17, 18, 21, 24.

350 _Calytrix depressa_

351 **_Calytrix ecalycata_** Craven [syn. _Calythropsis aurea_
C.A.Gardner]
Small shrub to 1 m high; leaves 5–7 mm long; flow-
ers 2 cm across without sepals; formerly placed in
Calythropsis, because of the absence of the long, usu-
ally awn-tipped sepals found in most _Calytrix_
species.
Habitat: sandy kwongan.
Dist: 16.

351 _Calytrix ecalycata_

352 *Calytrix eneabbensis*

352 *Calytrix eneabbensis* Craven

Shrub to 50 cm high; leaves 4–11 mm long; flowers to 2 cm across, purple with pale yellow patch at base of petals which changes to reddish purple as the flowers age.

Habitat: kwongan in sand or shrubland in sand over laterite; known only from the Eneabba district.

Dist: 16.

Chamelaucium (waxflower), a genus of shrubs restricted to the south-west of WA. The common name refers to the waxy appearance of the petals. In many species the flower, when fully open, exposes the shiny surface of the top of the ovary. The calyx is also distinctive, not hidden by bracts, usually tubular or bell-shaped and usually ribbed. Waxflowers grow in a wide variety of habitats and soils but most are found in heathland communities.

353 *Chamelaucium megalopetalum*

353 *Chamelaucium megalopetalum* F.Mueller ex Bentham

Large Waxflower

Upright, rigid, usually few-stemmed shrub 0.5–2 m high; leaves glabrous, 6–8 mm long; flowers to 15 mm across, white ageing to a distinctive deep red.

Habitat: southern kwongan.

Dist: 21, 22, 23, 24.

354 *Chamelaucium micranthum* Turczaninow

Much-branched shrub to 3 m high; leaves 1.3–5 mm long; buds pink; flowers c. 5 mm across, white but becoming reddish with age.

Habitat: sandy soil, usually saline.

Dist: 15, 16, 22, 23.

354 *Chamelaucium micranthum*

355 *Chamelaucium uncinatum* Schauer

Geraldton Wax

Shrub 2–5 m high; leaves almost terete, to 4 cm long; flowers 15–25 mm across, varying from white to pink, mauve or dull red; a very floriferous species. In recent years its distribution appears to be extending southwards and it is becoming an unwelcome intruder into native bushland reserves in suburban Perth. It is widely cultivated and popular as a cut flower, particularly in the eastern states.

Habitat: near-coastal sandplain north of Perth.

Dist: 16, 17.

355(a) *Chamelaucium uncinatum*

356 **Conothamnus aureus** (Turczaninow) Domin
Dwarf, intricately branched shrub to 1 m high;
branchlets often spine-tipped; leaves c. 1 cm long,
flower heads c. 1 cm across.
Habitat: low, near-coastal shrubland in deep white
sand.
Dist: 21.

357 **Conothamnus trinervis** Lindley
Shrub to 1 m high; stems thick, rigid; leaves 1–3
cm long with 3 parallel veins and pungent apex;
flower heads to 3 cm across; flowers occasionally
purple.
Habitat: kwongan in deep sand.
Dist: 16, 17.

Darwinia is named after Dr Erasmus Darwin, grandfa-
ther of the famous naturalist Charles Darwin. It is an
endemic genus of which about 60 species have been described, most of which are confined to south-western
Western Australia. They are all dwarf to medium-sized
shrubs with flowers in small terminal heads; in many
species the flowers are enveloped by large colourful bell-
like bracts.

356 *Conothamnus aureus*

357 *Conothamnus trinervis*

355(b) *Chamelaucium uncinatum*

358 Darwinia neildiana

359 Darwinia oldfieldii

361 Darwinia speciosa

360 Darwinia oxylepis

362 Darwinia vestita

358 **_Darwinia neildiana_** F.Mueller
Fringed Bell
Dwarf, spreading or semi-prostrate shrub 0.5–1 m high; leaves c. 1 cm long; flower heads 2–3 cm across containing up to 60 very small flowers; bracts green ageing to dark red, inner bracts softly ciliate-plumose.
Habitat: sand or gravelly sand.
Dist: 16, 17, 23.

359 **_Darwinia oldfieldii_** Bentham
Dwarf, twiggy shrub 0.5–1 m high with many short branches; leaves aromatic, 2–6 mm long; flower heads 2.5 cm across, cream to greenish, changing with age to deep red. The flower clusters are surrounded by small bracts that do not obscure the flowers as in some species.
Habitat: sand or limestone outcrops.
Dist: 16.

360 **_Darwinia oxylepis_** (Turczaninow) N.G.Marchant and G.Keighery
Gillam Bell
Shrub to 2 m tall with erect branches; leaves c. 10 x 1 mm; flower heads 3 x 2–3 cm.
Habitat: dense mallee heath in rough rocky soil in the western Stirling Range.
Dist: 21.

361 **_Darwinia speciosa_** (Meisner) Bentham
Dwarf spreading, often decumbent shrub 10–30 cm high; leaves 4–9 mm long; flower heads c. 3 cm long, bell-shaped; flowers greenish, surrounded and hidden by several dark red or brownish bracts.
Habitat: sandy kwongan.
Dist: 16.

362 **_Darwinia vestita_** (Endlicher) Bentham
Pom-pom Darwinia
Shrub to 1 m high; leaves c. 4 mm long, close together and appressed to the stem; flowers with finely ribbed calyx tube, in heads to 3 cm across, white ageing to pink or red. _D. diosmoides_ is similar but is usually a larger plant and can be distinguished by the rows of closely packed papillae on the calyx tube.
Habitat: sandy soil in kwongan or woodland, coastal and slightly inland.
Dist: 19, 21, 23.

363 **_Darwinia purpurea_** (Endlicher) Bentham
Rose Darwinia
Dense, spreading shrub to 70 cm high; leaves 2–4 mm long; flower heads green and red, 1.5–2 cm across, individual flowers with minute sepals.
Habitat: in sandy loam and granitic soil, in kwongan and shrubland.
Dist: 23.

364 **_Darwinia wittwerorum_** N.G.Marchant and
G.Keighery
Wittwer's Mountain Bell
Dwarf single-stemmed shrub 30–80 cm high; leaves
5–10 mm x less than 1 mm; flower heads c. 2 cm long.
Habitat: sandy soil in kwongan of the north-central Stirling Range.
Dist: 21.

365 **_Eremaea brevifolia_** (Bentham) Domin
Densely branched, spreading shrub 1–1.5 m high;
leaves c. 7 x 7 mm; flowers 8–10 mm across.
Habitat: deep sand.
Dist: 16.

366 **_Eremaea fimbriata_** Lindley
Shrub to 1 m high; leaves 4–8 mm long, hairy on
margins and undersides; flowers in heads 1–2 cm
across; stamens c. 8 mm long.
Habitat: kwongan or low woodland in sand or
lateritic gravel.
Dist: 16, 17.

Eucalyptus (gum trees), named from the Greek _eu_
(well) and _kalyptos_ (covered) in reference to the
operculum which covers the stamens in bud.

Eucalyptus is one of Australia's most important plant genera, with over 800 species and others still to be described. Most species are endemic in Australia but several extend to parts of Malesia and the Philippines, and two are confined to that region. Eucalypts were first introduced to cultivation in 1771 and have since become established in over 90 countries where their main use is for building timber and fuel. One of the most famous uses of _Eucalyptus_ overseas was in the draining of the Pontine Marshes near Rome. Planting _E. globulus_ (Southern Blue Gum) began there in 1870 in the belief that the production of aromatic oil in the atmosphere would solve the malaria problem. Research subsequently revealed that it was the ability of the trees to dry out the marshes and hence eliminate the breeding grounds of the mosquito that solved the problem. Cultivation of eucalypts overseas has not been without problems, including their capacity to dry out soil and to become tree weeds. South-western WA, together with near-coastal regions of New South Wales, contain the greatest diversity of species; many western species are renowned for their colourful flowers and extraordinary fruits. The eucalypts known as bloodwoods (broadly speaking, those with flowers in large corymbs and urn-shaped fruits) are now placed in the genus _Corymbia_ (bloodwoods), named for the form of the inflorescence. There are more than 100 species, all confined to Australia.

363 _Darwinia purpurea_

364 _Darwinia wittwerorum_

365 _Eremaea brevifolia_

366 _Eremaea fimbriata_

367 *Corymbia ficifolia*

367 ***Corymbia ficifolia*** (F.Mueller) K.D.Hill and L.A.S.Johnson [syn. *Eucalyptus ficifolia* F. Mueller] Red-flowering Gum

Tree to 10 m; bark rough, fibrous, adult leaves 7.5–15 cm long without conspicuous oil glands, the upper surface darker than lower; flowers to 4 cm across; capsules urn-shaped, to 3.5 x 3 cm, commonly contracted at the top; seeds winged.

Habitat: restricted to areas between Walpole and Denmark in sandy soil in low forest.

Dist: 20.

Typically a small, often irregular tree but one of the most widely planted of the ornamental eucalypts. In favourable conditions it becomes a large, spreading, dense-crowned tree with many colour

368 *Eucalyptus accedens*

forms from white depicted here to deep red. It is closely related to *C. calophylla* (R.Brown ex Lindley) K.D.Hill and L.A.S.Johnson (Marri) which has a wider distribution and differs in having tessellated bark, obvious oil glands in the leaves, white or rarely pink flowers, slightly larger fruits with a distinct neck at the top and wingless seeds.

368 *Eucalyptus accedens* W.V.Fitzgerald
Powderbark

Tree to 25 m, superficially similar to *E. wandoo* but distinguished by the blunt bud caps and the powder on the white or pink bark that brushes off on the hand; patches of exfoliating flakes of brown bark are also present on the trunk. The wood is heavy, strong and tough but of limited availability.
Habitat: lateritic hilltops in open forest.
Dist: 16, 18, 23.

369 *Eucalyptus albida* Maiden and Blakely
White-leaved Mallee

Mallee to 4 m, bark smooth, white or grey-brown, adult leaves lanceolate, thin, 4–7 cm long, juvenile leaves glaucous, ovate, cordate; bud caps broadly conical, 3–4 mm long and wide; fruit hemispherical, 4–5 mm long and wide. A decorative tree which commonly retains grey-leaved juvenile coppice growth on mature trees.
Habitat: yellow sand in open kwongan and shrubland from near Tammin south-east to the Hamersley River area.
Dist: 16, 22, 23.

370 *Eucalyptus caesia* Bentham subsp. *caesia*
Gungurru

Upright or spreading mallee shrub or small tree to 10 m high with reddish brown bark peeling in narrow, curling strips to reveal greenish brown new bark; adult leaves 7–12 x 1.2–2.5 cm; flowers c. 4 cm across; a rare species popular in cultivation.
Subsp. *magna* Brooker and Hopper, often marketed as 'Silver Princess', has larger flowers and fruits.
Habitat: on or around granite outcrops.
Dist: 18, 23, 24.

371 *Eucalyptus coronata* C.A.Gardner
Crowned Mallee

Mallee to 2 m high; bark grey; leaves 9–12 x 1.8–3 cm; fruits deeply corrugated, 18–25 x 25–35 mm.
Habitat: open shrubland among boulders on steep quartzite hills.
Dist: 21.

369 *Eucalyptus albida*

370 *Eucalyptus caesia* subsp. *caesia*

371 *Eucalyptus coronata*

373 *Eucalyptus diversicolor*

372 *Eucalyptus diptera* C.R.P.Andrews
Two-winged Gimlet

Slender mallee shrub or small tree to 8 m high; adult leaves 6–9 x 0.8–1.5 cm; flowers to 2 cm across. The name refers to the distinctive winged capsules. The slender trunks are usually fluted and become a rich coppery brown in late summer after the old bark is shed.
Habitat: sand or clay-loam, in thickets and shrubland.
Dist: 21, 22, 23, 24.

373 *Eucalyptus diversicolor* F.Mueller
Karri

Tree to almost 90 m; leaves to 12 cm long, discolorous. One of Australia's tallest trees, having been recorded at 87 m; an important timber species yielding longer lengths of wood than any other hardwood species; also important in honey production.
Habitat: forms tall forest in deep loam on hilly country between Manjimup and Denmark, with outliers west to Karridale and east to the Porongurup Range and Mt Manypeaks.
Dist: 19, 20.

374 *Eucalyptus sporadica* Brooker and Hopper
Mallee 4-6m high, bark smooth, red-brown, greyish or silvery white; leaves to 9 cm long, glossy green; fruit to 1.5 cm long, cylindrical to slightly campanulate.
Habitat: sandy soils of southern wheatbelt.
Dist: 22, 23, 24.

372(a) *Eucalyptus diptera*

372(b) *Eucalyptus diptera*

374 *Eucalyptus sporadica*

375 *Eucalyptus megacornuta*

375 *Eucalyptus megacornuta* C.A.Gardner
Warted Yate
Tree to 12 m; bark smooth, grey-brown to grey-red;
leaves 6–9.5 x 1.3–2 cm; fruit bell-shaped, up to 4 x
3.5 cm. One of several similar species with very long
finger-like buds; *E. megacornuta* is distinguished
by its tree habit, very warty buds and restricted distribution in the Ravensthorpe Range.
Habitat: lateritic hillsides.
Dist: 21.

376 *Eucalyptus preissiana* Schauer
Bell-fruited Mallee
Small to medium mallee 2–5 m high; leaves
7–12 cm long, thick, leathery, with prominent venation; flowers to 5 cm across; capsules 2.5 x
2–4 cm, usually bell-shaped.
Habitat: kwongan and rocky hills on or near the
coast.
Dist: 19, 21.

377 *Eucalyptus pyriformis*

377 *Eucalyptus pyriformis* Turczaninow
Pear-fruited Mallee
Mallee to 4.5 m high; bark smooth, grey to light
brown; leaves 6–8 cm long; buds corrugated, to
7 cm long including the long, pointed cap; flowers
to 10 cm across, pink, yellow or creamy.
Habitat: sandy soil in heathland.
Dist: 15, 16, 23.

378 *Eucalyptus rhodantha* Blakely and Steedman
Rose Mallee
Mallee 2–4 m high with slender, spreading trunks;
juvenile leaves opposite, grey-green; mature leaves
opposite or alternate, 6–13 x 6–8 cm, thick-textured,
glaucous or powdery-grey. This very showy species is becoming rare in the wild due to loss of habitat, but is widely cultivated.
Habitat: well-drained sand over clay.
Dist:16, 23.

376 *Eucalyptus preissiana*   378 *Eucalyptus rhodantha*

379 *Eucalyptus salmonophloia* F.Mueller
Salmon Gum
Tree to 24 m; bark smooth, pink, grey, or grey-
brown; leaves glossy, 6–12 cm long with hooked
tips. The wood has been used for mining timbers
and railway sleepers. The bark changes colour with
the seasons and becomes a rich bronze colour in
autumn.
Habitat: widespread throughout wheatbelt and
goldfields areas on plains and low hills in red clay,
loam and clay soil.
Dist: 22, 23, 24.

379 *Eucalyptus salmonophloia*

380 *Eucalyptus salubris* F.Mueller
Gimlet
Tree to 15 m or occasionally to 24 m; trunk strongly
spirally fluted; adult leaves narrowly lanceolate, 4.5–
10.5 cm long; flowers cream, c. 2 cm across, profuse
and valued for honey production. The wood is dense
and strong and was widely used in mining areas for
poles, posts and firewood; after felling regrows into
a multi-trunked tree.
Habitat: widespread in the drier areas of the south-
west in sandy loam to clay soil.
Dist: 15, 16, 22, 23, 24.

380 *Eucalyptus salubris*

381 *Eucalyptus ravida* L.A.S.Johnson & K.D.Hill
Differs from *E. salubris* in having glaucus leaves and
buds.
Habitat: flat or undulating areas of open woodland
in the eastern goldfields.
Dist: 24.

382 *Eucalyptus sepulcralis* F.Mueller
Weeping Gum
Mallee or slender tree to 8 m high with pendulous
branches and white bark; leaves 7–9 x 0.8–1.2 cm;
flowers pale yellow; fruit broadly urn-shaped, 25–
35 x 18–25 mm.
Habitat: quartzite sandy soil on eastern hills of the
Fitzgerald River National Park.
Dist: 21.

Above: 381 *Eucalyptus ravida*
Below: 382 *Eucalyptus sepulcralis*

383 *Eucalyptus staeri* (Maiden) Kessell and C.A.Gardner
Albany Blackbutt
Tree to 15 m; leaves 7.5–12.5 x 2.5–3.8 cm, thick, with conspicuous hooked tips; bud caps 10–13 mm long; fruit globular, 17–22 x 17–25 mm. Similar to *E. marginata* (Jarrah) but a smaller, rather stunted tree with more deeply fissured bark and larger fruits.
Habitat: sandy soil, in near-coastal scrub.
Dist: 19, 20, 21.

384 *Eucalyptus stoatei* C.A.Gardner
Scarlet Pear Gum
Slender tree to 6 m high; leaves 6–8 cm long, dark green, shining; flowers to 2 cm across; fruits 2.5–3.5 cm long.
Habitat: gravelly sand or sandy loam in shrubland.
Dist: 21.

385 *Eucalyptus synandra* Crisp
Mallee to 6 m; bark smooth, white to grey; leaves grey-green, 4–20 cm long; flowers c. 2.5 cm across, creamy yellow ageing to pink or red. This species is unusual in having the staminal filaments united in the lower half.
Habitat: sandy lateritic soil in tall shrubland.
Dist: 10, 23, 24.

386 *Eucalyptus tetraptera* Turczaninow
Four-winged Mallee
Sparsely branched, spreading, open mallee c. 2 m high; leaves very thick, leathery 13–18 x 4–7 cm; fruits quadrangular, 4–5 x 3.5–5 cm.
Habitat: sandy loam in kwongan.
Dist: 19, 21, 22.

383 *Eucalyptus staeri*

384 *Eucalyptus stoatei*

385 *Eucalyptus synandra*

386 *Eucalyptus tetraptera*

387 **Eucalyptus wandoo** Blakely
Wandoo
Tree to 25 m, leaves 8–12 x 1–2 cm, dull green to grey-green; inflorescence with up to 15 flowers; peduncle flattened; buds horn-shaped, to 2 cm long; capsule 10 x 8 mm, cylindrical to pear-shaped.
Habitat: widespread in agricultural areas from near Three Springs south to the Kalgan River and extending inland to near Karalee; grows in valleys, on ridges, plateaus and plains. Depicted here near the Stirling Range.
Dist: 16, 18, 20, 21, 22, 23, 24.

387 *Eucalyptus wandoo*

388 **Eucalyptus yalatensis** Boomsma
Yalata Mallee
Medium to tall, spreading mallee shrub or small tree; adult leaves 6–11 cm x 1–2 cm; flowers profuse, c. 1.5 cm across; confined to the south-east of the state, particularly along the Great Australian Bight.
Habitat: in shallow soil over limestone.
Dist: 11, 24; also SA.

389 **Homalocalyx coarctatus** (F.Mueller) Craven [syn. *Wehlia coarctata* F.Mueller]
Dwarf shrub to 70 cm high; leaves 2–8 mm long; flowers c. 1.5 cm across.
Habitat: kwongan in yellow sand or among taller scrub in clay-loam.
Dist: 16, 23, 24.

Above: 388 *Eucalyptus yalatensis*
Below: 389 *Homalocalyx coarctatus*

390 *Hypocalymma angustifolium*   391 *Hypocalymma cordifolium*

392 *Hypocalymma robustum*   393 *Hypocalymma speciosum*

394 *Hypocalymma xanthopetalum*

390 ***Hypocalymma angustifolium*** Endlicher
White Myrtle
Erect, many stemmed, glabrous shrub to 1.5 m high; leaves 1–4 cm long; flowers c. 8 mm across, opening white, maturing to deep pink; occasionally always white or cream.
Habitat: low-lying sandy soil over clay subsoil in damp areas, occasionally seasonally inundated.
Dist: 17, 18, 19, 20, 21, 23.

391 ***Hypocalymma cordifolium*** (Lehmann) Schauer
Shrub to 1.5 m high, densely branched; leaves 4–13 mm long; flowers 4–10 mm across.
Habitat: swampy, sandy soil in open forest or shrubland.
Dist: 18, 19, 20.

392 ***Hypocalymma robustum*** Endlicher
Swan River Myrtle
Shrub to 1.5 m high; leaves to 3 cm long; flowers c. 1 cm across, profuse, with spicy fragrance.
Habitat: deep sand in banksia woodland and in gravel in Jarrah forest.
Dist: 17, 18, 19, 20, 23.

393 ***Hypocalymma speciosum*** Turczaninow
Dwarf shrub to 70 cm high; leaves to 1.5 cm long, sometimes reddish in winter; flowers c. 1 cm across on slightly pendent stalks, with a spicy fragrance.
Habitat: endemic in the Stirling Range in sandy or gravelly loam over clay subsoil.
Dist: 21.

394 ***Hypocalymma xanthopetalum*** F.Mueller
Small tufted, dense shrub to 1 m high; stems covered in dense, short hairs; leaves 1–2 cm x 4–8 mm with ciliate margins; flowers c. 12 mm across. *H. tetrapterum* Turczaninow is similar but has glabrous stems and leaves and is much less common.
Habitat: kwongan, in sand or gravel soil.
Dist: 16, 17.

395 ***Kunzea affinis*** S.Moore
Erect shrub to 2.5 m high; leaves 4–6 mm long; calyx tube bell-shaped, glabrous; flowers 10–12 mm across. Similar to *K. preissiana* but usually of more erect habit and with glabrous calyx tube.
Habitat: sand and gravelly soil in kwongan and shrubland.
Dist: 19, 20, 21.

Far left: 395 *Kunzea affinis*
Left: 396 *Kunzea preissiana*

396 *Kunzea preissiana* Schauer

Spreading shrub to 1.5 m high; branches often arching; leaves 4–10 mm long; calyx tube densely hairy, flowers c. 12 mm across. A very floriferous shrub, plentiful along roadsides between Bremer Bay and Ravensthorpe; similar to *K. affinis* but can be distinguished by the densely hairy calyx tube.
Habitat: sand and gravel in kwongan and shrubland.
Dist: 21, 22, 23.

397 *Kunzea pulchella* (Lindley) A.S.George
Granite Kunzea

Shrub to 4 m high; leaves to 2.5 cm long, silky hairy on both surfaces; flowers to 3 cm across clustered in leafy spikes. When in full flower this is a strikingly beautiful plant. Var. *albiflora* S. Moore has white flowers and is found in the Southern Cross–Coolgardie district.
Habitat: granite outcrops.
Dist: 15, 22, 23, 24.

398 *Leptospermum incanum* Turczaninow

Erect, rounded shrub to 2 m high; leaves to 2 cm long; flowers 1–1.5 cm across.
Habitat: usually in sand associated with granite outcrops.
Dist: 21, 22.

399 *Leptospermum spinescens* Endlicher

Rigid, spiny shrub to 2 m high with corky bark; leaves 5–15 x 2–5 mm; flowers 10–15 mm across; fruiting capsules persistent, c. 2 cm across, partially buried in the corky bark.
Habitat: in kwongan or shrubland, in sandy or lateritic soil near the coast.
Dist: 16, 17, 18, 21, 22, 23.

400 *Melaleuca filifolia* F.Mueller
Wiry Honey-myrtle

The plant depicted here was photographed near Kalbarri and was a large shrub 4 m high. The name *M. filifolia* is currently applied to several distinct but very similar taxa; all have slender, linear leaves 4–12 cm long and globular or ovoid flower heads up to 3 cm across with mauve-pink to deep pink stamens and golden anthers. Several very showy forms are in cultivation.
Habitat: sandy soil or loam in kwongan or among tall scrub.
Dist: 15, 16, 23, 24.

397 *Kunzea pulchella*

398 *Leptospermum incanum*

399 *Leptospermum spinescens*   400 *Melaleuca filifolia*

402 *Melaleuca calothamnoides*

403 *Melaleuca longistaminea* subsp. *longistaminea*

404 *Melaleuca longistaminea* subsp. *spectabilis*

401 *Melaleuca acuminata* subsp. *websteri*

405 *Melaleuca cliffortioides*

401 ***Melaleuca acuminata*** F.Mueller subsp. ***websteri*** (S.Moore) Barlow
Erect, rather open shrub to 2.5 m high; leaves 12–14 x 1–2 mm; flowers in lateral clusters in interrupted spikes c. 2 cm wide.
Habitat: eucalypt or mallee woodland, in calcareous or saline loam or clay.
Dist: 21, 22, 23, 24.
Subsp. *acuminata* is similar but has shorter, wider leaves. It is widespread in similar habitats in southern WA, SA and western Vic.

402 ***Melaleuca calothamnoides*** F.Mueller
Large shrub 2–3 m high; leaves 1–2 cm long; flower spikes 4–5 cm long, commonly reflexed, on the old wood; restricted to the Murchison Range district but locally common.
Habitat: gullies and dry creek beds.
Dist: 16.

403 ***Melaleuca longistaminea*** (F.Mueller) Craven subsp. ***longistaminea***
[syn. *M. cardiophylla* var. *longistaminea* F. Mueller]
Widely spreading shrub to 1.5 m high, rarely erect and up to 2.5 m; leaves grey-green, 8–12 × 4–6 mm; flowers on old wood in clusters of seven to 15; stamens 15–22 mm long in bundles of nine to 15.
Habitat: open kwongan in calcareous soil.
Dist: 16, 23.

404 ***Melaleuca longistaminea*** subsp. ***spectabilis*** Barlow
Shrub similar to *M. longistaminea* subsp. *longistaminea* but with leaves 7–8 mm wide and shorter stamens in bundles of 20–24.
Habitat: open kwongan in calcareous soil.
Dist: 16.

405 ***Melaleuca cliffortioides*** Diels
Shrub to 1.5 m high; leaves 6–12 mm long with a pungent apex; flowers usually recurved, 10–15 mm across, sweetly scented, scattered along the branches but rarely profuse.
Habitat: sand, sandy loam or gravel, usually coastal.
Dist: 21, 22, 24.

406 ***Melaleuca concreta*** F.Mueller
Erect shrub to 2 m high; leaves 3–8 cm long with a prominent mid-nerve; flower heads 10–15 mm across.
Habitat: sandy soil including alkaline coastal situations.
Dist: 16, 23.

407 *Melaleuca conothamnoides* C.A.Gardner
Much-branched shrub to 1 m tall; leaves 25–40 mm long with three to five parallel nerves and conspicuous, glandular dots; flower heads to 3 cm diameter.
Habitat: sandy gravel soil of the wheatbelt.
Dist: 15, 16, 23, 24.

408 *Melaleuca cucullata* Turczaninow
Rounded shrub or small tree to 4.5 m high; leaves stem-clasping, c. 3 mm long; flowers in terminal spikes c. 2 x 1.5 cm.
Habitat: sand or sandy clay in woodland.
Dist: 21, 22.

407 *Melaleuca conothamnoides*

409 *Melaleuca diosmifolia* Andrews
Dense shrub 1–4 m high; leaves ovate, 10 mm long; flower spike c. 5 x 4 cm.
Habitat: coastal, usually among granite rocks.
Dist: 19, 20.

410 *Melaleuca elliptica* Labillardière
Granite Honey-myrtle
Erect shrub 2–3 m high; leaves elliptic, 5–15 mm long; flower spike c. 8 x 5 cm.
Habitat: usually on or near granite outcrops.
Dist: 21, 22, 24.

408 *Melaleuca cucullata*

409 *Melaleuca diosmifolia*

406 *Melaleuca concreta*

410 *Melaleuca elliptica*

411 *Melaleuca eurystoma*

413 *Melaleuca fulgens* subsp. *steedmanii*

412 *Melaleuca fulgens*
subsp. *fulgens*

414 *Melaleuca hamulosa*

415 *Melaleuca haplantha*

411 *Melaleuca eurystoma* Barlow
Spreading shrub to 1.5 m high; leaves 4–7 mm long, crowded, slightly recurved; flower heads c. 2 cm long.
Habitat: low kwongan in sand over clay.
Dist: 19, 20.

412 *Melaleuca fulgens* R.Brown subsp. *fulgens*
Scarlet Honey-myrtle
A shrub 1-2m high; leaves 2-4cm long; flowers in cylindrical spikes 3-6cm long, in shades of pale pink to scarlet; stamens joined to the sides of the claw; differs from subsp. *steedmanii* mainly in arrangement of the stamens and also in having slightly longer, narrower leaves and wider distribution.
Habitat: gravelly or granitic soil.
Dist: 21, 22, 23, 24.

413 *Melaleuca fulgens* R.Brown subsp. *steedmanii*
(C.A.Gardner) Cowley
Scarlet Honey-myrtle
Open shrub 0.5–2.6 m high; leaves opposite, 0.8–3.5 cm long; flower spikes 4–6 cm long; stamens joined to front of claw. The typical form of this taxon is bright scarlet; a pink form occurs in the Murchison River gorge and may be the result of hybridisation, probably with *Melaleuca radula*.
Habitat: sand on rocky slopes and creek beds.
Dist: 16, 22, 23.

414 *Melaleuca hamulosa* Turczaninow
Dense, broom-like shrub to 4 m high with many stiff, erect stems branching from the base; leaves 4–15 mm long with recurved tips and prominent oil glands; flower spikes 2–5 cm long, white, pink or pale mauve.
Habitat: shrubland or kwongan in sandy soil usually over clay, especially in saline depressions or swampy areas.
Dist: 16, 21, 22, 23, 24.

415 *Melaleuca haplantha* Barlow
Shrub to 4 m high with white papery bark; leaves 4–10 mm long, linear to elliptic; flowers c. 1 cm across, usually solitary but often profuse.
Habitat: kwongan or woodland in loam soil that is usually winter-wet.
Dist: 21, 22, 23.

416 *Melaleuca pungens* Schauer
Small shrub to 1.5 m high; leaves 1.5–3.5 cm long, pungent; flower heads globular or ovoid, to 2.5 cm long and 1.5 cm wide.
Habitat: in sand or gravelly sand in kwongan.
Dist: 16, 21, 22, 23, 24.

417 *Melaleuca radula* Lindley
Graceful Honey-myrtle
Small to medium open shrub to 3 m high; leaves 1.5–4 cm long; flowers in loose spikes to 5 cm long; colour varies through shades of pink, mauve, violet, purple and occasionally white; hybrids with *Melaleuca fulgens* are common and many of these have been brought into cultivation.
Habitat: in sandy loam or gravel over laterite or granite, usually in shrubland.
Dist: 15, 16, 17, 18, 23, 24.

418 *Melaleuca rhaphiophylla* Schauer
Swamp Paperbark
Large shrub or small tree with papery bark; leaves 1–2 cm long; flower spikes to 5 cm long.
Habitat: along water courses and in swamps.
Dist: 16, 17, 18, 19, 20, 21, 23: also SA.

419 *Melaleuca scabra* group
Rough Honey-myrtle
The *Melaleuca scabra* group comprises several taxa yet to be clearly distinguished, but which are widespread and common in woodland and kwongan. All are shrubs below 2 m high with linear leaves to 2.5 cm long and flower heads 1–1.5 cm across. The plant pictured was photographed near Eneabba and was a low, dense shrub c. 30 cm high.
Habitat: sand or gravelly sand in kwongan.
Dist: 16, 17, 18, 19, 21, 22, 23, 24.

416 *Melaleuca pungens*

417 *Melaleuca radula*

419 *Melaleuca scabra*

418 *Melaleuca rhaphiophylla*

420 *Melaleuca sparsiflora*

420 **Melaleuca sparsiflora** Turczaninow
Shrub to 2.5 m high; leaves 3–7 mm long; flowers to 1 cm across, solitary or in clusters of up to three flowers at the tips of shoots.
Habitat: eucalypt woodland, usually in sandy loam over clay subsoil.
Dist: 22, 24.

421 **Melaleuca suberosa** (Schauer) C.A.Gardner
Corky Honey-myrtle
Low, spreading shrub to 50 cm high; branches very corky and furrowed; leaves 4–6 mm long with raised oil glands; flowers in long spikes on old wood; stamens c. 6 mm long in bundles of seven to eleven.
Habitat: sandy or sand over laterite in mallee kwongan and shrubland.
Dist: 19, 21, 22.

422 **Pericalymma crassipes** (Lehmann) Schauer [syn. *Leptospermum crassipes* Lehmann]
Shrub to 30 cm high, with thickened trunk; leaves to 6 mm long; flowers to 5 mm across, white flushed with pale pink.
Habitat: seasonally wet sandy clay soil between the Scott River and Albany.
Dist: 20.

421 *Melaleuca suberosa*

422 *Pericalymma crassipes*

Phymatocarpus is a genus of 3 species confined to south-western WA. The generic name, from Greek *phymatos* (a swelling) and *karpos* (a fruit), refers to the warty outgrowths on the fruit of *P. porphyrocephalus* (not illustrated). Both flowers and fruits are similar to *Melaleuca*, differing only in the form of the anthers and ovules.

423 **Phymatocarpus maxwellii** F.Mueller
Woody shrub to 2.5 m high; leaves to 6 mm long; flower heads c. 1 cm across; the fruit is a cluster of smooth capsules, each c. 2.5 mm in diameter and similar to the fruits of some *Melaleuca* species.
Habitat: kwongan and banksia shrubland.
Dist: 21, 22.

423 *Phymatocarpus maxwellii*

424 *Pileanthus peduncularis*

425 *Regelia velutina*

424 **_Pileanthus peduncularis_** Endlicher
Copper cups
Erect, spreading shrub to 1 m high; leaves linear,
thick, 2–4 mm long; flowers 1–1.5 cm across on slen-
der pedicels up to 2 cm long.
Habitat: sandy soil in kwongan or shrubland.
Dist: 14, 16, 23.

425 **_Regelia velutina_** (Turczaninow) C.A.Gardner
Barrens Regelia
A shrub to 3 m tall; leaves 1–1.5 cm long; flower
spikes 3–4 cm diameter; one of five species endemic
in the south-west.
Habitat: among quartzite rocks on hillsides.
Dist: 21.

426 **_Rinzia carnosa_** (S.Moore) Trudgen
Woody sub-shrub to 1.3 m tall, much-branched,
with slender, often long branchlets; leaves appressed,
thick, sub-orbicular to elliptic, 0.5–2.5 x 0.5–1 mm,
pitted; flowers 5–7 mm across, clustered near tips
of branchlets.
Habitat: thickets of acacia scrub in loam or granitic
loamy sand.
Dist: 23, 24.

426 *Rinzia carnosa*

427 **_Scholtzia involucrata_** (Endlicher) Druce
Spiked Scholtzia
Erect or decumbent shrub to 1.5 m high; leaves 4–
9 mm long; flowers to 8 mm across, appearing in
late summer.
Habitat: sandy soil in kwongan and banksia wood-
land on western coastal plain.
Dist: 16, 17, 18, 23.

427 *Scholtzia involucrata*

428 **_Scholtzia parviflora_** F.Mueller
Spreading shrub to 2.5 m high with pendulous
branches; leaves 1–2 mm long, flowers c. 5 mm
across; superficially similar to and more widespread
than S. *uberiflora* but with smaller leaves lacking
prominent veins and flowers on short pedicels no
longer than the leaves.
Habitat: sandy kwongan.
Dist: 15, 16, 23, 24.

429 **_Scholtzia uberiflora_** F.Mueller
Open shrub to 2.5 m high with long arching branches,
usually overtopping associated heathland plants;
leaves orbicular, up to 6 mm across, prominently
veined; flowers 4–5 mm across.
Habitat: sandy kwongan.
Dist: 16.

428 *Scholtzia parviflora*   429 *Scholtzia uberiflora*

430 *Aluta appressa*

431 *Thryptomene racemulosa*

430 **Aluta appressa** (C.R.P.Andrews) B.L.Rye & M.E. Trudgon [syn. *Thryptomene appressa* C.R.P.Andrews] Erect shrub to 2 m high with willowy branches; leaves to 1 cm long with recurved tip; flowers 5 mm across, profuse.
Habitat: sand or gravelly sand in shrubland.
Dist: 21, 22, 24.

431 **Thryptomene racemulosa** Turczaninow
Erect shrub to 1 m high, sparsely branched; leaves 2–3 mm long; flowers 5–8 mm across, calyx lobes ciliate and as long as petals.
Habitat: shrubland in sandy soil with lateritic gravel.
Dist: 21, 22.

432 **Verticordia aurea** A.S.George
Shrub to c. 2 m high; leaves terete, 1–2 cm long; flowers c. 1 cm across.
Habitat: kwongan and low open banksia woodland within 30 km radius of Eneabba.
Dist: 16.
V. nitens is rather similar but has smaller, bright orange flowers and occurs further south.

432 *Verticordia aurea*

433 **Verticordia brachypoda** Turczaninow
Shrub c. 1 m high; leaves 3–5 mm long, mostly clustered near tips of short, widely spaced branchlets; flowers 1–1.5 cm across, white, cream or tinged pink.
Habitat: sandy soil over granite or lateritic loam, in kwongan.
Dist: 16, 21, 22, 23.

434 **Verticordia chrysanthella** A.S.George
Erect shrub to 1.3 m high; leaves terete, often warty, 3–8 mm long with a small hooked tip; flowers c. 7 mm across; a wide ranging, variable species.
Habitat: usually in granitic soil.
Dist: 16, 17, 18, 19, 22, 23.

433 *Verticordia brachypoda*

434 *Verticordia chrysanthella*

435 *Verticordia grandiflora*

435 *Verticordia grandiflora* Endlicher
Claw Featherflower
Erect shrub 40–60 cm high; leaves 3–6 mm long;
flowers c. 1.5 cm across.
Habitat: sandy soil in kwongan and shrubland, oc-
casionally in woodland.
Dist: 18, 21, 22, 23.

436 *Verticordia grandis* Drummond
Scarlet Featherflower
Erect, sparsely branched shrub to 1.5 m high; leaves
orbicular, blue-green, 1–1.5 cm diameter; flowers
to 2.5 cm across. This is one of the largest-flowered
species of *Verticordia*.
Habitat: in sand in kwongan.
Dist: 16.

436 *Verticordia grandis*   437 *Verticordia habrantha*

437 *Verticordia habrantha* Schauer
Hidden Featherflower
Slender shrub to 50 cm high; leaves linear, thick,
2–4 cm long; flowers 7–10 mm across; the fringed
calyx lobes are shorter than and hidden by the
petals.
Habitat: sandy loam in kwongan and woodland.
Dist: 17, 18, 19, 21, 22, 23.

438 *Verticordia helichrysantha*

438 *Verticordia helichrysantha* F.Mueller ex Bentham
Barrens Featherflower
Erect or spreading shrub to 75 cm high; leaves 3–7
mm long; flowers 6–8 mm across, partly hidden in
the dense foliage.
Habitat: rocky loam soil in very low kwongan.
Dist: 21.

439 *Verticordia huegelii* Endlicher var. ***huegelii***
Variegated Featherflower
Spreading shrub to 50 cm tall; leaves linear-terete,
3–6 mm long; flowers 12–15 mm across. Young
flowers are white or cream and gradually age to
shades of red.
Habitat: sandy, usually granitic soil.
Dist: 16, 17, 18, 22, 23.

439 *Verticordia heugelii* var. *huegelii*

440 *Verticordia insignis* subsp. ***compta*** (Endlicher)
A.S.George
Erect or straggly shrub to 1 m high; upper leaves
1.5–3 mm long; flowers c. 10 mm across, smaller
than the other subspecies.
Habitat: sandy soil in open woodland and kwongan
of the wheatbelt from Manmanning, south to
Ongerup and east to Kulin and Newdegate.
Dist: 22, 23.

440 *Verticordia insignis* subsp. *compta*

441 *Verticordia mitchelliana*

442 *Verticordia monadelpha* subsp. *callitricha*

443 *Verticordia nobilis*

444 *Verticordia oculata*

Typical *V. insignis* has white flowers and occurs in granitic soil in open woodland on the Darling Scarp and inland to Northam. Subsp. *eomagis* has larger flowers than the other subspecies and occurs between Eneabba and Badgingarra.

441 *Verticordia mitchelliana* C.A.Gardner
Rapier Featherflower
Spreading shrub 10–80 cm high; leaves linear, c. 1 cm long. The flower petals form a tube from which the very long style protrudes.
Habitat: sandy soil in shrubland.
Dist: 22, 23.

442 *Verticordia monadelpha* subsp. ***callitricha***
(Meisner) A.S.George
Woolly Featherflower
Dense, rounded shrub to 1 m high; leaves triquetous, 10–15 mm long; flowers c. 1.5 cm across. A very showy species. Subsp. *monadelpha*, found between Geraldton and Koorda, has slightly smaller petals but longer stamens.
Habitat: deep sand in kwongan.
Dist: 16, 23.

445 *Verticordia ovalifolia*

443 *Verticordia nobilis* Meisner

Single or few-branched shrub, 40–70 cm high; leaves linear, 5–15 mm long; flowers 15 mm across. This species is common between Gingin and Kalbarri; it is closely allied to *V. grandiflora* which occurs further south between Brookton and Ravensthorpe and has much shorter stamens.
Habitat: sandy soil in kwongan, occasionally in open woodland.
Dist: 16, 17.

444 *Verticordia oculata* Meisner

Shrub to 1 m high, leaves orbicular, 5 mm diameter, glaucous, stem-clasping; flowers 20–25 mm across.
Habitat: sandy kwongan.
Dist: 16.

445 *Verticordia ovalifolia* Meisner

Sparsely branched shrub to 50 cm high; leaves broadly elliptic to obovate, 8–15 mm long, stem-clasping, overlapping; flowers 2–2.5 cm across; petals pale pink or purple.
Habitat: sand or gravelly sand in kwongan or shrubland.
Dist: 16, 17, 22, 23.

446 *Verticordia picta* Endlicher
Painted Featherflower

Small, open, few-stemmed shrub 0.5–1 m high; flowers 8–l0 mm across; petals entire, more prominent than the much-divided, feathery calyx lobes.
Habitat: sandy soil in kwongan.
Dist: 16, 17, 18, 22, 23.

447 *Verticordia roei* Endlicher subsp. ***roei***

Shrub to 1 m high; leaves ovate to elliptic, 2–3 mm long; flowers c. 10 mm across.
Habitat: widespread inland from Southern Cross to Dumbleyung and Peak Charles in sandy loam over gravel and clay loam in kwongan.
Dist: 21, 22, 23, 24.
Subsp. *meiogona* differs in having shorter stamens and style and broader staminodes. It is confined to a few areas near Bonnie Rock and Dalwallinu.

448 *Verticordia staminosa* subsp. ***cylindracea*** var. ***erecta*** A.S.George

A small, spreading or occasionally upright shrub to 1 m high; leaves c. 1 cm long; flowers 6–10 mm across with conspicuous, protruding stamens.
Habitat: shallow soils on or near granite outcrops.
Dist: 22, 23.

446 *Verticordia picta*

447 *Verticordia roei* subsp. *roei*

448 *Verticordia staminosa* subsp *cylindracea* var. *erecta*

449 *Olax aurantia*

450 *Olax benthamiana*

451 *Olax phyllanthi*

OLACACEAE

The Olacaceae is a tropical family of shrubs, scramblers and occasionally trees. It is poorly represented in Australia with only 13 species of a world-wide total of c. 250.

The genus *Olax* has 11 species in Australia of which four occur in south-western Western Australia. They all have distinctive distichous, rather soft, pale yellow-green or grey-green leaves which contrast with the often harsh, rigid leaves of the heathland plants among which they grow. The flowers are pale yellow or white and the fruit a fleshy drupe.

449 ***Olax aurantia*** A.S.George
Slender shrub to 2 m high with pendulous branches and small cream flowers 6–7 mm long followed by shining orange drupes 10–14 mm long x 8–9 mm wide.
Habitat: sand, usually over limestone, in kwongan or shrubland.
Dist: 14, 16.

450 ***Olax benthamiana*** Miquel
Open shrub to 1 m high; leaves 2–20 mm long, very variable; flowers 4–6 mm long; fruit an oval drupe 5–7 mm long. A very widespread, variable species extending from the lower Murchison River to Busselton and east to Esperance.
Habitat: sand or gravelly sand, sometimes on dunes, also in laterite in shrubland and open woodland.
Dist: 16, 17, 18, 19, 21, 22, 23.

451 ***Olax phyllanthi*** (Labillardière) R.Brown
Shrub to 1.5 m high, pale green, often bushy; branches curved or pendulous; leaves 5–15 x 4–8 mm; flowers c. 5 mm across, creamy white and inconspicuous followed by a fleshy ovoid drupe 3–5 mm long.
Habitat: common on consolidated dunes along the south coast, sometimes slightly inland in deep sand and occasionally on granite or quartzite.
Dist: 19, 20, 21.

ORCHIDACEAE

The Orchidaceae is the world's largest plant family, containing over 30 000 species. The tropical rainforests are by far the richest orchid habitats where most species are epiphytic on trees, but the family occurs throughout the world in a great variety of habitats. About 700 species are known in Australia, with around 200 species in south-western Western Australia, all of which are terrestrial.

The remarkable structure of orchid flowers reflects their evolutionary adaptation to highly specialised insect pollination. The male and female reproductive organs are fused to form a structure called the column. The floral segments consist of three sepals and three petals which are variously modified, sometimes extremely so. In the simplest orchid at least one petal forms a landing stage for the pollinating insect. Some species mimic specific insects, both visually and by scent, forming a total dependence on the chosen insect for pollination.

The edible tubers of many Australian terrestrial species were an important food source for the Aborigines; they also used seeds of the epiphytic *Cymbidium madidum* as a contraceptive. Some recent taxonomic studies have made extensive changes in generic concepts by splitting both *Caladenia* and *Pterostylis* into a number of new genera. The broader concepts as retained in the WA Census have been followed here.

453 *Caledenia cairnsiana*

452 *Caladenia bryceana* R.S.Rogers
Dwarf Spider Orchid
Stem to 10 cm tall; one or two flowers 10–20 mm across; leaf to 5 x 4 mm, sparsely hairy. A rare orchid, difficult to see because of its cryptic colouring and one of the smallest species in WA.
Habitat: open woodland.
Dist: 16, 21.

453 *Caladenia cairnsiana* F.Mueller
Zebra Orchid
Stem to 20 cm or more tall bearing one or two flowers c. 20 mm across; leaf to 10 x 5 mm, slightly hairy above and below. The left flower illustrated is typical, the right hand flower is possibly a hybrid with *Caladenia denticulata* which was growing nearby.
Habitat: sandy coastal soil and open forest and woodland in gravel and laterite.
Dist: 16, 17, 18, 19, 20, 21, 22, 23, 24.

454 *Caladenia denticulata* Lindley
Wispy Spider Orchid
Stem to 20 cm tall, bearing one or two flowers up to 10 cm across; leaf to 13 x 1 cm, hairy above and below. Colour is variable. Often found in clusters.
Habitat: diverse, from Kalbarri south to Israelite Bay and inland to the wheatbelt and goldfields.
Dist: 14, 15, 16, 18, 21, 22, 23, 24.

452 *Caledenia bryceana*

454 *Caladenia denticulata*

455 *Caladenia discoidea*   456 *Caledenia doutchiae*

457 *Caladenia falcata*

458 *Caladenia flava*

455 ***Caladenia discoidea*** Lindley
Dancing Orchid
Stem to 40 cm tall bearing up to three flowers about 40 mm across; leaf to 15 x 7 mm, hairy above and below. Widespread in the south-west but appears to be absent from tall closed forest.
Habitat: sandy soil in open forest and woodland and shrubland.
Dist: 16, 17, 18, 21, 22, 23.

456 ***Caladenia doutchiae*** O.H.Sargent
Purple-veined Spider Orchid
Stem to 30 cm tall bearing a solitary flower c. 35 mm across; leaf to 10 x 8 mm, sparsely hairy. This species is closely related to *Caladenia roei* which lacks the purple veins on the labellum and has shorter rounded calli. A variable species.
Habitat: Wheatbelt in woodland and tall scrub.
Dist: 21, 22, 23, 24.

457 ***Caladenia falcata*** (Nicholls) Clements and Hopper [syn. *C. dilatata* var. *falcata*]
Fringed Mantis Orchid
Stem to 40 cm tall bearing one or two flowers about 9cm across; leaf to 15 cm x 18 mm, hairy above and below. The upward-sweeping lateral sepals are distinctive.
Habitat: open forest and woodland in a variety of soils.
Dist: 18, 21, 22, 23.

458 ***Caladenia flava*** R.Brown
Cowslip Orchid
Flowering stem 10–30 cm high with one to five flowers; basal leaf hairy 5–15 x 5–20 mm. The amount of red in the flowers is variable; widespread and common from Kalbarri to Israelite Bay. Hybrids with *Caladenia latifolia* have been recorded.
Habitat: sandy soil in woodland, shrubland or kwongan, and lateritic or granitic areas on the Darling plateau.
Dist: 16, 17, 18, 19, 20, 21, 22, 23, 24.

459 ***Caladenia latifolia*** R.Brown
Pink Fairies
Stem to 35 cm or more tall, bearing one to three flowers up to 20 mm across; leaf to 15 x 3 cm, very hairy above and below. This species may be confused with *Caladenia reptans* which is generally smaller.
Habitat: in sand in coastal scrub and further inland in woodland.
Dist: 16, 17, 19, 20, 21, 23; also SA, NSW, Vic, Tas.

460 *Leptoceras menziesii* (R. Brown) Lindley
[syn. ***Caladenia menziesii*** R. Brown]
Stem to 25 cm tall, usually bearing one or two flowers; leaf to 8 x 3 cm, ovate, bright green. Common in the south-west but flowers freely only after fire, when spectacular displays may be seen.
Habitat: in winter-moist places in coastal woodland and forest and inland to the wheatbelt.
Dist: 17, 18, 19, 20, 21, 23; also SA, NSW, Vic, Tas.

461 *Paracaleana nigrita* (Lindley) Blaxell [syn. *Caleana nigrita* Lindley]
Flying Duck
Stem to 15 cm high, bearing one to three flowers; leaf 20 x 10 mm, ovate, green above, purple beneath. The flowers attract and temporarily capture insects to effect pollination. An 'open' flower and a flower closed after capturing a pollinating insect are shown.
Habitat: open sandy flats, and in woodland in sandy gravel.
Dist: 17, 18, 21, 22, 23.

462 *Drakaea* sp.
Hammer Orchid
Stem to 40 cm tall, bearing a solitary, insectiform flower of unique structure; leaf heart-shaped 25 x 20 mm, pale green. Pollination is effected by male thynnid wasps when attempting to copulate with the hinged labellum.
Habitat: in sand in open forest and woodland.
Dist: 17.

463 *Elythranthera brunonis* (Endlicher) A.S.George
Purple Enamel Orchid
Stem to 40 cm tall with up to four glossy flowers, deep purple when fresh; fading, dull flowers are sometimes confused with *E. emarginata*. In *E. brunonis* the labellum is abruptly recurved and tapers gradually to an obtuse apex; the flowers are also usually smaller than those of *E. emarginata*. It is one of the commonest and most widespread orchids from the extreme south-west to the eastern wheatbelt.
Habitat: woodland and kwongan in sand or lateritic gravel.
Dist: 16, 17, 18, 19, 20, 21, 22, 23.

459 *Caladenia latifolia*   460 *Leptoceras menziesii*

461 *Paracaleana nigrita*   462 *Drakaea* sp.

463 *Elythranthera brunonis*

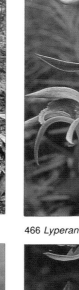

465 *Pyrorchis nigricans*

466 *Lyperanthus serratus*

467 *Disa bracteata*

468 *Prasophyllum regium*

469 *Pterostylis* sp.

470 *Pterostylis sanguinea*

464 **Elythranthera emarginata** (Lindley) A.S.George
Pink Enamel Orchid
Stem to 20 cm tall, bearing up to four glossy pink flowers c. 35 mm across, blotched deep pink to purple outside. The labellum is distinctively S-shaped in side view. Leaf to 10 x 7 cm, dark green, with glandular hairs.
Habitat: sandy soil of coastal and near-coastal scrub, heavy soil of the Darling Plateau and inland to the wheatbelt.
Dist: 16, 17, 18, 19, 20, 21, 23.

465 **Pyrorchis nigricans** (R.Brown) D.L.Jones & M.A.Clements [syn. *Lyperanthus nigricans* R.Brown]
Red Beaks
Stem to 20 cm high, bearing up to seven flowers c. 40 mm across. Although common within its range, this orchid flowers freely only after fire, but the large fleshy, ovate leaves up to 8 cm in diameter are often seen in dense colonies, including under trees such as Marri.
Habitat: open forest, woodland, kwongan and coastal scrub.
Dist: 16, 17, 18, 19, 20, 21, 23, also SA, Qld, NSW, Vic, Tas.

466 **Lyperanthus serratus** Lindley
Rattle Beaks
Flowering stem to 35 cm high, bearing up to seven flowers about 40 mm across; leaf to 35 x 1.5 cm, leathery, dark green, erect. Plants often grow through low, dense vegetation. A powdery bloom covers the whole plant excepting inner surfaces of flower parts.
Habitat: forest and woodland in heavy but well-drained soil.
Dist: 17, 18, 19, 20, 21, 23.

464 *Elythranthera emarginata*

467 **Disa bracteata** Swartz [syn. *Monadenia bracteata* Swartz) Dur and Schinz
South African Orchid
Flower spikes to 40 cm, flowers c. 5 mm across; leaves to 15 x 1.5 cm, overlapping at base. Introduced from South Africa and first recorded in 1944 near Albany. It is now wide-spread in south western WA.
Habitat: cleared or disturbed areas, road verges and open forest.
Dist: 17, 18, 19, 20, 21; also SA and Vic.

468 **Prasophyllum regium** R.S.Rogers
King Leek Orchid
A very tall orchid growing to nearly 2 m high, bearing up to 150 flowers c. 25 mm long by 15 mm wide; leaf to 90 cm long, fleshy, onion-like. Locally common but flowers freely only after fire the previous summer.
Habitat: swamps and semi-swamp depressions, also open forest in its southern range.
Dist: 17, 20.

469 **Pterostylis** sp.
Stem 20 cm, bearing four flowers each c. 25 mm high; leaves 3 x 1 cm, ovate, dull green in rosette of four to eight. A species belonging to the *Pterostylis rufa* aggregate.
Habitat: gravel slopes in open woodland.
Dist: 23.

470 **Pterostylis sanguinea** Jones and Clements
[syn. *Pterostylis vittata* Lindley]
Banded Greenhood
Stem to 40 cm tall, bearing up to eight flowers c. 20 mm long; leaves to 3 x 1.8 cm, ovate, greyish green, up to seven in a basal rosette. Green forms are common.
Habitat: open forest, scrub and woodland.
Dist: 16, 17, 18, 19, 21, 22, 23; also SA, Vic, Tas.

471 **Thelymitra campanulata** Lindley
Bell Sun Orchid
Stem to 50 cm, bearing up to ten flowers c. 20 mm across; leaf to 25 x 0.5 cm, dark green, channelled.
Habitat: near-coastal kwongan and low woodland.
Dist: 16, 17, 19, 21.

472 **Thelymitra crinita** Lindley
Blue Lady Orchid
Stem to 75 cm high, flowers up to ten, c. 40 mm across; leaf to 16 x 4.5 cm, ovate–lanceolate, dark green. The forward-projecting column arms bear distinctive purple hair tufts.
Habitat: in gravelly or granitic soil, in woodland and forest.
Dist: 17, 18, 19, 20, 21.

471 *Thelymitra campanulata*

472 *Thelymitra crinita*

473 *Thelymitra variegata*

474 *Orobanche minor*

473 **Thelymitra variegata** (Lindley) F. Mueller
Queen of Sheba
Stem to 40 cm high, bearing one to four flowers c.
40 mm across; leaf solitary to 10 x 1 cm, usually
spirally twisted. The flower colour is rather variable
but always striking.
Habitat: sandy to lateritic soil in woodland and
kwongan.
Dist: 16, 17, 19, 20, 21.
T. apiculata has narrow points on the column 'ears'
and grows between Eneabba and Mogumber,
flowering in winter.

OROBANCHACEAE

Orobanchaceae is a family of about 180 species of herbs
without chlorophyll, parasitic on the roots of other plants
and mainly confined to the northern hemisphere. The
genus *Orobanche* (broomrape) is the family's only
representative in Australia, with one or possibly two species
naturalised. Some European species parasitise clover and
may be a pest in pasture and vegetable crops.

474 **Orobanche minor** J.E. Smith.
Lesser Broomrape.
This species is introduced and widespread throughout
the agricultural areas of WA, SA, Vic. and Tas. A native
species, *O. cernua* is superficially similar and usually
found in sandy, mallee habitats.
Dist: 16, 17, 18, 19, 20, 21, 22, 23.

PHILYDRACEAE

The Philydraceae is a small family of three genera with a
centre of diversity in Australia where five of its six species are represented. They are generally confined to wa-
terlogged areas on swamp margins, or in soaks on rocky
outcrops and cliffs. The plants have rhizomatous roots
and leaves in two rows as in *Iris*. The flowers are yellow
and have only one stamen.

475 **Philydrella pygmaea** (R.Brown) Caruel
Lesser Butterfly Flower
Small single-stemmed herbs to 20 cm high arising
from a corm; spike two- to eight-flowered, flowers
usually opening singly, to 15 mm long.
Habitat: fresh-water swamps and seepage areas from
Geraldton south to 100 km west of Esperance.
Dist: 16, 17, 18, 19, 20, 21, 23.

PITTOSPORACEAE Native Frangipani

The Pittosporaceae family contains nine genera, all represented in Australia with two extending into New Zealand, Africa and South-east Asia.

The family shows much variation in Australia, from trees and shrubs to climbers and small shrublets. Several species of *Pittosporum* are grown as decorative shrubs. *Pittosporum angustifolium* (Weeping Pittosporum) is widespread in the drier areas of all mainland States.

Several species of *Billardiera* occur in south-western Western Australia; all are twiners with white, red, orange or mauve flowers.

Sollya heterophylla, with blue flowers and known as Australian Bluebell, is widespread and commonly cultivated as a screening creeper.

476 **Billardiera candida** (Huegel ex Endlicher) E.Bennett
Twining shrub; leaves narrowly oblong, ovate or elliptic, 25–90 x 2–21 mm; flowers 2–3 cm across in dense clusters.
Habitat: moist loam in forest.
Dist: 16, 18, 19.

477 **Billardiera erubescens** (Putterlick) E.Bennett
Shrubby or slender climber with reddish stems; leaves 2–3.5 cm long; flowers 2–2.5 cm long in loose clusters.
Habitat: sandy loam in shrubland or mallee.
Dist: 16, 18, 19, 21, 23.

475 *Philydrella pygmaea*

477 *Billardiera erubescens*

476 *Billardiera candida*

478 *Pittosporum angustifolium*

479 *Spinifex hirsutus*

480 *Spinifex longifolius*

478 ***Pittosporum angustifolium*** C.L.Loddiges
Weeping Pittosporum
Small tree to 17 m tall with grey, flaky or deeply fissured bark; branches pendulous; leaves glabrous 2.5–12.5 cm long; flowers white to yellow, sweetly scented; fruit 10–20 mm long with sticky red seeds.
Habitat: widespread in drier areas, including mallee woodland and open shrubland.
Dist: 8, 9, 10, 11, 12, 14, 15, 16, 17, 22, 23, 24; also NT, SA, Qld, NSW, Vic.
P. phylliraeoides has leaves silvery hairy on underside. It is confined to limestone plains N. of Kalbarri.

POACEAE Grasses

The Poaceae is one of the largest and most important plant families. They range in habit from small, delicate annuals to rhizomatous perennials and tree-like bamboos. Grasses are cosmopolitan and occur in most habitats; they contribute some 20% of the world's vegetation cover. Native grasses are not well represented, however, in many plant communities of south-western WA and the few that grow there are largely overshadowed by the colourful herbs and flowering shrubs. Some weedy species such as *Ehrharta* (Veldt grasses), introduced from South Africa, have become troublesome weeds in many bushland reserves in the south-west.

479 ***Spinifex hirsutus*** Labillardière
Hairy Spinifex
Spreading perennial with creeping stems rooting at the nodes; leaf blades flat, 10–40 cm x 9–17 mm, densely hairy on both sides. Photographed on the dunes at Jurien Bay and showing the large globular inflorescence of the female plants; these may break loose and roll along before the wind, giving rise to the alternative name Rolling Grass.
Habitat: beach sand and dunes.
Dist: 17, 19, 20, 21, 24.

480 ***Spinifex longifolius*** R.Brown
Beach Spinifex
Tussock-forming dioecious perennial with stout culms; leaf blades sub-terete 15–30 cm x 1.5–3 mm, glabrous; male inflorescence a raceme of solitary spikelets within a long, leaf-like spathe.
Habitat: beach sand and dunes.
Dist: 4, 12, 14, 16, 17; also NT, Qld.

481 ***Austrostipa elegantissima*** (Labillardière) S.W.L.Jacobs & J.Everett [syn. *S. elegantissima* Labillardière]
Feather Speargrass
Slender perennial 2-3 m tall; panicle open and

loose, to 25 cm long; branches and elongated pedicels plumose with spreading hairs; often seen in clumps overtopping surrounding shrubs and appearing like a drift of smoke.

Habitat: widespread on a variety of soils in kwongan and woodland.

Dist: 6, 8, 11, 13, 15, 16, 18, 21, 22, 23, 24; also SA, NSW and Vic.

482 *Triodia scariosa* N. Burbidge
Spinifex

Coarse tussock or hummock-forming perennial, old hummocks sometimes form rings as the centre plants die. Australia has 45 species, all endemic. Almost all have rigid needle-pointed leaves; flowering stems are up to 2.5 m high. Hummocks of *Triodia* and a similar genus *Plechtrachne* comprise the bulk of the vegetation cover of large areas of inland Australia. Although widely known by the common name 'spinifex', true *Spinifex* is a quite different genus restricted to coastal sands.

Habitat: sandy soil, particularly the deep red sand of the hummock grass plains and in mallee associations.

Dist: widespread except the wetter areas of the south-west; also NT, SA, Qld, NSW, Vic.

PODOCARPACEAE

The Podocarpaceae is a very ancient coniferous family of trees and shrubs of tropical and subtropical montane habitats, mainly in the southern hemisphere. It is related to the Taxaceae (Yew) of the northern hemisphere.

Most species are dioecious, with scale-like or linear evergreen leaves and small terminal cones. Some are cultivated as ornamentals, including *Phyllocladus aspleniifolius* (Celery Top Pine) and one species, *Dacrydium franklinii* (Huon Pine), is highly prized for its close-grained, long-lasting timber.

483 *Podocarpus drouynianus* F.Mueller
Wild Plum, Kula

A shrub 0.75–3 m tall with underground creeping stems rooting at the nodes and giving rise to clumps of erect, leafy stems; leaves 4–11 cm long; male cones 5–12 mm long; female cones c. 15 mm long subtended by an enlarged receptacle c. 20 mm long. At maturity the receptacle enlarges to an edible but almost tasteless 'fruit' 2–3 x 1–2.5 cm, dark blue with a glaucous bloom. It is the only member of the Podocarpaceae in WA. Plate 483(a) shows immature fruit.

Habitat: sandy, lateritic soil in Jarrah forest; fertile the first year after fire.

Dist: 17, 18, 19, 20.

481 *Austrostipa elegantissima*

482 *Triodia scariosa*

483(a) *Podocarpus drouynianus* (see also page 152)

483(b) *Podocarpus drouynianus (see page 151)*

484 *Comesperma confertum*

485 *Calandrinia liniflora*

POLYGALACEAE milkworts

The Polygalaceae is a widespread family occurring throughout warm and temperate regions of the world except for the South Pacific Islands and New Zealand. World-wide it contains c. 900 species with c. 40 in Australia.

The flowers are pea-like in appearance, and quite small in Australian species. *Comesperma* is the largest genus in WA with 19 species; the flowers are blue, pink or yellow. The rootstock is of economic importance in the production of oil of evergreen.

484 ***Comesperma confertum*** Labillardière
  Shrub to 1 m high; leaves narrowly linear, closely spaced, to 2.5 cm long; flowers c. 19 mm across in a dense, pyramidal spike up to 12 cm long.
  Habitat: alkaline soil over limestone, usually in damp situations.
  Dist: 16, 17, 19, 20, 21.

PORTULACACEAE

The Portulacaceae is a small family of mainly succulent herbs widespread in the southern hemisphere with a few genera in the northern. Some species are widely cultivated; *Portulaca oleracea* (purslane) is used as a salad plant and *Portulacaria afra* (Jade plant) is a popular small garden shrub in warm areas. Seeds of Australian *Portulaca* and *Calandrinia* species, although very small, were ground and made into cakes by Aborigines. The fleshy leaves were also eaten and are particularly attractive to cattle in times of drought but may be toxic when young.

485 ***Calandrinia liniflora*** Fenzl
  Very similar to *C. remota* but of more restricted distribution and confined to WA; Both species often cover large areas on the margins of shallow lakes and on sandy flats following rain.
  Habitat: sand plains and lake margins.
  Dist: 14, 15, 16, 17, 21.

486 ***Calandrinia remota*** J.M.Black
  Round-leaved Parakeelya
  Annual or perennial herb to 30 cm high; leaves fleshy, 1–5 cm long, mostly basal; flowers about 2.5 cm across.
  Habitat: red sand, often round salt lakes.
  Dist: 10, 14, 16, 23; also SA, Qld, NSW.

PROTEACEAE

The Proteaceae is probably Australia's most admired plant family; it reaches a peak of diversity in south-western Western Australia.

World-wide the family contains over 1400 species, mostly confined to the southern hemisphere with a few species north of the equator in south-east Asia, Africa and America. In Western Australia there are about 550 species of which about 500 are endemic in the State. Most of these are found to the south and west of a line between Shark Bay and Israelite Bay.

Their most favoured habitats are heathlands on mineral-deficient sand and gravel, but many also grow in Jarrah forest and a few in Karri forest. They are generally absent from saline and permanently wet situations.

All the Proteaceae are perennial evergreen plants and usually woody; they vary from small prostrate shrubs to tall trees and most have stiff, harsh, often prickly leaves. Many have lignotubers and regenerate well after fire; others rely on seed for regeneration and need fire to stimulate seed germination.

An increasing number of the Proteaceae of WA are being brought into cultivation although much is still to be learnt about propagation. Many are particularly sought after as cut flowers, and as garden plants they are valuable attractors of birds.

Adenanthos Labillardière The generic name is derived from the Greek *aden* (a gland) and *anthos* (a flower), referring to the prominent nectaries inside the floral tube. Glands also occur either at the apex of the leaf lobes or on the leaf surface.

Most species are woody shrubs, prostrate or erect. Two species, *A. cygnorum* and *A. acanthophyllus*, may form small trees. Some have lignotubers and hence regenerate rapidly after fire. The genus is endemic in Australia and contains 32 species of which only two extend beyond south-western WA.

487 ***Adenanthos barbiger*** Lindley
Hairy Glandflower
Low, erect or spreading shrub to 1 m high with many stems arising from a lignotuber; leaves 3–5 cm long; flowers to 4 cm long.
Habitat: loam or gravelly soil in Jarrah forest.
Dist: 17, 18, 19, 20.

486 *Calandrinia remota*

487 *Adenanthos barbiger*

488 *Adenanthos cuneatus*

489 *Adenanthos drummondii*

490 *Adenanthos flavidiflorus*

492 *Adenanthos obovatus*

488 ***Adenanthos cuneatus*** Labillardière
Coastal Jug-flower
Shrub to 3 m high; leaves to 2.5 cm long, silky hairy, old leaves greyish, young growth pinkish to red and often conspicuous; flowers to 4 cm long, pink to purple.
Habitat: sandy, near-coastal kwongan.
Dist: 19, 20, 21, 22, 24.

489 ***Adenanthos drummondii*** Meisner
Dense spreading shrub to 1.5 m high; leaves c. 3 cm long, clustered and usually divided into about three segments; flowers c. 3 cm long, often hidden among the foliage.
Habitat: sand in kwongan.
Dist: 16, 17, 23.

490 ***Adenanthos flavidiflorus*** F.Mueller
Low, diffuse shrub to 1 m high; leaves to c. 2 cm long, divided into five to seven segments; flowers to 3 cm long.
Habitat: in kwongan in deep sand near the south coast and hinterland.
Dist: 22,22, 23.

491 ***Adenanthos gracilipes*** A.S.George
Multi-stemmed, spreading shrub to 1.5 m high; leaves 1–3 cm long, divided several times; flowers solitary, c. 3 cm long.
Habitat: deep sand in the eastern Roe region, locally common.
Dist: 22.

492 ***Adenanthos obovatus*** Labillardière
Basket Flower
Erect shrub to 1.5 m high; leaves c. 2 cm long; flowers to 4 cm long, glabrous except for short hairs on lower half of style.
Habitat: sandy soil in woodland and margins of swamps.
Dist: 17, 18, 19, 20, 21.

491 *Adenanthos gracilipes*

493 **Adenanthos venosus** Meisner
Shrub 1–2 m high; leaves to 2 x 1 cm; flowers c. 4 cm long, red to pink-purple.
Habitat: quartzite areas round the Barren Ranges.
Dist: 21.

493 *Adenanthos venosus*

Banksia Linnaeus f. was named in 1782 after Sir Joseph Banks who collected the first known members of the genus at Botany Bay in 1770. Banksias are among WA's best known and most spectacular plants; apart from one species in Papua New Guinea the genus is restricted to Australia and 59 of the 76 species are endemic in south-western WA. Plants vary in size from robust trees to small, erect or prostrate shrubs.

The flower spikes consist of numerous (often hundreds) of very small flowers but very few of these are fertilised or produce mature seed. The fruiting cones come in a wide variety of shapes and sizes. The peak flowering season for most banksias is summer, autumn or winter rather than spring. Recent studies have placed the genus *Dryandra* among the descendants of the more widespread genus *Banksia*. New combinations for all *Dryandra* names in *Banksia* have been published but pending the general acceptance of this we have retained *Dryandra* as a separate genus.'

494 *Banksia attenuata*

494 **Banksia attenuata** R.Brown
Slender Banksia
A shrub to 2 m or tree to 10 m high, leaves 4–27 cm x 5–16 mm; flower spikes to 25 cm long.
Habitat: deep sand in kwongan, shrubland and woodland.
Dist: 16, 17, 18, 19, 20, 21, 22, 23.

495 **Banksia baueri** R.Brown
Woolly Banksia
A branched, bushy shrub to 2 m high; leaves narrowly obovate, 4–13 x 0.5–3.5 cm; flower spikes 15–40 x 12–20 cm, colour may be yellow, rusty brown or grey-mauve.
Habitat: deep white or grey sand and shallow sand over laterite or quartzite, in kwongan or shrubland.
Dist: 21, 22, 23.

495 *Banksia baueri*

496 **Banksia blechnifolia** F.Mueller
Spreading, prostrate shrub; stems horizontal, sometimes creeping slightly underground; leaves to c. 50 cm long, deeply lobed and with prominent midrib; flower spikes 6–16 cm long.
Habitat: white sand in kwongan or mallee heath.
Dist: 21, 22.

496 *Banksia blechnifolia*

497 *Banksia coccinea*

498 *Banksia gardneri*

499 *Banksia grandis*

500 *Banksia hookeriana*

497 **Banksia coccinea** R.Brown
Scarlet Banksia
Erect shrub or small tree to 8 m high, often spindly and with few stems; leaves truncate, broadly oblong, 3–9 x 2–7 cm; flower spikes to 12 x 15 cm, often broader than long; styles usually scarlet, occasionally yellow.
Habitat: white or grey sand in tall shrubland or woodland.
Dist: 19, 20, 21.

498 **Banksia gardneri** A.S.George var. **gardneri**
Prostrate shrub; leaves erect, 10–40 x 2–6 cm, deeply lobed; flower spikes to 6–15 x 5–6 cm, flowers in September to November.
Habitat: sand, sandy loam or gravel in shrubland and low woodland.
Dist: 19, 20, 21, 22, 23.
Two other varieties are recognised: var. *brevidentata* A.S. George has shortly dentate leaves and flowers in winter; it is restricted to the Stirling Range and a small area near Albany; var. *hiemalis* A.S. George has very deeply lobed pale green leaves and pinkish flowers in winter.

499 **Banksia grandis** Willdenow
Bull Banksia
A tree to 10 m, in coastal areas sometimes a shrub; leaves 10–45 x 3–11 cm, divided to the midrib into triangular lobes; flower spikes 25–40 x c. 10 cm.
Habitat: sand on the coastal plain in woodland; common on laterite in Jarrah forest, particularly in the Darling Range.
Dist: 16, 17, 18, 19, 20, 21, 23.

500 **Banksia hookeriana** Meisner
Hooker's Banksia
Dense, rounded shrub to 3 m high, leaves 10–25 cm x 8–10 mm; flower spikes to 12 x 8 cm.
Habitat: deep white or yellow sand in kwongan; locally common.
Dist: 16.

501 **Banksia ilicifolia** R.Brown
Holly-leaved Banksia
Tree to 10 m high; leaves 3–10 cm long, acutely serrate or occasionally entire; flowers in terminal hemispherical clusters 6–7 cm across; fruit a cluster of 1–3 ovoid follicles. This species lacks the typical long cone of most banksias and the flowers are somewhat similar to *Dryandra*.
Habitat: woodland or tall shrubland on deep white or grey coastal sand and in the Stirling Range.
Dist: 16, 17, 18, 19, 20, 21.

502 *Banksia laevigata* Meisner subsp. *laevigata*
Tennis Ball Banksia
Shrub to 3.5 m tall; leaves 5–14 cm x 4–20 mm;
flower spikes c. 10 cm across; flowers pale yellow
with grey hairs.
Habitat: rocky soil in shrubland and open woodland in the Ravensthorpe Range and along the lower
Fitzgerald River.
Dist: 21.
One other subspecies is recognised; subsp. *fuscolutea*
has bright yellow flowers with rusty-brown hairs; it
occurs in scattered localities in sandy soil in regions
22 and 24.

501 *Banksia ilicifolia*

503 *Banksia lemanniana* Meisner
Large shrub to 5 m high; leaves 3–9 x 1.2–3.5 cm;
new growth rusty brown and velvety; mature flower
spikes 5–11 x 8–10 cm, pendulous, borne usually
on stems five to eleven years old.
Habitat: rocky quartzite sand on lateritic loam in
low woodland or tall shrubland.
Dist: 21.

504 *Banksia menziesii* R.Brown
Firewood Banksia
Tall shrub or small tree to 10 m high; leaves 8–25 x 1–
4 cm; flower spikes 10–15 x 8–12 cm, flowers are usually pink but occasionally cream or brown; a common component of the remnant vegetation in parks
and reserves in suburbs to the north and south of Perth,
extending north to Kalbarri.
Habitat: deep sand in low woodland or kwongan
near the coast.
Dist: 16, 17, 18, 23.

502 *Banksia laevigata* subsp. *laevigata*

503 *Banksia lemanniana*

504 *Banksia menziesii*

505 *Banksia oreophila*

506 *Banksia praemorsa*

508 *Banksia pulchella*

507 *Banksia prionotes*

509 *Banksia quercifolia*

511 *Banksia speciosa*

505 **Banksia oreophila** A.S.George
Western Mountain Banksia
Shrub to 3 m high, usually much branched; leaves
2–11 cm long, usually entire, sometimes with a few
serrations; flower spikes 2–9 cm long on short
branchlets from older stems.
Habitat: rocky or shale soil, quartzite or sandstone
in shrubland in Stirling Range and Fitzgerald River
National Park, usually on hillsides and peaks.
Dist: 21.
Related to *B. quercifolia* which differs in the thin,
always serrate, deep green leaves and which is usually less robust than *B. oreophila* and always grows
in wet situations.

506 **Banksia praemorsa** Andrews
Cut-leaf Banksia
Shrub to 4 m high; leaves 2–6 cm long; flower spikes
10–27 cm long, often hidden among foliage, colour
varies from red-maroon when exposed, to greenish-yellow or gold.
Habitat: coastal dunes overlying granite or limestone, often overhanging the sea.
Dist: 20, 21.

507 **Banksia prionotes** Lindley
Acorn Banksia
Shrub or tree to 10 m high; leaves 15–27 x 1–2 cm;
flower spikes 10–15 x c. 8 cm.
Habitat: deep yellow or white sand in tall shrubland
and low woodland, mainly in coastal areas but also
in a few scattered inland localities.
Dist: 16, 17, 18, 22, 23.

508 **Banksia pulchella** R.Brown
Teasel Banksia
Shrub to 1 m tall; leaves 4–13 x 1 mm; flower spikes
c. 5 x 5 cm.
Habitat: deep white sand in tall shrubland and
kwongan near the coast.
Dist: 21.

509 **Banksia quercifolia** R.Brown
Oak-leaved Banksia
Erect, much-branched shrub to 3 m high; leaves 3–
15 x 1–4 cm, acutely serrate; flower spikes c. 5–10 x
4–6 cm on short lateral branches within the shrub;
flowers orange or brown with rusty brown hairs.
Habitat: sandy wet depressions and swamp margins in shrubland-sedge formations, sometimes in
low woodland. Restricted to coastal areas between
Windy Harbour and Cheyne Beach.
Dist: 19, 20.

510 **Banksia repens** Labillardière
Creeping Banksia
Shrub with prostrate underground stems; leaves
erect, scattered, 25–40 cm long; flower spikes 6–10
cm long, cream and pink, emerging at ground level
usually beyond the leaves.
Habitat: in sand or sandy loam, sometimes with
gravel, in kwongan or occasionally coastal dunes.
Dist: 21.

511 **Banksia speciosa** R.Brown
Showy Banksia
A large, spreading, much-branched shrub or small
tree to 6 m high; leaves 20–40 cm long; flower spikes
to 15 cm long; new growth pale brown on rusty
brown branches.
Habitat: deep coastal sand, forming large thickets.
Dist: 21, 22, 24.

512 **Banksia sphaerocarpa** var. **caesia** A.S.George
Spreading shrub to 4 m tall; leaves glaucous, 2.5–
10 cm x 1.5 mm; flower spikes 5–8 cm across
Habitat: laterite or shallow sandy loam over laterite
in the central and southern wheatbelt.
Dist: 18, 22, 23.

Two other varieties are recognised; var. *sphaerocarpa*
is a smaller plant, up to 2 m tall with non-glaucous
foliage and purplish brown or rusty coloured flowers; it occurs in scattered inland and near-coastal
areas of regions 16, 17, 18, 19 and 21.

Var. *dolichostyla* A.S.George has the large habit, glaucous foliage and golden flowers of var. *caesia* but is
distinguished by a long perianth, (49–55 mm long)
and long style (50–65 mm long); it is confined to a
small area east of Hyden in region 22.

513 **Banksia violacea** C.A.Gardner
Violet Banksia
Shrub to 1.5 m tall; leaves 1–4 cm x 1.5 mm; flower
spikes 6–8 cm across
Habitat: white sand or sandy loam over laterite in
kwongan.
Dist: 21, 22, 23.

Conospermum Smith, named from the Greek *konos* (a
cone); *sperma* (a seed); referring to the shape of the nut.
These shrubs or small perennial herbs are known generally as smokebushes because of the likeness of some of the
larger, very woolly species to drifts of smoke. Many species
also appear in large numbers after fire. The genus is restricted to Australia with about 36 species at present named.
The small tubular flowers are often woolly and usually
white, blue or grey. The fruit is a small nut with a fringe of
hairs at the base.

510 *Banskia repens*

512 *Banksia sphaerocarpa* var. *caesia*

513 *Banksia violacea*

514 *Conospermum acerosum*
subsp. *hirsutum*

515 *Conospermum boreale*
subsp. *boreale*

516 *Conospermum brownii*

517 *Conospermum caeruleum*

514 **_Conospermum acerosum_** Lindley subsp. **_hirsutum_**
E. M. Bennett
Needle-leaved Smokebush
Shrub 1–2 m high with several, usually unbranched stems arising from the base of the plant; leaves terete, pungent, to 5 cm long; leaf bases and upper stems pubescent; flowers c. 8 mm long.
Habitat: sandy kwongan between Northampton and Kalbarri.
Dist: 16.
Subsp. *acerosum* has usually glabrous stems and fine red hairs on perianth. It occurs from Northampton south to Perth and in a few places in the Busselton-Nannup area.

515 **_Conospermum boreale_** E.M.Bennett subsp. **_boreale_**
Shrub to 1 m high, multi-stemmed from base; leaves variable, 5–10 cm x 6–10 mm spreading, and with three nerves; flowers c. 6 mm long. Previously regarded as a form of the Tree Smokebush, *C. triplinervium* (q.v.)
Habitat: sandy kwongan and woodland between Eneabba and Kalbarri.
Dist: 16.
Subsp. *accedens* E.M. Bennett differs in having ascending leaves and lower inflorescence branches glabrous. It occurs from Eneabba north to Geraldton.

516 **_Conospermum brownii_** Meisner
Blue-eyed Smokebush
Herbaceous shrub, leafy at base; leaves to 7 cm long, flowering stalks up to 30 cm long; flowers 8 mm long, white or cream, buds blue.
Habitat: sand or gravel in shrubland and kwongan.
Dist: 22, 23, 24.

517 **_Conospermum caeruleum_** R.Brown
Shrub to 1 m high; leaves basal, to 15 cm long, including a long petiole; flowers 5–8 mm long in small clusters terminating leafless branched stems.
Habitat: sandy soil in open forest.
Dist: 17, 18, 19, 20, 21.

518 **_Conospermum coerulescens_** F. Mueller subsp. **_dorrienii_** (Domin) E.M. Bennett
Stirling Range Smokebush
Erect shrub to 1m high, usually with one main stem branching in the middle; leaves 1–2 cm long; incurved or 'S'-shaped flowers c. 8 mm long, borne in dense terminal clusters.
Habitat: sandy or rocky soil of the Stirling Range.
Dist: 21.
Subsp. *coerulescens* has grey-blue flowers and occurs near Albany and Bremer Bay. Subsp. *adpressum* has ascending but not incurved leaves and mid-blue flowers; it occurs south of the Stirling Range between Albany and Mt. Manypeaks.

519 *Conospermum ephedroides* Kippist ex Meisner
Shrub to 1 m high; stems erect; leaves to 15 cm long, rush-like, on lower part of stem only, reduced to scales on upper parts; flowers 6–7 mm long in clusters at intervals along stems.
Habitat: sand or gravel in kwongan or mallee shrubland.
Dist: 22, 23.

520 *Conospermum flexuosum* R.Brown subsp. *flexuosum*
Tangled Smokebush
Spreading shrub, branches flexuose, tangled and prominently four-angled; leaves 15–30 cm long including the long petiole; flowers 7–9 mm long in clusters of two to six flowers.
Habitat: sandy soil in woodland and heath commonly in swampy depressions in the Albany area and east to Wellstead.
Dist: 19, 20, 21.
Subsp. *laevigatum* E.M. Bennett has eight to twelve ribbed branches and occurs in the Capel-Busselton-Nannup area.

521 *Conospermum nervosum* Meisner
Small spreading shrub 30–60 cm high; leaves variable, 1.5–3 cm long, perianth glabrous or slightly hairy, blue or rarely pale pink.
Habitat: kwongan north of Perth.
Dist: 16, 17.

522 *Conospermum teretifolium* R.Brown
Spider Smokebush
Shrub to 1.5 m high; leaves rush-like, to c. 30 cm long; flowers 1.5–2 cm long, tubular with long lobes, glabrous.
Habitat: sandy coastal kwongan.
Dist: 19, 20, 21.

520 *Conospermum flexuosum* subsp. *flexuosum*

522 *Conospermum teretifolium*

518 *Conospermum coerulescens*

519 *Conospermum ephedroides*

521 *Conospermum nervosum*

523 *Conospermum triplinervium*

524 *Conospermum unilaterale*

526 *Dryandra carlinoides*

525 *Dryandra arborea*

527 *Dryandra comosa*

528 *Dryandra corvijuga*

523 *Conospermum triplinervium* R.Brown
Tree Smokebush
Tall shrub or small tree to 7 m high; leaves usually with three nerves, 5–20 cm x 2–40 mm; flowers c. 6 mm long.
Habitat: sand in shrubland and woodland; now common only around Perth.
Dist: 16, 17, 18, 19, 21, 22, 23.

524 *Conospermum unilaterale* E.M.Bennett
Plume Smokebush
Shrub 1–2 m high with glabrous incurved leaves to 2.5 cm long which gradually become shorter and appressed to the stem below the inflorescence; flowers c. 5 mm long, white with a lavender tip. Previously included with *C. incurvum* which is a shorter plant with terete leaves.
Habitat: sandy soil in kwongan in the Badgingarra-Eneabba area.
Dist: 16, 17, 23.

Dryandra R.Brown, named after Jonas Dryander, first librarian of the Linnean Society. It is a purely Western Australian genus with about 91 species, most of which occur in south-western WA. It is closely related to *Banksia* but with flowers in heads surrounded by bracts; the fruiting follicles are hard but not formed into woody cones as in *Banksia*.

525 *Dryandra arborea* C.A.Gardner
Yilgarn Dryandra
Tree to 5 m high with thick, rough, black bark; leaves 6 cm long, deeply serrated; flower heads 4–5 cm across. this species occurs further inland than any other *Dryandra*.
Habitat: shallow soil over hard clay on ironstone hills north of Southern Cross.
Dist: 24.

526 *Dryandra carlinoides* Meisner
Pink Dryandra
Dense, erect shrub to 1 m high; leaves to 3 cm x 5 mm; flower heads c. 3 cm across; the pink-tinged flowers are uncommon in the genus.
Habitat: kwongan and dry ridges.
Dist: 16, 17.

527 *Dryandra comosa* Meisner
Dense single or multi-stemmed shrub 1–3 m high; leaves 15–30 cm x 5 mm; flower heads 3–4 cm across, often hidden among a tangled mass of very long leaves.
Habitat: in shrubland on lateritic hills of the Wongan Hills district.
Dist: 23.

528 *Dryandra corvijuga* A.S.George
Spreading shrub to 1.5 m high with dense tangled foliage; leaves to 30 cm long; flower heads 6–8 cm wide.
Habitat: lateritic gravel in open kwongan or dense shrubland.
Dist: 21, 22.

529 *Dryandra formosa* R.Brown
Showy Dryandra
Shrub 3–8 m tall; leaves 5–20 cm long, not rigid; flower heads to 10 cm across. A very showy species widely cultivated, well-known in the cut-flower trade.
Habitat: Rocky or peaty soil in open forest.
Dist: 19, 20, 21.

530 *Dryandra glauca* A.S.George
Glaucous shrub to 2 m high; leaves to 6 cm long, truncate, the marginal teeth terminating in long pungent points; flower heads c. 5 cm across.
Habitat: sandy soil in kwongan.
Dist: 16, 23.
Superficially similar to *D. sessilis* (Knight) Domin, which has shorter, less deeply serrated leaves with rounded tips. *D. falcata* R.Brown has rather similar but non-glaucous leaves; it is confined to southern heathlands.

531 *Dryandra kippistiana* Meisner
Small, erect shrub to 1 m; leaves to 2.5–6 cm x 5–10 mm; flower heads 4–5 cm across, light yellow to pinkish-yellow.
Habitat: in kwongan, in laterite or sand over laterite.
Dist: 16.

532 *Dryandra lindleyana* subsp. *lindleyana* var. *mellicula* A.S.George
Sprawling shrub with underground stems and branches to 30 cm high; leaves to 20 cm long; flower heads 2–4 cm across with a distinctive cup-like appearance before the styles straighten.
Habitat: common in open Marri–Jarrah forest in lateritic soil on the Darling Plateau from Perth to Cape Naturaliste.
Dist: 17, 18, 19, 20.

533 *Dryandra nobilis* Lindley subsp. *nobilis*
Golden Dryandra
Upright, untidy, many-branched shrub to c. 3 m high; leaves 12–25 cm long; flower heads 5–7 cm across.
Habitat: gravelly soil on ridges, usually in forest.
Dist: 16, 18, 23.

529 *Dryandra formosa*   531 *Dryandra kippistiana*

530 *Dryandra glauca*

532 *Dryandra lindleyana* subsp. *lindleyana* var. *mellicula*

533 *Dryandra nobilis* subsp. *nobilis*

534 *Dryandra pulchella*

535 *Dryandra speciosa* subsp. *speciosa*

536 *Dryandra squarrosa*

537 *Dryandra wonganensis*

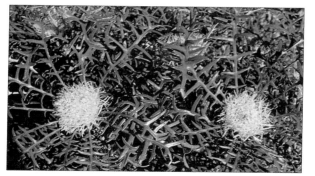

538 *Dryandra xylothemelia*

534 **_Dryandra pulchella_** Meisner
Sprawling shrub to c. 1.7 m high; leaves to 20 cm long, narrow, finely toothed, glaucous, crowded; flower heads 2–3 cm across.
Habitat: in shrubland on lateritic hillsides in the Wongan Hills region.
Dist: 23.

535 **_Dryandra speciosa_** Meisner subsp. **_speciosa_**
Shaggy Dryandra
Spreading shrub to 1.5 m high with erect branches and pendulous flowers; leaves linear, 8 cm x 2 mm; one of the few species with entire leaves; flower heads to 7 cm across.
Habitat: sandy or gravelly soil in kwongan near Tammin.
Dist: 23.
Subsp. *macrocarpa*, with larger fruit, occurs on lateritic hillsides between Eneabba and Badgingarra.

536 **_Dryandra squarrosa_** R.Brown subsp. **_squarrosa_**
Pingle
Erect shrub to 2.5 m high, lower leaves 10–25 cm long; upper leaves shorter ; flower heads c. 3.5 cm across.
Habitat: gravelly lateritic soil in Jarrah and Wandoo open forest.
Dist: 18, 19.
Subsp. *argillacea* is a rare plant of winter-wet flats near Busselton.

537 **_Dryandra wonganensis_** A.S.George
Erect, dense shrub to 2 m high; leaves not glaucous, to 20 cm long with long, widely spaced teeth; flower heads c. 4 cm across.
Habitat: rocky, lateritic soil in the Wongan Hills area.
Dist: 23.

538 **_Dryandra xylothemelia_** A.S.George
Suckering shrub to 1 m high; leaves with widely spaced, pungent lobes; flower heads 2–3 cm across.
Habitat: sand over laterite in kwongan.
Dist: 22.

Franklandia R.Brown, named after the English Botanist Thomas Frankland, is a genus of two species endemic in south-western WA. *F. triaristata* (not illustrated) is similar to *F. fucifolia*, but is much less common. It has slightly larger, white and purple flowers and one of the strangest fruits in the Proteaceae. The nut is surmounted by a long twisted column which terminates in three slender hairy awns; the whole fruit is c. 15 cm long.

539 *Franklandia fucifolia* R.Brown
Lanoline Bush
Shrub to 1.5 m high; leaves to 15 cm long, several
times divided into terete segments; flowers per-
fumed, to 5 cm long and 3–4 cm across in racemes
up to 15 cm long.
Habitat: sandy soil in kwongan and woodland.
Dist: 18, 19, 21, 22, 23.

Grevillea R.Brown ex Knight, named from a manuscript
name of Robert Brown honouring Charles Greville, one
of the founders of the Royal Horticultural Society. It is a
genus of over 340 species occurring throughout Australia
in a wide variety of habitats and ranging from small
shrubs to large forest trees. A few species are found outside Australia in Malaysia, New Guinea and New Caledonia; over half of the Australian species occur in WA.

The flowers are tubular and split open at anthesis to
release the style which is often very long; the anthers
adhere to the concave tips of the tepals. The fruit is a
thin-walled follicle containing two seeds, usually with
membranous, usually encircling wings. The fruit matures within a few weeks of flowering, and in most species the follicles fall from the plant soon after shedding
the seed. The genus is widely cultivated and particularly valued as a bird attractor; it hybridises freely and
many fine cultivars have been developed. Some species
were used by the Aborigines for medicinal purposes and
many were a source of sweet nectar, either sucked directly from the flowers or made into a sweet drink.

539 *Franklandia fucifolia*   540 *Grevillea acacioides*

540 *Grevillea acacioides* C.A.Gardner ex McGillivray
Shrub 1–2 m high with many erect branches; leaves
4–7 cm long, usually terete, rarely linear to narrowly
obovate; flowers c. 5mm long.
Habitat: usually in shrubland in red or yellow sand
on sandplain, sometimes in gravelly loam over granite or on laterite.
Dist: 10, 15, 21, 22, 23, 24.

541 *Grevillea biformis* Meisner subsp. ***biformis*** [syn.
G. integrifolia subsp. *biformis* McGillivray]
Erect shrub 1.5–2.5 m high; leaves linear, to 16 cm
long, both sides silky; flower spikes up to 13 cm long,
occasionally pale pink.
Habitat: sand or sandy clay loam in shrubland or
mallee in the northern central and southern
wheatbelt.
Dist: 22, 23.
Subsp. *cymbiformis* P. Olde and N. Marriott differs
in having obovate, boat-shaped leaves with upper
surface glabrous; confined to a small area near
Eneabba.

541 *Grevillea biformis* subsp. *biformis*

542 *Grevillea bipinnatifida*

542 ***Grevillea bipinnatifida*** R.Brown
Fuchsia Grevillea
Spreading shrub to 1.5 m high; leaves bipinnatifid, 8–15 cm long; the pendulous flowers are conspicuous and vary from pale orange to deep red, with racemes up to 16.5 cm long and 3–5 cm wide. *G. bipinnatifida* is one parent of several hybrid cultivars including the popular 'Robyn Gordon'.
Habitat: woodland, usually in lateritic loamy soil, and in granitic soil in shrubland.
Dist: 17, 18, 19.

543 *Grevillea coccinea* subsp. *coccinea*

543 ***Grevillea coccinea*** Meisner subsp. ***coccinea***
Spreading shrub to 2.5 m high; leaves to 12.5 cm x 2–4 mm, often hairy and appearing greyish; flower spikes to c. 6.5 cm long.
Habitat: near-coastal in sand or gravelly sand.
Dist: 21.
Subsp. *lanata* P. Olde and N. Marriott differs in having a slightly broader perianth with a woolly outer surface. It is restricted to small areas in the Fitzgerald River National Park.

544 ***Grevillea commutata*** F. Mueller
Spreading, much-branched shrub 1–3 m high; leaves 5–10 cm x 2–10 mm, occasionally lobed; inflorescence 1–2.5 cm long. The flowers are sweetly scented, and are greenish-white to cream or pale pink.
Habitat: on sandhills or kwongan.
Dist: 16.

545 ***Grevillea didymobotrya*** Meisner subsp. ***didymobotrya***
Erect shrub 1–3 m high; leaves 2.5–14 cm x 0.5–1.3 mm; inflorescence 4–12 cm long, simple or with up to 5 branches. Two subspecies are recognised; subspecies *involuta* D.J. McGillivray differs in having shorter, obovate leaves with recurved apex; both have flowers with a strong sweet scent.
Habitat: kwongan, shrubland or open mallee associations on sand plain.
Dist: 15, 16, 22, 23, 24.

544 *Grevillea commutata*

545 *Grevillea didymobotrya* subsp. *didymobotrya*

546 *Grevillea dryandroides* subsp. *hirsuta*

546 *Grevillea dryandroides* subsp. *hirsuta* Olde and Marriott

Tufty, vigorously root-suckering shrub to 30 cm high, usually forming large colonies; leaves 7–14 cm long, deeply divided with up to 35 pairs of leaflets, each 12–35 mm long and covered with persistent crisped hairs; flower spikes 6–10 cm long.

Habitat: yellow sand in kwongan, sometimes with eucalypts.

Dist: 23.

Subsp. *dryandroides* differs in having shorter glabrous leaf-lobes 5–10 mm long and flower spikes only 3–4 cm long; it is confined to small areas near Ballidu.

547 *Grevillea erectiloba* F.Mueller

Shrub 1–3 m high; leaves 5–12 cm long, several times divided into narrow, closely aligned, erect lobes; inflorescence c. 3–4 cm long with three to eighteen flowers.

Habitat: tall shrubland in semi-arid areas north of Southern Cross in gravelly loam.

Dist: 24.

548 *Grevillea eriostachya* Lindley

Shrub to 4 m high, often with one or two prominent horizontal branches; leaves 5–25 cm long divided into linear lobes and often with conspicuous hairs on the upper surface; flower spikes 8–35 cm long, borne well clear of foliage, subconical with the lowest flowers opening first; fruit 15–22 mm long x 9–13 mm wide and 4–7 mm thick, crustaceous.

Habitat: acacia, sheoak, spinifex and kwongan associations, usually on sandhills or sandy situations.

Dist: 4, 5, 6, 7, 8, 9, 12, 13, 14, 15, 16, 17, 18, 23, 24; also NT and SA.

549 *Grevillea excelsior* Diels

Flame Grevillea

Single stemmed shrub or small pine-like tree to 8 m high; leaves 5–25 cm long, usually divided into linear lobes but simple leaves often present below the inflorescence which is 7–25 cm long and usually borne among the leaves and with most flowers in the spike opening together; fruit 15–22 mm long x 13–17 mm wide and 9–12 mm thick, bony.

Habitat: in sandy loam in mallee scrub, tall shrubland and kwongan.

Dist: 21, 22, 23, 24.

547 *Grevillea erectiloba*

548 *Grevillea eriostachya*

549 *Grevillea excelsior*

550 *Grevillea hookeriana*

552 *Grevillea insignis* subsp. *insignis*

553 *Grevillea intricata*

551 *Grevillea huegelii*

555 *Grevillea kenneallyi*

550 ***Grevillea hookeriana*** Meisner
Spreading to erect, often stiff shrub; leaves 1–12 cm long, usually divided with rigid, pungent lobes 1–20 mm long; inflorescence up to 8 cm long x 3 cm wide. Colour of the style varies from very deep reddish purple to black.
Habitat: kwongan or shrubland in sandy soil.
Dist: 22, 23, 24.

551 ***Grevillea huegelii*** S.Moore
Shrub to 2.5 m high, occasionally prostrate; leaves 1–3 x 1.5–3 cm, deeply divided into two to seven pungent tipped segments; flowers in a raceme up to 6 cm across with few to many flowers; perianth 1.5–2.5 cm long, pink to deep red.
Habitat: widely distributed in arid areas in both acid and alkaline soils, usually in woodland.
Dist: 18, 21, 22, 23, 24; also SA, NSW, Vic.

552 ***Grevillea insignis*** Kippist ex Meisner subsp. ***insignis***
Wax Grevillea
Shrub 2–4 m high; leaves glabrous, to 9 x 4 cm, holly-like with sinuate prickly toothed margins, flowers glabrous, 15–20 mm long.
Habitat: mallee and shrubland in gravelly lateritic or ironstone soil.
Dist: 22, 23.
Subsp. *elliotii* Olde and Marriott differs in its non-glaucous branches and usually smaller, more deeply divided leaves with cuneate bases. It is confined to lateritic outcrops north-east of Lake King.

553 ***Grevillea intricata*** Meisner
Spreading shrub 1–3 m high and up to 3 m across with tangled branches; leaves to 16 cm long and up to three times ternately divided; inflorescence 5–20 cm long.
Habitat: kwongan or tall shrubland in sandy soil.
Dist: 16.

554 ***Grevillea juncifolia*** Hook. subsp. ***temulenta*** Olde and Marriott
Honeysuckle Grevillea
Shrub with erect branches to 4 m high; leaves 5–22 cm long, deeply divided; inflorescence a sticky raceme of well-spaced flowers each 2–3 cm long.
Habitat: red sand on dunes, plains and mallee communities.
Dist: 7, 9, 10, 13, 14, 15, 23, 24.
Subsp. *juncifolia* differs in having no glandular hairs on the flowers and undivided leaves. It is widespread in desert regions including NT, SA, Qld and NSW.

555 *Grevillea kenneallyi* McGillivray

Dense, spreading shrub 1.2–3 m high; leaves 4–8 cm long, divided several times into terete, pungent tipped lobes; inflorescence 3–5 cm long, usually branched.
Habitat: open woodland or shrubland, often on gravelly loam.
Dist: 23.

556 *Grevillea leptopoda* McGillivray

Spreading to erect shrub 0.6–1.5 m high; leaves 4–8 cm long, usually biternate; inflorescence 4–9 cm long; usually branched.
Habitat: mallee or woodland in sandy soil or lateritic gravel.
Dist: 16, 23.

557 *Grevillea leucopteris* Meisner

White Plume Grevillea
Spreading shrub 2–5 m high; leaves pinnatisect, to 30 cm long with eight to 30 narrowly linear segments, greyish green above, densely hairy below; inflorescence terminal, 20–80 cm long, with 5–14 branches, borne on long stems held well clear of the foliage; buds are enclosed by conspicuous, silky red-brown bracts. This is a striking plant whose flowers have a distinctive fetid scent. Although of limited distribution in the wild, it is widely used in roadside plantations and parks around Perth.
Habitat: in sand in kwongan.
Dist: 16.

558 *Grevillea oligantha* F.Mueller

Shrub 0.5–2 m high, usually with erect branches, leaves to 8 cm long; flowers bright red to pale orange, 15–22 mm long.
Habitat: mallee scrub or shrubland in clay-loam or gravelly soil.
Dist: 21, 22.

559 *Grevillea paradoxa* F.Mueller

Bottlebrush Grevillea
Bushy, rigid shrub 0.5–2 m high; leaves divided several times into slender pungent segments; inflorescence dense, 4–10 cm long; buds covered with silky-hairy bracts.
Habitat: mallee scrub and sclerophyllous shrubland; in sandy to gravelly soil over laterite.
Dist: 16, 22, 23, 24.

554 *Grevillea juncifolia* subsp. *temulenta*

556 *Grevillea leptopoda*

557 *Grevillea leucopteris*

558 *Grevillea oligantha*   559 *Grevillea paradoxa*

561 *Grevillea pilosa* subsp. *pilosa*

562 *Grevillea pterosperma*

563 *Grevillea tenuiflora*

560(a) and(b) *Grevillea petrophiloides*

560 *Grevillea petrophiloides* Meisner
Pink Pokers

Upright, sparsely branched shrub 2–4 m high; leaves erect, several times divided into long, linear pungent segments; inflorescence 7–20 cm long, usually branched and terminating leafless stems held well above the foliage; fruit deeply pitted, conspicuous. When young the fruits exude a sticky, caustic fluid which was used by the Aborigines to score the flesh prior to rubbing in ash which resulted in permanent scars.

Habitat: gravelly soil in shrubland.

Dist: 16, 22, 23.

G. magnifica and *G. oligomera* are closely related taxa sometimes considered subspecies of *G. petrophiloides*.

561 *Grevillea pilosa* A.S. George subsp. *pilosa*
Spreading semi-prostrate shrub to 2 m high; leaves to 6 cm long, the undersurface with rusty hairs, upper surface with prominent reticulate veining; flowers to 2.7 cm long, including style; perianth covered with rusty hairs.

Habitat: kwongan, shrubland or mallee scrub, in gravelly soil.

Dist: 21, 22.

Subsp. *redacta* Olde and Marriott differs in having smaller leaves and smaller perianth with fewer hairs on the outer surface.

562 *Grevillea pterosperma* F.Mueller
Erect shrub 2–4 cm high; leaves linear, 6–18 cm long, simple or occasionally divided with up to 6 linear lobes; inflorescences erect, 8–16 cm long, crowded at ends of branches. This species is widespread in scattered populations across southern Australia.

Habitat: mallee scrub, open shrubland or spinifex associations, in yellow or red sand.

Dist: 7, 9, 10, 15, 22, 23, 24; also NT, SA, NSW and Vic.

563 *Grevillea tenuiflora* (Lindley) Meisner
Tassel Grevillea

Spreading shrub to 1.5 m high; leaves to 5 x 5 cm, pinnatifid or occasionally undivided on flowering stems; flowers in racemes up to 4 cm long, usually pendent.

Habitat: kwongan, shrubland or eucalypt woodland in gravelly, lateritic soil; uncommon.

Dist: 18, 23.

564 *Grevillea tetragonoloba* Meisner
Erect to spreading shrub 1–2.6 m high, sometimes the branches almost horizontal; leaves generally lobed but varying considerably in length, width and number of lobes; inflorescence 4.5–11.5 cm long. Five races are recognised in this species based on variation in leaf characters.
Habitat: kwongan, open mallee and shrubland usually in deep sand.
Dist: 21, 22.

564 *Grevillea tetragonoloba*

565 *Grevillea tripartita* Meisner
Shrub 1.5–3 m high; leaves usually three-lobed but highly variable in length, width and number of lobes; flowers 4–5 cm long in racemes up to 8 cm across.
Habitat: kwongan or shrubland, in sandy to clayey soil.
Dist: 21, 22.

566 *Grevillea umbellulata* Meisner
Spreading or occasionally prostrate shrub 0.3–1 m high; leaves 1–5 cm long, acute, commonly pungent; flowers in dense clusters 1–2 cm long, sweetly scented.
Habitat: woodland in sandy or gravelly soil on granite or laterite.
Dist: 16, 17, 18, 19, 21, 22, 23.

565 *Grevillea tripartita*   566 *Grevillea umbellulata*

567 *Grevillea uncinulata* Diels subsp. *uncinulata*
Hook-leaf Grevillea
Bushy shrub to 1.5 m high; leaves c. 1.5 cm long with small, hooked tips and recurved margins; flowers including protruding style c. 1 cm long, densely hairy.
Habitat: sandy to gravelly lateritic soil in kwongan, shrubland or shrubby woodland.
Dist: 17, 18, 19, 21, 22.
Subsp. *florida* McGillivray differs in having flower stalks about as long as styles and leaves with revolute margins but lacking a hooked point. It is confined to a few areas between Perth and New Norcia.

567 *Grevillea uncinulata* subsp. *uncinulata*

568 *Grevillea wilsonii* Cunningham
Bushy, spreading shrub to 2 m high; leaves to 6 x 6 cm, divaricately divided; flowers c. 3–3.5 cm long, very showy, intense red.
Habitat: in gravelly or sometimes sandy soil, in Jarrah forest.
Dist: 17, 18.

568 *Grevillea wilsonii*

569 *Hakea bucculenta*

570 *Hakea corymbosa*

571 *Hakea costata*

573 *Hakea denticulata*

572 *Hakea cucullata*

Hakea Schrader, named after the German, Baron von Hake, a patron of botany. The genus is endemic in Australia and contains about 100 species of which over 70 occur in WA. Plants range from small shrubs to medium-sized trees but are always woody with harsh, usually prickly, leaves. Flower structure is very similar to *Grevillea* but the fruit differs in being always woody, often strangely shaped and occasionally very massive. The fruiting follicles are retained on the plant; in some species they open naturally as soon as the seed is mature, but most require a period of drying or even exposure to fire before the seed is shed.

Hakea flowers were used by the Aborigines as a source of nectar, and the roots of *H. leucoptera* could be cut to yield water, as was done with mallee eucalypts. A number of species are in cultivation and recently developed techniques of grafting have enabled some of the more difficult but very showy species to be grown more easily. Several *Hakea* species are naturalised in South Africa and New Zealand where they have become serious pest plants.

569 ***Hakea bucculenta*** C.A.Gardner
Red Pokers
Erect, multi-stemmed shrub or small tree; leaves 12–20 cm x 1.5–2 mm with one distinct central vein; flowering racemes up to 15 cm long.
Habitat: yellow or red sand; often forms thickets.
Dist: 16.

570 ***Hakea corymbosa*** R.Brown
Shrub to 2 m high; leaves 3–9.5 cm long, very thick and stiff with a pungent tip; individual flowers are c. 1.3 cm long.
Habitat: gravelly lateritic sand in the southern and northern kwongan.
Dist: 16, 17, 21, 22, 23.

571 ***Hakea costata*** Meisner
Ribbed Hakea
Shrub to 2.5 m high; branches ascending with short, rigid, erect branchlets; leaves to 1.5 cm long, thick, rigid, pungent; racemes to 1.5 cm across; flowers white or pale pink.
Habitat: kwongan or shrubland in white sand.
Dist: 16, 17.

572 ***Hakea cucullata*** R.Brown
Scallops
Shrub 2–5 m high with erect or ascending branches; young growth has pale green, densely hairy, toothed

leaves; flower clusters to 3.5 cm across, sometimes cream. *H. conchifolia* Hook, (Shell Hakea) from near-coastal areas around Perth and northwards is similar but all leaves have prickly teeth.
Habitat: usually in sand, but also in loam, gravel and rocky soil, in shrubland.
Dist: 19, 20, 21.

573 *Hakea denticulata* R.Brown
Stinking Roger
Divaricately branched shrub 2–3 m high; stems flexuose, prominently angled; leaves 2–5 cm long, base decurrent and wedge or heart shaped; flowers in racemes c. 3 cm across with an unpleasant odour.
Habitat: kwongan or shrubland in sand or seasonally wet gravelly clay.
Dist: 21, 22.

574 *Hakea erecta* Lamont
Shrub to 2.5 m high with short trunk and many stems, branchlets erect; leaves 6.5–12 cm long, twisted through 90° at base with one longitudinal vein above and three below; flowers in axillary clusters c. 3 cm across, pink or rarely cream; fruit 1.5–3 cm long with short beak and covered with raised pustules. Part of a complex of five WA taxa formerly known as either *H. falcata* or *H. ambigua*. *H. erecta* can be recognised by its distinctive fruits with short beak and raised pustules.
Habitat: sandy soil over laterite.
Dist: 15, 22, 23, 24.

575 *Hakea francisiana* F.Mueller
Emu Tree
Shrub or small tree to 8 m high with ascending branches; leaves to 26 cm x 4–6 mm with 5–7 parallel veins; inflorescence to 10 cm long x 5 cm wide at base.
Habitat: sand or gravel in shrubland or woodland.
Dist: 15, 22, 23, 24; also S.A.

576 *Hakea invaginata* B.L.Burtt
Shrub to 2.5 m high; branches ascending to erect; leaves undivided to 22 cm long with five sunken longitudinal grooves; flower heads 2–3 cm across, pink, rarely cream; fruit faintly warty with a prominently pointed beak.
Habitat: yellow or red sand in mallee or acacia scrub.
Dist: 15, 16, 23, 24.

574 *Hakea erecta*

575 *Hakea francisiana*

576 *Hakea invaginata*

577 *Hakea laurina*

578 *Hakea lissocarpha*

579 *Hakea multilineata*

580 *Hakea preissii*

581 *Hakea platysperma*

577 ***Hakea laurina*** R.Brown
Pincushion Hakea
Shrub or small tree to 8 m high; leaves 7–15 cm long, leathery with prominent longitudinal veins; flowers in ball-like clusters to 7 cm across. A handsome, widely cultivated plant, introduced into England in 1830.
Habitat: sandy soil in kwongan and shrubland.
Dist: 19, 21, 22, 23.

578 ***Hakea lissocarpha*** R.Brown
Honey Bush
Shrub 0.6–2 m high, densely branched, often flat-topped; leaves to 3.5 cm long, usually divided into several short, pungent segments; flowers sweetly scented, in clusters c. 2 cm across.
Habitat: kwongan, forest and woodland on sand or lateritic soil.
Dist: 16, 17, 18, 19, 21, 22, 23.

579 ***Hakea multilineata*** Meisner
Grass-leaf Hakea
Medium to tall shrub or small tree 3–5 m high with ascending branches; leaves to 18 cm long with about 15 longitudinal veins; flowers in racemes to 4 cm long in axils, sometimes clustered on older wood; fruit has a distinctive dorsal groove on each valve.
Habitat: gravelly shrublands and often a prominent species in remnant roadside vegetation in the wheatbelt.
Dist: 21, 22, 23, 24.

580 ***Hakea preissii*** Meisner
Needle Tree
Erect shrub to 5 m high; leaves 1–6.5 cm long with pungent yellow tips; flowers c. 7 mm long, sweetly fragrant in racemes c. 3 cm across, profuse and conspicuous; fruit to 2 x 1 cm, smooth.
Habitat: deep sand in kwongan.
Dist: 16, 17, 21, 22, 23.

581 ***Hakea platysperma*** Hooker
Cricket-ball Hakea
Spreading shrub 1.5–3 m high, leaves to 17 cm long x 2 mm wide; flower clusters c. 2.5 cm across. It is best known for the very large round fruits. The circular seed is surrounded by a thin, papery wing; one surface of the central portion is flat, the other surface is slightly raised and covered with soft, pointed spikes. It is thought that

these anchor the seed to the soil allowing it to germinate without blowing away.

Habitat: deep sand and gravelly soil in kwongan and shrubland.

Dist: 16, 22, 23, 24.

582 *Hakea prostrata* R.Brown
Harsh Hakea

Shrub 0.5–5 m tall, very variable; coastal forms (as illustrated) are prostrate, but inland plants are erect, substantial shrubs and their flowers are often tinged with red.

Habitat: sandy or loam soil including near coastal dunes, in shrubland or woodland.

Dist: 16, 17, 18, 19, 20, 21, 22, 23, 24.

582 *Hakea prostrata*

583 *Hakea scoparia* Meisner

Shrub to c. 3 m; young growth silky-hairy; leaves becoming glabrous, to 20 cm long, five-grooved, star-shaped in cross-section; flowers in clusters 3–4 cm across; fruit c. 2.5 x 1 cm. warty, with prominent narrow beak.

Habitat: in sand or gravelly sand in kwongan.

Dist: 16, 22, 23, 24.

583 *Hakea scoparia*   584 *Hakea trifurcata*

584 *Hakea trifurcata* (Smith) R.Brown
Two-leaf Hakea

Shrub 2–3 m high and up to 5 m across with many ascending to erect branches; leaves to 7.5 cm long, highly variable from terete and simple or with two or three lobes to flat and oblong, up to 1 cm wide; most plants have a mixture of leaf forms.

Habitat: widely distributed on a variety of soils including sand, sandy loam and granitic loam.

Dist: 16, 17, 18, 19, 21, 22, 23.

585 *Hakea nitida* R. Brown
Frog Hakea

Spreading shrub to 4 m high; leaves 3-10 x up to 2 cm, veins inconspicuous, margins with or without a few teeth or short spines, usually some leaves on the plant are toothed; flowers glabrous, heavily scented, in clusters 2-3 cm across: fruit with two outward curving horns.

Habitat: sand in kwongan.

Dist: 11, 21, 22, 23, 24.

585 *Hakea nitida*

586 *Hakea victoria*

588 *Isopogon baxteri*

587 *Isopogon adenanthoides*

589 *Isopogon cuneatus*

590 *Isopogon divergens*

586 **Hakea victoria** Drummond
Royal Hakea
An erect, robust, few-stemmed shrub up to 2 m high. The colourful floral leaves are up to 20 cm x 12 cm and enclose a cluster of cream or pinkish flowers. The leaves persist for several years and their colours deepen with age.
Habitat: sandy or quartzite soil in southern kwongan.
Dist: 21.

Isopogon R.Brown ex Knight, named from the Greek *isos* (equal) and *pogon* (a beard); referring to the uniformly hairy nut. Plants are usually shrubs up to 2 m tall, often spreading widely. The flowers are in heads or short, dense spikes, cream, yellow, pink or mauve and often very showy. The fruit is a small, usually silky nut enclosed in bracts that fall away when the nut is ripe. *Petrophile* is very similar but the bracts are persistent on the fruit.

587 **Isopogon adenanthoides** Meisner
Spider Coneflower
Small shrub to 1.5 m high; leaves slender, 1–2.5 cm x 8–10 mm, terete and trifid, crowded and hairy; usually a very floriferous plant with flower heads 4–5 cm across.
Habitat: gravelly sand in kwongan.
Dist: 16, 17.

588 **Isopogon baxteri** R.Brown
Stirling Range Coneflower
Small shrub to 1.5 m high; leaves 2–4 x 2–4 cm, divided into lobes with wavy margins and prickly tips; flower heads c. 3.5 cm across. A very showy, distinctive plant confined to the Stirling Range and Mt Barker.
Habitat: gravelly soil in kwongan and mallee woodland.
Dist: 21.

589 **Isopogon cuneatus** R.Brown
Shrub to 2.5 m high; leaves 4–10 cm x up to 2.5 cm; flower heads to 5 cm across.
Habitat: kwongan and woodland in gravelly or sandy soil, often with clay subsoil.
Dist: 19, 21.

590 **Isopogon divergens** R.Brown
Spreading Coneflower
Spreading shrub to 1.5 m high; leaves 5–15 cm long, terete, variably divided into spreading segments;

flower heads to 5 cm across; colour varies from very pale pink to deep carmine.
Habitat: widespread on gravelly sand in kwongan and shrubland.
Dist: 16, 17, 18, 22, 23.

591 **Isopogon dubius** (R.Brown) Druce
Pincushion Coneflower
Dense, rounded shrub to 1 m high; leaves 2–7.5 cm long, twice or three times divided into threes; flower heads to c. 5 cm across.
Habitat: gravelly soil in Wandoo or Jarrah forest and occasionally in mallee.
Dist: 16, 17, 18, 23.

591 *Isopogon dubius*

592 **Isopogon formosus** R.Brown subsp. **formosus**
Rose Coneflower
Spreading, erect shrub to 1.5 m high; leaves 2–6 x 4-5 cm terete, ternately divided one to three times into short, narrow segments; flower heads c. 6 cm across; flowers to 25 mm long.
Habitat: sand or gravelly sand in woodland centred around Albany and extending into the Stirling and Porongurup Ranges.
Dist: 19, 21.
Subsp. *dasylepis* differs in being a smaller plant with leaves often held close to the stem, with narrow lamina and incurved margins; also smaller flowers to 20 mm long; found around Busselton, Bunbury and south to the Scott River.

593 **Isopogon heterophyllus** Meisner
Erect shrub to 1.5 m high, very similar to and formerly confused with *I. formosus*. It has slightly flattened rather than terete leaves and flowers with a slightly mauve tinge. A common species occurring from near Cranbrook to Albany, in the Stirling Range and east to Esperance.
Habitat: sand or gravelly sand in woodland.
Dist: 19, 21, 22.

594 **Isopogon latifolius** R.Brown
Shrub to 3 m high; leaves 6–10 cm x up to 3 cm; flower heads to 8 cm across are the largest in the genus. This species is superficially similar to *I. cuneatus* which differs in having usually shorter leaves with rounded tips and less prominent veining and also smaller flowers.
Habitat: gravelly lateritic soil in shrubland in the Stirling Range.
Dist: 21.

592 *Isopogon formosus* subsp. *formosus*

593 *Isopogon heterophyllus*

594 *Isopogon latifolius*

595 *Isopogon scabriusculus*
subsp. *stenophyllus*

596 *Isopogon sphaerocephalus*

595 ***Isopogon scabriusculus*** Meisner subsp. ***stenophyllus*** Foreman

Shrub to 1.5 m high; branches mainly ascending or erect; leaves to 18 cm long, simple and terete; flower heads to c. 3.5 cm across, terminal or sometimes on short branchlets, perianth tube glabrous.

Habitat: kwongan or shrubland, in lateritic sand or gravelly sand.

Dist: 22, 23, 24.

Subsp. *scabriusculus* has flat leaves, sometimes with one to three lobes and a globrous perianth. Subsp. *pubiflorus* has terete leaves and pubescent perianth.

596 ***Isopogon sphaerocephalus*** Lindley
Drumstick Isopogon

Shrub to 1.5 m high; leaves 5–25 cm x 2–10 mm with soft hairs; young growth reddish; flowers to 4 cm across; a variable species, particularly in habit and leaves.

Habitat: sandy, lateritic soil, usually in Jarrah forest, occasionally on rocky slopes.

Dist: 16, 17, 18, 19, 20.

599 *Isopogon trilobus*

597 ***Isopogon teretifolius*** subsp. ***petrophiloides*** (R.Brown) Foreman

Shrub to 1.5 m high; leaves 6–20 cm long, pungent, smooth, always undivided; flower heads often pendulous, 2–3 cm across.

Habitat: shrubland on sandy, lateritic soil, between the Stirling Range, Newdegate, Lake King, Holt Rock and Marvel Lock.

Dist: 21, 22, 23, 24.

598 ***Isopogon teretifolius*** R.Brown subsp. ***teretifolius***
Nodding Coneflower

Shrub to 1.5 m high; leaves 4–8 cm long, some simple but always a few leaves in the upper parts divided into short, pungent segments; flower heads usually pendulous, up to 4 cm across; colour varies from pale pink to pale yellow.

Habitat: kwongan in sand or gravelly clay loam, from Mt Lesueur to Cranbrook, Stirling Range, Albany to East Mt Barren.

Dist: 16, 17, 18, 19, 21, 22, 23.

599 ***Isopogon trilobus*** R.Brown
Barrel Coneflower

Shrub to 2.5 m high; leaves 4–8 cm long, wedge or fan-shaped with 3–5 lobes at the tip; flower heads to 3 cm across.

Habitat: kwongan on deep white sand, usually near the coast.

Dist: 19, 21, 22.

597 *Isopogon teretifolius*
subsp. *petrophiloides*

598 *Isopogon teretifolius*
subsp. *teretifolius*

600 *Isopogon villosus* Meisner

Dwarf, spreading shrub to 60 cm high; leaves to 25 cm long, intricately divided into short, pungent segments; flower heads c. 3 cm across, towards base of plant and often partially hidden by foliage.
Habitat: kwongan or shrubland on white sand.
Dist: 22, 23.

Lambertia Smith, named after English horticulturist Aylmer Lambert who also had a large herbarium. There are nine species of these very decorative shrubs, known as 'wild honeysuckle', of which eight are restricted to south-west WA. Most are shrubs but several are small trees; the flowers are usually in heads of seven or, rarely, one flower, in shades of orange, yellow, pink or red.

600 *Isopogon villosus*

601 *Lambertia ericifolia* R.Brown

Heath-leaved Honeysuckle
Shrub to 4 m high; leaves 12–20 mm long; flowers c. 2 cm long with style protruding c. 3 cm; flower heads composed of five to eight flowers, but usually seven; colour varies from bright orange-red to brick red.
Habitat: sandy loam, often with rocks or gravel in tall shrubland and woodland.
Dist: 21.

602 *Lambertia inermis* R.Brown

Chittick
Shrub or small tree to 8 m high; leaves to 2.5 cm long; flower heads of five to seven flowers, perianth to c. 4 cm long; colour varies from orange-red to pale yellow. Yellow-flowered forms are recognised as var. *drummondii* (Fielding and Gardner) Hnatiuk.
Habitat: sand or gravelly sand in coastal or near coastal kwongan and shrubland.
Dist: 19, 20, 21, 22.

601 *Lambertia ericifolia*

603 *Lambertia multiflora* Lindley

Many-flowered Honeysuckle
Shrub to 2 m high; leaves 2.5–5 cm long; flowers to 4 cm long, usually in clusters of seven; colour varies from yellow or pinkish to pale red.
Habitat: the pinkish or red-flowered form depicted here occurs in gravelly soils in kwongan from Gingin to Eneabba. South of Muchea a yellow-flowered form (var. *darlingensis* Hnatiuk) occurs on sandy, gravelly or granitic soil in woodland.
Dist: 16, 17, 18.

602 *Lambertia inermis*   603 *Lambertia multiflora*

604 *Lambertia ilicifolia*

605 *Persoonia helix*

606 *Acidonia microcarpa*

608 *Persoonia rufiflora*

607 *Persoonia pungens*

604 **Lambertia ilicifolia** Hook.
Holly-leaved Honeysuckle
Compact, often dense shrub to 1.5 m; leaves c. 1.5 cm long with pungent lobes; flowers usually in clusters of seven; perianth c. 2 cm long; fruit spiny, about 1.4 x 1.2 cm. The smallest-flowered species.
Habitat: low-lying, but not swampy, sandy kwongan.
Dist: 19, 20, 21.

Persoonia Smith, named after the botanist Christian Persoon who studied fungi in Paris. It is the only member of the Proteaceae family in WA whose fruit is a drupe. Many species have brighter green foliage than is common in Australian plants and some of them have striking reddish coloured flaky or papery bark.

605 **Persoonia helix** P.H.Weston
Dense spreading shrub to 1 m high; leaves 2–4 cm long, spirally twisted; flowers yellow followed by greenish fruits with dark purple streaks. This taxon was previously known as *P. tortifolia* Meisner.
Habitat: sandy or gravelly loam in kwongan and shrubland.
Dist: 21, 22, 24.

606 **Acidonia microcarpa** (R.Brown)
L.A.S.Johnson & B.Briggs [syn. *Persoonia microcarpa* R.Brown]
Broom-like shrub 1–2 m high; leaves 5–11 cm long, terete or thick and slightly flattened; flowers c. 10 mm long, opening to 2 cm across.
Habitat: heath swamp in poorly drained sand round bogs or creeks.
Dist: 19, 20, 21, 23.

607 **Persoonia pungens** W.V.Fitzgerald
Low, spreading shrub to c. 40 cm high with spine-tipped branchlets; leaves 5–12 mm long; flowers 10–12 mm long, solitary in leaf axils.
Habitat: in Wandoo woodland or shrubland in white sand over laterite, occasionally in granitic sand.
Dist: 16, 23.

608 **Persoonia rufiflora** Meisner
Erect shrub to 1 m high; leaves 3–4 cm long; flowers c. 1 cm long; fruit an ovoid, greenish, fleshy drupe.
Habitat: sandy kwongan.
Dist: 16, 17, 23.

Petrophile Knight, from the Greek *petra* (a rock) and *phileo* (to love); because many are found in rocky habitats. The flowers are very similar to those of Isopogon but the ripe nuts are retained within persistent bracts that resemble a small cone.

609 ***Petrophile brevifolia*** Lindley
Erect, spreading shrub to 2 m high; leaves to 6 cm long with rigid pungent tips; flower heads 3–4 cm across.
Habitat: kwongan in sand.
Dist: 16, 17, 18, 23.

610 ***Petrophile divaricata*** R.Brown
Much-branched, tangled, prickly shrub to c. 1 m high; leaves several times divided, the ultimate segments pungent tipped; flower heads 3–4 cm long.
Habitat: open forest in gravelly soil or yellow sand.
Dist: 18, 19, 21, 22, 23.

611 ***Petrophile ericifolia*** R.Brown var. ***subpubescens*** (Domin) Foreman
Erect, rather rigid shrub 0.5–1.5 m high; leaves 3–6 x 1 mm; flower hairy in heads c. 20 cm across. The typical variety has flowers both hairy and sticky.
Habitat: sandy or gravelly soil in kwongan.
Dist: 16, 21, 22, 23, 24.

609 *Petrophile brevifolia*

610 *Petrophile divaricata*

611 *Petrophile ericifolia* var. *subpubescens*

612 *Petrophile glauca*

612 **Petrophile glauca** D.Foreman
Dense dome-shaped shrub 0.5–1 m x 2 m with many tangled branches; leaves to 20 cm long with very long petiole, upper part of leaf several times divided; flower heads 2–2.5 cm across.
Habitat: kwongan in gravelly lateritic soil.
Dist: 17, 18, 21, 22, 23.

613 **Petrophile helicophylla** D.Foreman
Prostrate spreading shrub; leaves 15–30 cm long, spirally twisted; flowers on very short stems at ground level, white or cream to pale pink.
Habitat: sandy kwongan.
Dist: 21.

614 **Petrophile heterophylla** Lindley
Open, straggly shrub to 2.5 m high; leaves 4–15 cm x 3–10 mm, very variable, usually simple but occasionally divided into two or three linear segments; flowers in loose clusters 2–3 cm across.
Habitat: shrubland or open forest, in gravelly lateritic soil.
Dist: 17, 18, 21, 23.

615 **Petrophile linearis** R.Brown
Pixie Mops
Shrub to 70 cm high; leaves linear or narrowly obovate, 5–10 cm long, thick, usually curved; flowers 2.5–3 cm long in loose heads.
Habitat: sand in coastal banksia or Jarrah woodland.
Dist: 16, 17, 18, 19, 20.

616 **Petrophile longifolia** R.Brown
Prostrate shrub 30–50 cm high; leaves undivided, 16–30 cm long; flower heads 3–4 cm across, often

613 *Petrophile helicophylla*

614 *Petrophile heterophylla*

615 *Petrophile linearis*

tightly clustered at base of plant; flowers with a lemony fragrance.

Habitat: heath or mallee, in sand or gravelly sand.

Dist: 18, 19, 20, 21, 22, 23.

617 *Petrophile seminuda* Lindley

Spreading shrub 1–2 m high; leaves 5–8 cm long; several times divided, the ultimate segments short, pungent; flower heads c. 1.5 cm across. Young foliage is a distinctive reddish-brown colour.

Habitat: sand or gravelly sand in kwongan or woodland.

Dist: 16, 17, 18, 21, 22, 23, 24.

618 *Petrophile serruriae* R.Brown

Shrub to 1 m high; leaves 2–3 cm long, finely dissected; flowers in heads 2–3 cm across.

Habitat: open woodland and forest, in lateritic soil and also coastal limestone.

Dist: 16, 17, 18, 19, 20, 21, 23.

619 *Petrophile striata* R.Brown

Erect to semi-prostrate woody shrub; leaves to 8 cm long, many times divided into flat segments c. 2–4 mm wide; flower heads 1.5–2.5 cm long, each sepal with a distinctive hair-like appendage at the tip.

Habitat: sand or gravelly sand, in Jarrah forest and kwongan.

Dist: 16, 17, 23.

620 *Petrophile teretifolia* R.Brown

Shrub to 1 m high, occasionally semi-prostrate, leaves terete, to 20 cm long; flower heads 4–5 cm across.

Habitat: kwongan or shrubland, in sandy, lateritic soil and also on granite outcrops.

Dist: 21, 22, 24.

617 *Petrophile seminuda*

616 *Petrophile longifolia*

619 *Petrophile striata*

620 *Petrophile teretifolia*

618 *Petrophile serruriae*

621 *Stirlingia abrotanoides*

Stirlingia Endlicher, named after James Stirling, the first Governor of WA. It is a small genus of seven species restricted to south-western WA within 150 km of the coast. Three species have finely dissected leaves and are not very showy in flower. *S. latifolia* is very common, flowering particularly well after fire, and regenerates rapidly forming large floriferous clumps within a year of being burnt; fruiting branches are often used in dried flower arrangements.

621 ***Stirlingia abrotanoides*** Meisner
Soft shrub to 1 m high; leaves finely dissected, the ultimate segments 2–5 mm long; flowering stems branching low with leaves extending in clusters at least halfway between point of branching and flowers; flower heads 10–12 mm across.
Habitat: sandy kwongan.
Dist: 16, 23.

622 ***Stirlingia anethifolia*** Endlicher
Shrub to 70 cm high; leaves very fine with short curved segments; flowering stems much branched and exceeding the leaves; flower heads 5–10 mm across.
Habitat: sandy soil in near-coastal kwongan.
Dist: 19, 20, 21.

623 *Stirlingia latifolia*

623 **Stirlingia latifolia** (R.Brown) Steudel
Blueboy
Glaucous shrub to 1.5m high forming clumps;
leaves basal, 20–30 cm long divided into linear lobes;
flowers c. 5 mm long in large panicles on leafless stems.
The fruit is a very hairy, persistent small nut.
Habitat: sandy shrubland and woodland.
Dist: 16, 17, 18, 19, 21, 23.

Synaphea R.Brown is a genus of c. 60 species restricted
to south-western WA in forest, woodland and kwongan.
All are small shrubs, sometimes prostrate and suckering.
All have small yellow tubular flowers in spikes and leathery, usually divided and often prickly, leaves.

624 **Synaphea flabelliformis** A.S.George
Tufted shrub 40–60 cm high; leaves 8–13 cm long
including the long petiole; flowers 2–3 mm long.
Habitat: rocky lateritic soil in woodland.
Dist: 18, 23.

625 **Synaphea polymorpha** R.Brown
Erect shrub with a few reddish stems to 80 cm tall;
lowest leaves simple, upper much-divided; flowers
c. 6–7 mm long.
Habitat: sandy soil in woodland.
Dist: 19, 20, 21.

624 *Synaphea flabelliformis*

622 *Stirlingia anethifolia*

625 *Synaphea polymorpha*

626 *Synaphea spinulosa* subsp. *borealis*

627 *Synaphea tripartita*

628(a) *Xylomelum angustifolium*

628(b) *Xylomelum angustifolium*

626 ***Synaphea spinulosa*** subsp. ***borealis*** A.S.George
A much-branched erect or spreading shrub 0.5–1 m high; leaves variable but usually twice divided into three lobes.
Habitat: deep sand in kwongan or woodland.
Dist: 16.

627 ***Synaphea tripartita*** A.S.George
Spreading shrub 50 x 80 cm; leaves leathery, flat but deeply divided; flowers 5–6 mm long.
Habitat: in sandy gravel in kwongan.
Dist: 22.

Xylomelum Smith, from the Greek *xylon* (wood); *melon* (a tree fruit), has two species in south-western Australia, and three in New South Wales and Queensland. All are small trees with large, woody, pear-like fruits which remain on the plant unopened until burnt in a bush-fire.

628 ***Xylomelum angustifolium*** Kippist ex Meisner
Sandplain Woody Pear
Large shrub or small spreading tree to 7 m high, with smooth grey bark; leaves 7–14 x 5–10 cm; flowers in racemes 5–8 cm long, in summer; fruit c. 5 cm long, persistent and not opening readily.
Habitat: sandy soil in shrubland.
Dist: 16, 22, 23.
X. occidentale (not illustrated) occurs in sandy woodlands between Perth and Albany; it has rough flaky bark, often blackened by fire, and stiff oak-like leaves.

RANUNCULACEAE
buttercups, clematis, anemones

The Ranunculaceae is a large cosmopolitan family of c. 1800 species world-wide with c. 45 in Australia, mainly in temperate regions. *Ranunculus,* from Latin 'little frog' or 'tadpole', alludes to the aquatic or wet habitats of many species. Although widespread in eastern States, this genus is not well represented in WA. The family is regarded as primitive and has the rare characteristic of rain pollination. It includes many valuable, widely grown horticultural plants such as *Clematis*, *Ranunculus*, *Anemone*, *Helleborus*, *Aquilegia* and *Delphinium*.

Clematis are usually dioecious climbing perennials. Female plants have a persistent style which develops in fruit into a long plumose awn, making plants in fruit conspicuous and sometimes known as 'Old Man's Beard'.

629 **Clematis pubescens** Huegel ex Endlicher
Common Clematis
Twining plant with hairy stems; leaves with three leaflets each 3–6 x 1–1.5 cm, almost glabrous; flowers 2–4 cm across.
Habitat: widespread on coastal plain and Karri and Jarrah forests of the south-west.
Dist: 17, 18, 19, 20, 21.

629 *Clematis pubescens*

RESTIONACEAE

The Restionaceae is a southern hemisphere family of sedge-like plants, superficially similar to and often confused with the Cyperaceae. South-western WA is particularly rich in species and has about 13 endemic genera.

The family is also well represented in southern Africa and extends to New Zealand, Chile and Malesia.

The plants are usually dioecious and have leaves reduced to sheathing bracts that are split open on one side, unlike the Cyperaceae which has bracts or leaf sheaths fused into a complete tube round the stem.

630 *Anarthria prolifera*

630 **Anarthria prolifera** R.Brown
Perennial, rush-like plant up to 60 cm high; leaves to 10 cm long arising from nodes along the stems; flowers with brown, papery perianth segments; stamens c. 4 mm long, conspicuous but ephemeral.
Habitat: sandy soil in winter-wet depressions in sedge shrubland and Jarrah woodland.
Dist: 17, 18, 19, 20, 21.

631 **Ecdeiocolea monostachya** F.Mueller
Large tufting perennial herb with stems up to 1 m high; leaves absent but sheathing scales present at the base of stems; inflorescence a terminal spike of unisexual flowers with papery perianths, each flower subtended and almost hidden by a broad, brown bract. Male flowers (in the upper part of the spike) have three of the six perianth segments with densely woolly keels visible at flowering time emerging from the bract.
Habitat: sand, lateritic gravel or sandy clay in kwongan or shrubland.
Dist: 14, 16, 23, 24.

631 *Ecdeiocolea monostachya*

632 *Lepidobolus chaetocephalus*   633 *Tremulina tremula*

634 *Cryptandra aridicola*

635 *Cryptandra leucopogon*

632 **_Lepidobolus chaetocephalus_** F.Mueller
Tufted perennial herb; stems to 50 cm tall; leaves absent but caducous papery bracts present at intervals along stems, leaving ring-like scars after shedding; male spikes (depicted) two to four per stem, each c. 12 mm across, female spikes narrower, reddish.
Habitat: sand or sandy loam in kwongan or woodland.
Dist: 21, 22, 23.

633 **_Tremulina tremula_** (R.Brown) B.G.Briggs & L.A.S.Johnson [syn. *Restio tremulus* R.Brown]
Rush-like perennial, stems to 1 m tall; leaves reduced to sheathing bracts; flowers in the axils of scale-like bracts forming tight heads 5–8 mm long.
Habitat: sandy soil in moist situations in shrubland and woodland.
Dist: 17, 19, 20, 21.

RHAMNACEAE

The Rhamnaceae is a large family widely distributed throughout the world. Of the c. 900 species world-wide, c. 100 occur in Australia. The flowers are quite small but often borne in showy heads or panicles. The Aborigines used several Australian species for edible gum, wood for implements and for their edible fruits. A few members of the family are cultivated as ornamentals, including *Pomaderris* and the exotic genera *Rhamnus*, *Discaria* and *Ceonothus*. *Cryptandra* is a genus of small heath-like shrubs well represented in WA, mainly in drier kwongan and mallee communities. *Spyridium*, with c. 14 species in WA, *Pomaderris* with c. seven, and *Trymalium* with c. eight, are generally shrubs found in both kwongan and forest. Several of the larger, soft-leaved species are prominent in the moist, south-western forests.

634 **_Cryptandra aridicola_** Rye
Tangled shrub c. 50 cm high; leaves terete, 1–2 mm long; flowers 6–8 mm across.
Habitat: photographed in open shrubland at the base of a granite outcrop; a newly described species.
Dist: 15, 24.

635 **_Cryptandra leucopogon_** Meisner
Small, mat-forming shrub 5–10 cm high and up to 50 cm wide; leaves 2–4 mm long; flowers c. 5 mm across.
Habitat: sandy kwongan.
Dist: 21, 22, 23, 24.

636 **Cryptandra recurva** Rye
Dense spreading shrub c. 1 m high; leaves terete,
1–3 mm long; flowers 4–5 mm long.
Habitat: photographed in shrubland in red soil near
Norseman; a newly described species.
Dist: 24.

637 **Pomaderris forrestiana** F.Mueller
Shrub 1–1.5 m high with many twiggy branches;
leaves obovate to obcordate, 4–8 mm long; flowers
about 4 mm across. The small spathulate petals distinguish this from *P. obcordata* which has similar
leaves but lacks petals.
Habitat: coastal limestone.
Dist: 11, 14, also SA.

638 **Spyridium oligocephalum** (Turczaninow)
Bentham
Shrub to 80 cm high, stems and undersides of leaves
covered with rusty hairs; leaves 1–2 cm long; flow-
ers densely woolly in tight heads c. 1 cm across.
Habitat: shrubland in sandy soil with lateritic gravel.
Dist: 22.

639 **Trymalium myrtillus** S.Moore
Erect shrub up to 1.5m high; leaves 4–5 mm long;
flowers 3–4 mm long with a creamy calyx which is
more conspicuous and larger than the very small,
narrow linear petals.
Habitat: sand in shrubland or mallee woodland.
Dist: 10, 21, 22, 23, 24.

636 *Cryptandra recurva*

637 *Pomaderris forrestiana*

639 *Trymalium myrtillus*

638 *Spyridium oligocephalum*

RUTACEAE

The Rutaceae is a large, world-wide family of strongly scented trees or shrubs and, rarely, herbaceous perennials. The name derives from *Ruta graveolens*, a European herb known as the 'herb of grace' and cultivated since antiquity for its medicinal properties.

The family is important economically for its citrus fruits (orange, lemon, grapefruit). In Australia the family is represented by 320 species and over half the genera are endemic. Many native Rutaceae are horticulturally valuable and widely cultivated; two rainforest trees *Flindersia* and *Halfordia* are prized for their timber. Most of the species illustrated belong to one section of the family, the tribe *Boroniae*. It is almost exclusively Australian and is represented in Western Australia by a large number of diverse, highly ornamental species, some of which are cultivated to provide oils for the perfume industry.

640 *Boronia alata*

642 *Boronia coerulescens*

641 *Boronia capitata* subsp. *clavata*

643 *Boronia crassifolia*

640 **Boronia alata** Smith
Winged Boronia
Much-branched shrub to 3 m high; leaves pinnate, to 7.5 cm long, with usually 7–11 leaflets; flowers c. 2.5 cm across.
Habitat: moist, near coastal forest in sand or loam.
Dist: 17, 19, 20, 21.

641 **Boronia capitata** Bentham
Cluster Boronia
Bushy shrub to 1 m high; leaves up to 1.5 cm long; flowers c. 1 cm across.
There are three subspecies distinguished mainly by the type and degree of hairiness of leaves and flowers. Illustrated is subsp. *clavata* Paul G. Wilson which has thick fleshy, glabrous or ciliate leaves, ciliate sepals and glabrous petals.
Habitat: heath or shrubland in sandy soil.
Dist: 22, 23.

642 **Boronia coerulescens** F.Mueller
Blue Boronia
Erect shrub 0.5–l m high; leaves up to 10 mm long, thick and glandular; flowers to 15 mm across; colour varies from very pale bluish-white to lilac or rosy purple; pale forms are the most common in WA. This is a very variable plant, often with few stems and sparse leaves.
Habitat: sandy heath and mallee scrubland.
Dist: 16, 17, 19, 21, 22, 23, 24; also SA, NSW, and Vic.

643 **Boronia crassifolia** Bartling
Small shrub 25–50 cm high; leaves 1–1.5 cm long, pinnate with obovate leaflets; flowers bell-shaped, 10 x 10 mm; colour varies from yellow-green to brownish; the outside of the petals is often darker.
Habitat: sandy soil and often among rocks.
Dist: 11, 19, 21, 22, 23, 24.

644 *Boronia crenulata* Smith

Aniseed Boronia

Dense shrub to 1 m high; branches erect; leaves spathulate, to 1.5 cm long; flowers c. 1.5 cm across. A very variable species; a distinctive form from Margaret River, var. *pubescens* Bentham, has hairy branches and broadly elliptic, pubescent leaves. Habitat: very diverse, sand or clay soil in kwongan and forest.

Dist: 16, 17, 18, 19, 20, 21, 22, 23, 24.

645 *Boronia cymosa* Endlicher

Granite Boronia

Open shrub to 1 m high with erect twiggy branches; leaves entire, 2–3 cm long; flowers c. 1 cm across; superficially similar to *B. denticulata* which has toothed leaves. Habitat: shrubland, heath or open forest in sandy lateritic or granitic soil.

Dist: 16, 17, 18.

646 *Boronia fabianoides* (Diels) Paul G.Wilson

Compact shrub to 40 cm high; leaves crowded, 5 to 10 mm long; flowers 5–12 mm across, white or pink. The large flowered form is illustrated; the small-flowered form is a low plant with flowers 5 to 6 mm across, usually white. Habitat: mallee woodland.

Dist: 21, 22, 23, 24.

647 *Boronia inornata* Turczaninow subsp. *inornata*

Open, spreading shrub 0.4–1.2 m high; leaves densely hairy, three- or five-foliate, to 1 cm long; flowers to 15 mm across with a strong citrus odour; sepals hairy, and sometimes the petals which are also ciliate. Habitat: sandy soil in mallee woodland.

Dist: 21, 22, 24.

648 *Boronia inornata* subsp. *leptophylla*

(Turczaninow) Burgman

This subspecies has no hairs on the leaflets and sepals; the petals are glabrous and usually not ciliate on the margins. Habitat: sandy soil in eucalypt woodland.

Dist: 21, 22, 24; also SA, Vic.

644 *Boronia crenulata*　　　645 *Boronia cymosa*

647 *Boronia inornata* subsp. *inornata*

646 *Boronia fabianoides*　　　648 *Boronia inornata* subsp. *leptophylla*

649 *Boronia megastigma*

651 *Boronia spathulata*

650 *Boronia scabra*

652 *Boronia ternata* var. *ternata*

653 *Boronia ternata* var. *elongata*

654 *B.ternata* var *austrofoliosa*

649 **Boronia megastigma** Nees
Scented Boronia
Upright, often dense shrub to 3 m high; leaves compound, to 1.5 cm long with three or rarely five very slender leaflets; flowers c. 1 cm across, very fragrant, commonly brown outside and yellow inside, occasionally yellow-green outside. A widely cultivated species with many forms selected for colour variation.
Habitat: winter-wet woodland.
Dist: 18, 19, 20, 21.

650 **Boronia scabra** Lindley
Rough Boronia
Woody perennial to 60 cm high, usually hairy or scabrid; leaves 5–12 mm long; flowers c. 1 cm across.
Habitat: sand or gravelly soil in Jarrah forest and in kwongan.
Dist: 16, 17, 19, 21, 22, 23.

651 **Boronia spathulata** Lindley
Glabrous, woody perennial to 1 m high; leaves widely spaced, 5–20 mm long and usually shorter than internodes, lower leaves obovate, to 9 mm wide, upper leaves 1–2 mm wide, obovate to almost terete; flowers 10–15 mm across.
Habitat: lateritic sand and gravelly sand, common in Jarrah forest.
Dist: 17, 18, 19, 20, 21.

652 **Boronia ternata** Endlicher var. **ternata**
Open, erect shrub to 70 cm high; leaves densely covered with fine, grey, stellate hairs.
Habitat: sandy shrubland.
Dist: 16, 22, 23, 24.

653 **Boronia ternata** var. **elongata** Paul G.Wilson
Open shrub to 1.5 m high; leaves glabrous, 5–10 mm long; flowers on pedicels more than half the length of the leaves.
Habitat: mallee shrubland.
Dist: 21.

654 **Boronia ternata** var. **austrofoliosa** Duretto.
Shrub to 80 cm high; leaves appearing glaucous due to a covering of very fine, short, appressed hairs; flowers on pedicels less than half the length of the leaves; an uncommon variety.
Habitat: sandy soil in kwongan or shrubland.
Dist: 22,23.
Var. *foliosa* is similar but differs in having leaves without hairs.

655 *Chorilaena quercifolia* Endlicher
Shrub to 4 m high; leaves 2–4 x 1–3 cm, undersurface densely hairy; flower heads 1–1.5 cm across, surrounded by bracts which vary in colour from cream to yellow-green or reddish.
Habitat: deep loam soil in Karri forest.
Dist: 19, 20.

656 *Crowea angustifolia* var. *dentata* (Bentham) Paul G.Wilson
Crowea
Shrub to 3 m high; leaves 5–8 x 1–1.5 cm, finely toothed; flowers c. 2 cm across, white or very pale pink.
Habitat: moist peaty sand in forest and woodland.
Dist: 19, 20.
Var. *angustifolia* has narrower leaves, flowers usually deeper pink and a similar distribution.

655 *Chorilaena quercifolia*   656 *Crowea angustifolia*

657 *Diplolaena ferruginea* Paul G.Wilson
Rounded, compact shrub 0.5–1 m high, distinguished by the dense, rusty indumentum on the petals and bracts; leaves up to 2 cm long; flower heads about 2 cm across.
Habitat: sandy kwongan.
Dist: 16, 17.

657 *Diplolaena ferruginea*

658 *Diplolaena grandiflora* Desfontaines
Tamala Rose
Spreading shrub to 3 m high; leaves 2–5 cm long; flower heads 3–4 cm across, the largest in the genus; stamens about equal to innermost bracts.
Habitat: red sand in shrubland or calcareous rocky coastal areas.
Dist: 14, 16.

659 *Diplolaena drummondii* (Bentham) Ostenfeld
Lesser Diplolaena
Multi-stemmed shrub to 80 cm high; leaves broadly ovate, 1–1.5 cm long, both surfaces finely pubescent; flower heads c. 2.5 cm across with very long stamens.
Habitat: sandy shrubland in the Kalbarri area.
Dist: 16.
D. drummondii and *D. velutina* were formerly regarded as varieties of *D. microcephala*.

658 *Diplolaena grandiflora*

659 *Diplolaena drummondii*

660 *Diplolaena velutina*

661 *Drummondita hassellii*

662 *Drummondita longifolia*

663 *Philotheca brucei* subsp. *brucei*

660 **Diplolaena velutina** (Paul G.Wilson)
Paul G.Wilson
Spreading shrub to 1.5 m high; leaves 2–5 cm long,
pubescent; stems, underside of leaves and outer floral bracts with dense, rusty hairs; flower heads c.
2.5 cm across.
Habitat: diverse, including mallee woodland and
shrubland.
Dist: 16, 23.

661 **Drummondita hassellii** (F.Mueller) Paul
G.Wilson
Erect shrub 50–70 cm high; branches ascending;
leaves terete, 5–15 mm long with slender
recurved tip; flowers to 2 cm long; petals papery,
shorter than stamens which are united into a
tube from which the dark red stigma protrudes.
Habitat: widespread in southern areas, mainly in
kwongan and mallee.
Dist: 22, 23, 24.

662 **Drummondita longifolia** (Paul G.Wilson)
Paul G. Wilson
Peak Charles Drummondita
This species is distinguished by its longer leaves
(to 2 cm long) and larger flowers.
Habitat: among granitic rocks near Peak Charles.
Dist: 22.

663 **Philotheca brucei** (F.Mueller) Paul G.Wilson subsp.
brucei [syn. *Eriostemon brucei* F.Mueller subsp. *brucei*]
Noolburra
Shrub to 2 m high, glaucous; branchlets erect, very
warty; leaves to 2 cm long; flowers c. 1 cm across,
profuse, white to pink.
Habitat: diverse, in clay, granite, laterite or red sand
soil, in woodland and kwongan.
Dist: 15, 23, 24.
Subsp. *cinereus* Paul G.Wilson, has branchlets, leaves
and pedicels densely stellate-tomentose and occurs in
the Upper Murchison Range area (Region 15). Subsp.
brevifolius Paul G. Wilson, is also stellate-tomentose
with elliptic to suborbicular leaves 1.5 mm long and
wide; it occurs between Paynes Find and Sandstone
(Region 15).

664 **Philotheca gardneri** (Paul G.Wilson) Paul G.Wilson
[syn. *Eriostemon gardneri* Paul G.Wilson]
Densely branched shrub to 1.5 m high; leaves semi-
terete, glandular, to 10 mm long; flowers c. 12 mm
across.
Habitat: shrubland or mallee on rocky clay loam.
Dist: 21, 22.

665 ***Philotheca sericea*** (Paul G.Wilson) Paul G.Wilson
[syn. *Eriostemon sericeus* Paul G.Wilson]
Shrub to 2 m high; leaves to 4 mm long, elliptic to
obovate, fleshy; flowers c. 2 cm across, white to pale
pink; petals with fine, silky hairs on both sides.
Habitat: sandy soil in dry woodland.
Dist: 15, 16, 24.

666 ***Philotheca spicata*** (A.Richard) Paul G.Wilson
[syn. *Eriostemon spicatus* A.Richard]
Pepper and Salt
Slender shrub to 1 m high; leaves 6–20 mm long;
flowers 8–10 mm across, pink, white, mauve or bluish, in spikes up to 20 cm long. Widespread and
common from Geraldton south to near Albany.
Habitat: very diverse, in sand or gravelly soil in
kwongan and woodland.
Dist: 17, 18, 19, 20, 23.

667 ***Geijera linearifolia*** (A.P.de Candolle) J.Black
Sheep Bush; Oil Bush
Small to medium, usually dense-foliaged shrub 1.5–
3.5 m high; leaves 20–50 mm long, thick and rather
rigid; flowers c. 5 mm across.
Habitat: widespread in arid shrubland and wood-
land, both coastal and inland.
Dist: 11, 22, 24; also SA.

668 ***Geleznowia verrucosa*** Turczaninow
Erect shrub to 1 m high; stems warty; leaves obovate,
c. 12 x 4 mm, warty; flowers c. 10 mm across, surrounded by several rows of petal-like persistent
bracts. As the flower fades the bracts close over it
and become orange-brown. Extensive exploitation
of wild populations for the cut flower trade has
caused it to become a rare species, now known in
the wild from only small populations.
Habitat: sandy soil in low kwongan.
Dist: 14, 16, 23.

664 *Philotheca gardneri*

665 *Philotheca sericea*

666 *Philotheca spicata*

668 *Geleznowia verrucosa*

667 *Geijera linearifolia*

669 *Microcybe multiflora* var. *multiflora*

670 *Microcybe multiflora* var. baccharoides

671 *Nematolepis phebalioides*

673 *Phebalium canaliculatum*

672 *Rhadinothamnus anceps*

674 *Phebalium drummondii*

669 **Microcybe multiflora** Turczaninow var. **multiflora**
Dense rounded shrub to 50 cm high; leaves terete, spreading, 3–5 mm long; flowers white, perfumed.
Habitat: woodland in sand and loam soil.
Dist: 21, 22, 24; also SA.

670 **Microcybe multiflora** var. **baccharoides** (F.Mueller) Ewart and Tovey
Dense shrub to 80 cm high; leaves triangular, c. 2 mm long, erect or appressed to stem; flowers cream to pale yellow, strongly perfumed.
Habitat: in mallee in sandy soil, including shallow soil over limestone, and under eucalypts near salt lakes.
Dist: 22, 24; also SA.

671 **Nematolepis phebalioides** Turczaninow
Erect but spreading, multi-stemmed shrub 1–2 m high; leaves 1–2 cm long; flowers 12–15 mm long. This species is superficially similar to *Correa*.
Habitat: in clay-loam in mallee and woodland.
Dist: 21, 22, 23.

672 **Rhadinothamnus anceps** (A.P. de Candolle) Paul G. Wilson [syn. *Phebalium anceps* A.P. de Candolle] Blister Bush
Slender shrub to 3 m; young branches and leaves covered with fine, silvery scales; leaves 4–12 cm long; flowers 10–15 mm across. Contact with any part of the plant may cause the skin to blister.
Habitat: margins of creeks and swamps in near coastal regions from Yanchep south to Albany.
Dist: 16, 17, 19, 20.

673 **Phebalium canaliculatum** (F.Mueller and Tate) J.H.Willis
Shrub to 1.5 m high; leaves 10–20 mm long; flowers 7–10 mm across.
Habitat: red sand in open shrubland or mallee associations, occasionally on rock outcrops.
Dist: 15, 23, 24.

674 **Phebalium drummondii** Bentham
Shrub to 1.5 m high; leaves 3–5 x 1–2 mm, flat or slightly concave, smooth; flowers 12–15 mm across.
Habitat: sand in shrubland.
Dist: 23.

675 **_Phebalium elegans_** Paul G.Wilson
Spreading shrub 1–1.5 m high; leaves obovate, 3–7 mm long, 1–2 mm wide; flowers 1 cm across. This new species is yet to be formally named.
Habitat: granitic sand.
Dist: 24.

676 **_Phebalium filifolium_** Turczaninow
Slender Phebalium
Rounded shrub to 1.3 m high; leaves c. 15 mm long; flowers pale to deep yellow, rarely white, c. 8 mm across in terminal umbels.
Habitat: mallee shrubland.
Dist: 15, 23, 24.

677 **_Phebalium lepidotum_** (Turczaninow) Paul G.Wilson
Shrub to 90 cm high; leaves and stems smooth; leaves 10–20 mm long; flowers 10–13 mm across, white or cream.
Habitat: woodland or shrubland on sand and sandy clay.
Dist: 21, 22, 24.

678 **_Phebalium tuberculosum_** (F.Mueller) Bentham
Shrub to 1.5 m high; leaves and stems warty; leaves to 7 mm long, margins strongly recurved; flowers white to cream, 10–14 mm across; a very variable species. _P. megaphyllum_ is similar but has larger, cuneate-oblong leaves.
Habitat: shrubland in sand or gravel.
Dist: 22, 23, 24.

675 _Phebalium elegans_

676 _Phebalium filifolium_

678 _Phebalium tuberculosum_

677 _Phebalium lepidotum_

679 *Exocarpos aphyllus*

680 *Santalum murrayanum*

SANTALACEAE

The Santalaceae is a world-wide family of about 400 species of tropical and temperate climate herbs, shrubs and trees with about 50 species in Australia. Most are parasitic on the roots of other plants, at least in the initial stages of growth, but as all species contain chlorophyll they are probably better described as hemiparasitic. The genus *Santalum* yields timber suitable for wood carving, and *S. spicatum* is a source of incense. The outer fleshy tissue of the Quandong (*S. acuminatum*), was an important food for Aborigines throughout arid Australia, and is still used in rural areas for jam and desserts. Fruits of several other species in the family are edible. The wood of *Exocarpos cupressiformis* was used by Aborigines for making spear-throwers.

679 ***Exocarpos aphyllus*** R.Brown
Leafless Ballart
Rigid, divaricate shrub to 5 m high; leaves scale-like, c. 1 mm long; flowers greenish-yellow, very small, in clusters or spikes 2–4 mm long. The fruits illustrated consist of a swollen succulent receptacle surmounted by a drupe c. 3 mm long.
Habitat: diverse, including coastal dunes, eucalypt woodland and shrubland in rocky loam, clay loam and calcareous soil.
Dist: 10, 11, 13, 14, 15, 16; also SA, Qld, NSW and Vic.

680 ***Santalum murrayanum*** (Mitchell) C.A.Gardner
Bitter Quandong
Shrub or small tree to 4 m; branchlets pendulous; leaves in whorls, 1.5–3 cm long, yellowish-green, hooked; flowers cream, 2–4 mm across; fruit a fleshy drupe 15–25 mm diameter, very bitter.
Habitat: diverse, including gravelly plains and dunes, in tall shrubland and open woodland.
Dist: 10, 22, 23, 24; also SA, NSW and Vic.
S. acuminatum (quandong) is similar but the leaves are not hooked and the fruit has sweet edible flesh.

SAPINDACEAE Hop bushes

The Sapindaceae is a large, world-wide family of c. 2000 species of trees, shrubs and climbers with 150 species occurring in Australia. The family has a predominantly tropical and subtropical distribution and includes many important horticultural and food plants such as *Litchi chinensis* (lychee) and *Nephelium lappaceum* (rhambutan). *Dodonea* is the largest Australian genus with 68 species of which 30 occur in Western Australia.

681 *Diplopeltis huegelii* subsp. *huegelii*

682 *Diplopeltis petiolaris*

All are shrubs or small trees distinctive for the often colourful, capsular fruits with valves usually produced into vertical wings.

Diplopeltis is a small genus of five species, four restricted to WA, the fifth extending into the south-western Northern Territory.

681 *Diplopeltis huegelii* Endlicher subsp. *huegelii*

Pepperflower

Shrub to 1 m high; hairy with simple hairs and glandular hairs only on the inflorescence; leaves 1–4.5 cm long, divided into linear or cuneate lobes; flowers about 1–1.5 cm across, pepper-scented.
Habitat: sandy soil in kwongan or coastal shrubland, and in granitic soil in open forest.
Dist: 17, 18.
Var. *subintegra* A.S.George has less divided or entire leaves and occurs between Badgingarra and Geraldton.

682 *Diplopeltis petiolaris* F.Mueller ex Bentham

Pepperflower

Spreading shrub 0.5–1 m high, suckering; leaves obovate, crenate, 1–4 cm long; flowers c. 1.5 cm across. All species of the small genus *Diplopeltis* bear separate male and female flowers on the one plant. In the male flowers here depicted the ovary is rudimentary and the eight stamens are turned to one side. Most parts of the plant feel sticky due to a covering of mixed simple and glandular hairs.
Habitat: sandy, often alkaline soils between Kalbarri and Dongara.
Dist: 16.

683 *Dodonaea concinna*

683 *Dodonaea concinna* Bentham

Dioecious, erect, rounded, compact shrub, leaves pinnate, c. 2 cm long with four to 12 leaflets, each 5–9 mm long; capsule usually four-winged.
Habitat: mallee scrub.
Dist: 21, 22.
D. concinna resembles *D. stenozyga* (q.v.) which has longer leaves and fewer leaflets.

684 *Dodonaea inaequifolia* Turczaninow

Hopbush

Dioecious, erect shrub to 5 m high; leaves pinnate, 1.5–5.2 cm long with 17–23 leaflets; capsule usually three-winged.
Habitat: semi-arid mallee heath, mallee scrub or woodland.
Dist: 14, 15, 16, 23, 24.

684 *Dodonaea inaequifolia*

685 *Dodonaea ptarmicaefolia*   686 *Dodonaea stenozyga*

685 *Dodonaea ptarmicaefolia* Turczaninow
Erect, dioecious shrub to 4 m high; leaves up to 6 cm long, simple, with serrated margins; capsule with 3 or 4 wings about 10 mm x 16 mm.
Habitat: sandy or granitic loam.
Dist: 21, 22, 23, 24.

686 *Dodonaea stenozyga* F.Mueller
Erect, rounded dioecious shrub to 1.5 m high; leaves up to 4 cm long, pinnate with two to six narrow leaflets; flowers small, yellow or cream followed in female plants, as depicted here, by brightly coloured capsules about 15 x 17 mm with four prominent wings.
Habitat: semi-arid mallee scrub or eucalypt woodland.
Dist: 10, 11, 21, 22, 23, 24; also SA and Vic.

SOLANACEAE

The Solanaceae is a large, diverse family widely distributed in tropical and temperate regions, mostly native to Central and Southern America but also widespread in Australia.

The family contains important food plants such as potato (*Solanum tuberosum*), egg plant (*S. melongena*), tomato (*Lycopersicon esculentum*), Cape gooseberry (*Physalis peruviana*), chilli, peppers and capsicums (*Capsicum* spp.).

A large number of the family are cultivated as ornamentals such as *Browallia*, *Cestrum*, *Datura*, *Nierembergia* and *Petunia*.

Some species have a high alkaloid content and are poisonous or drug plants used medicinally or as narcotics, e.g. tobacco (*Nicotiana* spp.), Deadly nightshade (*Atropa belladonna*), Thornapple (*Datura* spp.) and Black Henbane (*Hyoscamus niger*).

In Australia several species were used by Aborigines for chewing or smoking and the fruits of several *Solanum* spp. were eaten by the Aborigines. *Duboisia* (Pituri) was also used by them as a narcotic and fish poison and is a source of alkaloids for the modern pharmaceutical industry.

687 *Anthocercis ilicifolia* subsp. *caldariola*

687 *Anthocercis ilicifolia* subsp. ***caldariola*** Haegi
Erect shrub to 2.7 m high with few main stems; lower parts of stems are prickly with toothed leaves, upper parts are unarmed with entire leaves 15–80 mm long; flowers tubular with spreading lobes 6–18 mm long. This subspecies is restricted to the coast near Kalbarri where it is an early coloniser after fire or

disturbance. The thick-textured, bulbous calyx tube distinguishes it from the subsp. *ilicifolia* which occurs south of Kalbarri. It is easily confused with *A. littorea*, also found in the Kalbarri area, but differs from the latter in having a large pyramidal, leafless inflorescence with brighter yellow flowers.
Habitat: calcareous coastal sand.
Dist: 16.

688 *Anthocercis littorea*

688 *Anthocercis littorea* Labillardière
Yellow Tailflower
Erect or sprawling many-stemmed shrub to 3 m high; leaves 2–6 cm long, usually thick and fleshy; inflorescence usually dense and leafy; flowers with narrow corolla lobes 10–25 mm long.
Habitat: calcareous coastal sand, a colonising species, common after fire.
Dist: 14, 16, 17, 19, 20, 21, 24.

689 *Anthocercis viscosa* subsp. *viscosa*

689 *Anthocercis viscosa* R.Brown subsp. ***viscosa***
Sticky Tailflower
Erect or spreading viscid shrub to 3 m; leaves 2–6 cm long; flowers 3–4 cm across with green or purplish striations; suspected of poisoning stock.
Habitat: on or near granite outcrops on the south coast close to the sea from Bremer Bay to Albany and Denmark.
Dist: 19, 20, 21.
Subsp. *caudata* has flowers with longer, narrower corolla lobes and occurs between Esperance and Mt Ragged and in the Nornalup-Walpole National Park.

690 *Anthotroche walcottii*

690 *Anthotroche walcottii* F.Mueller
Erect to sprawling shrub to 2 m high; leaves 7–20 mm long, densely hairy; flowers 10–15 mm across.
Habitat: yellow sandplain in scrub heath between Geraldton and Shark Bay.
Dist: 16.

691 *Cyphanthera microphylla* Miers
Small rounded shrub to 40 cm high; mature leaves 1–2 mm long but large, basal, obovate leaves 4–5 x 1 cm may be present on young plants; flowers 8–10 mm across.
Habitat: mallee or shrubland in sandy soil, often in disturbed habitats and common after fire.
Dist: 21, 22, 23, 24.

691 *Cyphanthera microphylla*

692 *Cyphanthera racemosa*

693 *Duboisia hopwoodii*

695 *Solanum orbiculatum*

694 *Solanum oldfieldii*

696 *Solanum plicatile*

692 **Cyphanthera racemosa** (F.Mueller) Haegi
Shrub to 1.2 m high; leaves elliptic, oblong or obovate 5–25 mm long; flowers c. 15 mm across.
Habitat: shrubland and scrub heath on sandplain and coastal dunes, often common after fire.
Dist: 16, 23.

693 **Duboisia hopwoodii** (F.Mueller) F.Mueller
Pituri
Erect soft shrub to 4 m tall; leaves 2–12 cm long, corolla 7–15 mm long, 5–11 mm wide when fully open.
Habitat: red or yellow sand or sandy loam on plains and dunes, often with spinifex.
Dist: 4, 6, 9, 10, 11, 13, 14, 15, 16, 22, 23, 24; also NT, SA, Qld, NSW.
Used by Aborigines as an animal poison and as a narcotic. Toxic to horses, goats, sheep and camels; toxicity varies with locality, age and part of the plant.

694 **Solanum oldfieldii** F.Mueller
Erect shrub to 1 m; young shoots often rusty-green; stems densely hairy, with scattered prickles up to 8 mm long; leaves ovate to oblong, 2–7 x 1–5 cm; flowers 2.5–4 cm across; fruit a pale yellow globular berry 5–10 mm across; suspected of poisoning stock.
Habitat: dry gravelly or sandy soil on slopes or plains.
Dist: 15, 16, 17, 18, 19, 21, 22, 23, 24.

695 **Solanum orbiculatum** Dunal ex Poiret
Wild Tomato
Erect or rounded shrub to 1.5 m, silvery rusty or grey-green with fine, dense hairs, usually without prickles; leaves 1.5–6 cm long; flowers 2–2.5 cm across; berry globular, ivory to yellow, 10–15 mm across; eaten fresh by Aborigines.
Habitat: widespread on coastal dunes and gravelly and sandy inland plains.
Dist: 8, 9, 10, 13, 14, 15, 16, 23, 24; also NT and SA

696 **Solanum plicatile** (S.Moore) Simon
Erect shrub to 60 cm high; stems densely hairy with scattered prickles to 5 mm long; leaves 10–20 mm long, shallowly lobed and with tightly folded and undulate margins; flowers 20–25 mm across.
Habitat: red sandy soil in eucalypt or acacia woodland, occasionally in hummock grassland.
Dist: 10, 15, 21, 22, 23, 24.

STACKHOUSIACEAE Stackhousias

The Stackhousiaceae is a small, almost entirely Australian family with one species extending to Malesia, Micronesia and New Zealand. The genus *Stackhousia* is widespread throughout temperate Australia. *Tripterococcus* is restricted to Western Australia. The usually white or cream flowers of *Stackhousia* have a sweet perfume which is stronger at night. Their pollinators are night-flying moths.

697 **Stackhousia dielsii** Pampanini
Perennial herb to 55 cm high; leaves reduced to scales up to 6 mm long, rarely also a few linear leaves; flowers with tube 5–6 mm long and lobes 2.5–3.5 mm long. Habitat: white to yellow sand in low heath or occasionally woodland between lower Murchison and Hill Rivers.
Dist: 16, 17.

698 **Stackhousia monogyna** Labillardière
Perennial to 70 cm high; leaves to 35 mm long; flowers tubular, 6–10 mm long with spreading lobes 3–5 mm long. A most variable plant, common over most of southern Australia. The form depicted here is particularly dense and showy, often found on or near granite platforms. Other forms are less leafy, open plants and may have cream or yellow flowers.
Habitat: very common in coastal and inland habitats, in sand to heavy soil in heath, woodland and forest.
Dist: 11, 15, 16, 17, 18, 19, 20, 21, 22, 23, 24; also SA, Qld, NSW, Vic, Tas.

699 **Stackhousia muricata** Lindley
Perennial or annual herb to 55 cm high; leaves linear, 7–30 x 1–2.5 mm; flowers yellow-green or pale or dark yellow, the tube 2–6 mm long, lobes 1–4 mm long.
Habitat: sand or loamy soil, often with rocks or gravel in woodland, open grassy areas and hummock grass plains, also associated with granitic outcrops.
Dist: 6, 9, 10, 12, 13, 14, 15, 16, 18, 21, 22, 23, 24; also SA, Qld and NSW.

700 **Tripterococcus brunonis** Endlicher
Perennial herb to 80 cm high; leaves narrowly linear to broadly ovate, to 20 mm long, sometimes scale-like; flowers yellow, green-yellow or brown-black, the tube 5–8 mm long, lobes 2.5–7.5 mm long.
Habitat: usually sand, sometimes loam, clay or stony soil, in heath, sclerophyll forest and woodland; abundant after fire and in semi-disturbed sites.
Dist: 16, 17, 18, 19, 20, 21, 22, 23, 24.

697 *Stackhousia dielsii*

698 *Stackhousia monogyna*

699 *Stackhousia muricata*

700 *Tripterococcus brunonis*

701 *Commersonia gaudichaudii*

702 *Commersonia pulchella*

703 *Guichenotia ledifolia*

704 *Guichenotia micrantha*

STERCULIACEAE

The Sterculiaceae is a large, world-wide family of mainly tropical trees, shrubs and herbs with a few genera extending into temperate regions. The family includes the Kurrajong, Flame Tree and Bottle Tree, all in the genus *Brachychiton*. In south-western WA, shrubs in genera such as *Lasiopetalum*, *Thomasia*, *Guichenotia* and *Keraudrenia* are a spectacular component of several plant communities. The flowers of these shrubs have an enlarged, papery, persistent and colourful calyx, whereas the petals are much reduced or absent. Distinctions between genera in this section of the family can be confusing and depend on a combination of floral characters. A third group in the family comprising *Commersonia* and *Rulingia* has generally white or pale yellow flowers with the calyx also the largest part of the corolla. Two economically important non-Australian species are *Theobroma cacao*, the seeds of which yield cocoa, and *Cola nitida*, cola nuts, used medicinally and for stimulating drinks.

701 ***Commersonia gaudichaudii* Gay**
Prostrate shrub with radiating flowering stems almost flat on the ground; flowers 6-8mm across; leaves 10-20 mm long.
Habitat: sandy kwongan.
Dist: 21, 22.

702 ***Commersonia pulchella* Turczaninow**
Compact shrub to 1.5 m high; leaves 1.5–2.5 cm long with irregularly lobed or toothed margins; flowers white or pink, c. 1 cm across; sepals larger and more conspicuous than the small pointed petals.
Habitat: lateritic sand or gravel and among rocks.
Dist: 16, 17, 23.

703 ***Guichenotia ledifolia* J.Gay**
Densely branched shrub up to 1.5 m high; leaves 2.5–3 cm long; flowers 1–1.5 cm across.
Habitat: diverse, including sandy kwongan and woodland, margins of salt flats and alkaline coastal areas and granitic sands.
Dist: 16, 17, 19, 21, 22.

704 ***Guichenotia micrantha* (Steetz) Bentham**
Open shrub to 1.5 m high; leaves 0.5–3 cm long; flowers c. 10–14 mm across; a very variable species.
Habitat: sand or gravel in kwongan and woodland.
Dist: 16, 17, 21, 22, 23, 24.

705 *Keraudrenia hermanniifolia* J.Gay
Crinkle-leaved Firebush
A spreading shrub c. 1 m high; leaves 5–12 mm long; flowers 10–20 mm across; the papery flower is formed from the joined sepals; there are no petals.
Habitat: gravelly or sandy kwongan.
Dist: 14, 15, 16, 17, 23.

706 *Keraudrenia integrifolia* Steudel
Rounded shrub to 1.5 m high; leaves 15–30 mm long, size, shape, and degree of hairiness very variable; flowers 20–30 mm across; a widespread and very colourful species. The calyx in *Keraudrenia* enlarges after flowering and retains its colour; each lobe has a distinct midrib; bracteoles are lacking.
Habitat: in kwongan and shrubland in sand or gravelly soil.
Dist: 13, 15, 16, 21, 22, 23, 24: also NT, SA.

The genus *Lasiopetalum* has calyx lobes divided almost or completely to the base with the underside covered with stellate hairs; the leaves lack stipules.

707 *Lasiopetalum compactum* Paust
Diffuse, spreading shrub to 2 m high; leaves and branches covered with fine, dense stellate hairs; leaves 3–4 cm long: flowers in tight heads up to 3 cm across.
Habitat: shrubland or woodland often in rocky places.
Dist: 21, 22.

708 *Lasiopetalum discolor* W.J.Hooker
Coast Velvet Bush
Shrub to 1.5 m high; leaves 2–9 cm long; inflorescence a dense, recurved head; flowers c. 1.4 cm across, mauve, pink or, rarely, white.
Habitat: coastal shrub communities in alkaline sand or limestone.
Dist: 21; also SA.

709 *Lasiopetalum molle* Bentham
Multi-stemmed shrub to 50 cm high; leaves heart-shaped, to 3.5 cm long; flowers 8–10 mm across.
Habitat: sandy kwongan.
Dist: 16, 22, 23.

705 Keraudrenia hermannifolia

707 *Lasiopetalum compactum*

709 *Lasiopetalum molle*

Right: 706 *Keraudrenia integrifolia*

Far right: 708 *Lasiopetalum discolor*

710 *Lasiopetalum oppositifolium*

711 *Lasiopetalum quinquenervium*

712 *Lasiopetalum rosmarinifolium*

713 *Rulingia densiflora*

714 *Rulingia luteiflora*

715 *Thomasia grandiflora*

710 **Lasiopetalum oppositifolium** F.Mueller
Low, spreading shrub 40–50 cm high; leaves opposite, to 10 cm long; flowers c. 1 cm across. Other members of the genus have alternate leaves.
Habitat: skeletal coastal soil, usually sandstone.
Dist: 14, 16, 17.

711 **Lasiopetalum quinquenervium** Turczaninow
Shrub to 1 m high; young growth with dense, rusty hairs; leaves 2–5.5 cm long; flowers c. 1.4 cm across.
Habitat: coastal heath or low shrubland, in sandy or gravelly soil.
Dist: 21.

712 **Lasiopetalum rosmarinifolium** (Turczaninow) Bentham
Spreading shrub 50–80 cm high; leaves 3–6 cm long; flowers 8–10 mm across.
Habitat: shrubland on hillsides and rocky places.
Dist: 21, 22.

713 **Rulingia densiflora** (Turczaninow) Bentham
Erect, densely hairy, few-branched shrub to 1.5 m high; upper leaf surface rugose; flowers 15 mm across; leaves 3–4 cm long.
Habitat: sandy shrubland.
Dist: 16, 23, 24.

714 **Rulingia luteiflora** E.Pritzel
Erect shrub to 2 m high with arching branches; leaves 10–20 mm long; flowers 18 mm across.
Habitat: acacia woodland in sandy soil.
Dist: 14, 15, 16.

715 **Thomasia grandiflora** Lindley
Multi-stemmed shrub 40–60 cm high; leaves 1.5–2.5 cm long; flowers 2–3 cm across; differs from *T. multiflora* in having calyx lobes with broad thin undulate margins.
Habitat: forest and shrubland in a variety of soils.
Dist: 16, 17, 18, 19, 20, 21, 22.

716 **Thomasia macrocarpa** Huegel
Erect, dense shrub to 2 m high; leaves 3–8 cm long, toothed or broadly lobed, undersurface with dense, stellate hairs; flowers 15–20 mm across, undersurface of calyx with large stellate hairs.
Habitat: rocky slopes in Jarrah forest, particularly on the Darling Scarp.
Dist: 17, 18.

717 *Thomasia microphylla* Paust

Erect, multi-stemmed shrub to 35 cm high; leaves
3–6 mm long; flowers 10–12 mm across.
Habitat: mallee shrubland.
Dist: 21, 22.

718 *Thomasia multiflora* E. Pritzel

Soft, spreading shrub to 1.5 m high; calyx lobes with
thickened margins.
Habitat: occurs in shrubland or woodland in sand
and often among rocks.
Dist: 20, 21.

The calyx of *Thomasia* is divided to about the middle with, usually, one thickened central rib per lobe
and three bracteoles; most species have leaves with
two leaf-like stipules.

719 *Thomasia pygmaea* (Turczaninow) Bentham
Tiny Thomasia

Low spreading shrub to 50 cm high; stems and undersides of leaves covered with minute, rusty-brown
scales; flowers 1–1.5 cm across; leaves 1 x 1 cm. Differs from most *Thomasia* species in having leaves
without stipules.
Habitat: sandy shrubland.
Dist: 21.

STYLIDIACEAE

The Stylidiaceae is a family of tropical to temperate annual or perennial herbs or, rarely, undershrubs. The family is predominantly Australian and is best developed in
south-western WA where over 100 endemic species in the
genera *Stylidium* and *Levenhookia* occur. Many species are
adapted to survive dry conditions but are usually found in
sandy heathland or around depressions on granite outcrops that are inundated in winter. Both *Levenhookia* and
Stylidium have specially developed floral mechanisms to
aid in the dispersal of pollen.

720 *Levenhookia leptantha* Bentham
Trumpet Stylewort
Plants 3-4 cm high; flowers 3-4 mm across.
Habitat: sandy depressions.
Dist: 15, 16, 17, 20, 23, 24.

716 *Thomasia macrocarpa*   718 *Thomasia multiflora*

717 *Thomasia microphylla*

719 *Thomasia pygmaea*

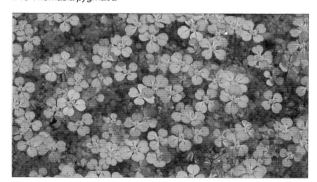

720 *Levenhookia leptantha*

722 *Stylidium breviscapum* subsp. *erythrocalyx*

721 *Stylidium albomontis*

723 *Stylidium brunonianum*

Stylidium triggerplants

The genus *Stylidium* has over 200 species and most are endemic in Australia with about 150 species in W.A. Like *Levenhookia* the flowers have five petals with one reduced to a small labellum. Stamens and style are fused and situated at the tip of a long, sensitive, reflexed column. A visiting insect causes the column to spring up and deposit the pollen on the insect's back, and later, when the stigma becomes receptive, to remove pollen received from another flower.

721 ***Stylidium albomontis*** Carlquist
Perennial herb; leaves linear, basal, c. 20 cm long; flowering stem 20–60 cm long; flowers c. 1.5 cm long.
Habitat: sandy soil in seasonally wet areas, restricted to southern heathlands.
Dist: 21.

722 ***Stylidium breviscapum*** subsp. ***erythrocalyx***
Bentham
Boomerang Triggerplant
Much-branched, spreading, stoloniferous perennial rooting at the nodes; leaves 5–15 mm long, flowers c. 10 mm across.
Habitat: heath and shrubland in sandy soil, usually coastal.
Dist: 21, 22.
The typical subsp. has shorter leaves and a denser inflorescence and is widely distributed inland.

723 ***Stylidium brunonianum*** Bentham
Pink Fountain Triggerplant
Tufted plant with 2 or 3 erect stems to 40 cm high; leaves basal, 2–5 cm long, with usually two clusters of leaf-like bracts along the stem; flowers 6–8 mm across, pink to pale mauve.
Habitat: sandy soil in forest and open heath.
Dist: 16, 17, 18, 19, 20, 21, 23, 24.

724 ***Stylidium bulbiferum*** Bentham
Circus Triggerplant
Creeping plant forming circular mats; leaves 5–15 mm long; flowers c. 10–12 mm across. A widespread species with several varieties recognised.
Habitat: sandy soil in kwongan and forest.
Dist: 16, 17, 18, 21, 22, 23, 24.

724 *Stylidium bulbiferum*

725 *Stylidium calcaratum* R.Brown
Book Triggerplant
Delicate annual 5–20 cm high (commonly c. 10
cm); usually with four basal leaves 2–6 mm long;
flowers c. 6–10 mm long, pink or white; often covers large areas around ephemeral pools.
Habitat: swampy or damp places including granite
outcrops.
Dist: 16, 17, 18, 19, 20, 21, 23, 24; also SA and Vic.

726 *Stylidium crossocephalum* F.Mueller
Posy Triggerplant
Robust perennial; flowering stems 10–20 cm long;
leaves 5–10 cm long; flowers 2 cm long, clustered
in heads and surrounded by reddish bracts with pa-
pery lacerated margins.
Habitat: in sand in kwongan.
Dist: 16, 17.

727 *Stylidium galioides* C.A.Gardner
Yellow Mountain Triggerplant
Trailing plant; stems to 50 cm long; leaves 2–4 cm
long, clusters of leaf-like bracts at intervals along
stems; flowers c. 1.5–2 cm across, cream or pale
yellow.
Habitat: confined to the rocky slopes of East
Mt Barren.
Dist: 21.

728 *Stylidium scandens* R.Brown
Climbing Triggerplant
Climbing plant; stems to 30 cm long; leaves 1.5–8
cm long; leaf-like bracts in clusters along stems; up-
per bracts with hooked tips; flowers 5–7 mm across,
pale to rosy pink.
Habitat: sandy soil in forest and woodland.
Dist: 19, 20, 21.

725 *Stylidium calcaratum*

726 *Stylidium crossocephalum*

728 *Stylidium scandens*

727 *Stylidium galioides*

729 *Stylobasium australe*

732 *Pimelea physodes*

731 *Pimelea imbricata*

SURIANACEAE

The Surianaceae is a small family comprising 6 uncommon species of trees and shrubs, only one of which extends beyond Australia. The family is not of economic importance although two eastern species, *Cadellia pentastylis* and *Guilfoylia monostylis*, endemic in Queensland and northern NSW, are attractive small trees which have been brought into cultivation. The genus *Stylobasium* contains two species of shrubs occurring in Western Australia and the Northern Territory. The genus is distinctive in having the style attached to the base of the ovary.

729 ***Stylobasium australe*** (W.J.Hooker) Prance
Erect shrub to 2 m high; leaves narrowly linear, 1.5–3 cm long; flowers 5–7 mm long with stamens protruding on long thread-like filaments.
Habitat: woodland or mallee in lateritic or granitic sand.
Dist: 16, 17, 23.

THYMELAEACEAE

The Thymelaeaceae is a small family of trees and shrubs widely distributed in tropical and temperate regions of both hemispheres. It includes the daphnes and pimeleas, both of which include many decorative plants.

Pimelea is a large, genus widespread in Australia and well represented in south-western WA. In eastern Australia the bark of some species was used by the early settlers as a substitute for twine.

730 ***Pimelea argentea*** R.Brown
Silvery-leaved Pimelea
Shrub to 1.8 m high; leaves densely hairy 4–47 mm long; flower heads ovate; individual flowers to 5.5 mm long. A very variable species, specimens from humid areas, including the Darling Range, being more lush than those from drier areas.
Habitat: sand or sandy clay, often associated with granite, watercourses or lakes.
Dist: 16, 17, 18, 19, 20, 21, 22, 23.

731 ***Pimelea imbricata*** R.Brown
Shrub 0.5–1 m high; leaves 1–16 mm long; flower heads 1.5–2.5 cm across, cream, white or very pale pink; a widespread, highly variable species with several varieties recognised. Illustrated is the south-coastal form from near Albany.
Habitat: granitic sand, sometimes winter-wet.
Dist: 21, 22.

732 *Pimelea physodes* Hooker
Qualup Bell
A slender, few-stemmed shrub 50–70 cm high;
leaves 12–32 mm long; bracts up to 60 mm long, at
first green but ageing to deep red, enclose a cluster
of small greenish-yellow flowers.
Habitat: kwongan and shrubland, on quartzitic or
lateritic hillsides.
Dist: 21.

733 *Pimelea rosea* R.Brown
Rose Banjine
Dense shrub to 1.5 m high; leaves elliptic, 6–30 mm
long; flowers hairy outside, to 15 mm long, in heads
to 3 cm across; peduncle 4–35 mm long.
Habitat: coastal sand dunes and plains, coastal limestone and granite rises.
Dist: 17, 19, 20, 21.
P. ferruginea Labill. is similar but has more rigid,
usually shorter leaves and shorter peduncle up to
3 mm long.

734 *Pimelea sessilis* Rye
Shrub to 40 cm high; leaves stem-clasping, elliptic
to almost circular, to 15 mm long; flowers to 11 mm
long in heads 2–3 cm across.
Habitat: sand in shrubland.
Dist: 16, 23.

735 *Pimelea suaveolens* subsp. *flava* Rye
Scented Banjine
Slender shrub to 1 m high; leaves glaucous, 15–30
mm long, 3–7 mm wide; flower heads 2–3 cm across
with individual flowers 8–14 mm long.
Habitat: mallee shrubland.
Dist: 22, 23, 24.
Subsp. *suaveolens* has green (not glaucous) leaves,
green or yellowish green floral bracts and generally
larger flowers. It occurs in forest and woodland and is
more widely distributed than subsp. *flava*.

730 *Pimelea argentea*

733 *Pimelea rosea*

735 *Pimelea suaveolens* subsp. *flava*

734 *Pimelea sessilis*

737 *Tetratheca hirsuta*

TREMANDRACEAE

The Tremandraceae is a small, endemic family of c. 43 species in three genera. They are small, heath-like shrubs sometimes with trailing stems. Flowers are usually pink, purple or, rarely, white. *Platytheca* has five species endemic in south-western Western Australia and *Tetratheca* extends across all southern States with 21 species in WA.

736 ***Platytheca galioides*** Steetz
Erect shrub to 50 cm high; leaves linear-terete, 10–15 mm long in whorls of 6–8; flowers 15–20 mm across.
Habitat: damp, sandy situations on the coastal plain.
Dist: 17, 18, 19, 20, 21.

737 ***Tetratheca hirsuta*** Lindley
Black-eyed Susan
Weak, erect shrub to 90 cm high but often smaller; stems frequently collapsing when in full flower; leaves opposite or in whorls of three or more, elliptic to ovate, 5–20 mm long; flowers deep pink 15–20 mm across.
Habitat: gravelly soil in kwongan or forest.
Dist: 17, 18, 19, 20.

738 ***Tremandra stelligera*** R.Brown ex A.P.de Candolle
Densely stellate-hairy shrub c. 1 m high; leaves 2.5–4 cm long; flowers 5–10 mm long, pink, purple or blue.
Habitat: moist forest.
Dist: 18, 19, 20.

VIOLACEAE Violets

The Violaceae, comprising herbs, shrubs and a few climbers, has worldwide distribution but is most common in temperate regions. Of the 900 species worldwide, only 26 occur in Australia. The family is of little economic importance except for *Viola* which is important in horticulture, perfumery and confectionery.

739 ***Hybanthus calycinus*** (A.P.de Candolle) F.Mueller
Wild Violet
Perennial herb 20–60 mm high; leaves 20–45 mm long; inflorescence a raceme of five or more flowers to 20 cm long; widespread in coastal areas.
Habitat: sandy soil in banksia woodland and shrubland.
Dist: 16, 17, 18, 19, 20.

738 *Tremandra stelligera*

740 **Hybanthus floribundus** (Lindley) F.Mueller subsp. **floribundus**
Shrub Violet
Shrub to 1.5 m high; leaves flat, 5–35 mm long; flowers 8–10 mm long.
Habitat: widespread in sand or gravelly soil in kwongan, shrubland or woodland.
Dist: 15, 16, 17, 18, 19, 20, 22, 22, 23, 24; also SA, NSW and Vic.
Subsp. *adpressus* differs in having straight, narrow, folded leaves appressed to the stem and is restricted to the Ravensthorpe area; subsp. *curvifolius* has spreading folded leaves and the sepals are dark blue to green; it occurs mainly in the Norseman area.

XANTHORRHOEACEAE

The Xanthorrhoeaceae is a family of ten genera and about 100 species, all but four endemic in Australia; south-western WA is particularly rich in species. Members of the family are highly drought-resistant, and many withstand fire and flower in profusion after burning. Most have woody stems and some have massive trunks surmounting a thick underground stem.

The genus *Calectasia* has 11 species, 10 of which are endemic in Western Australia. All are perennial herbs with rhizomes, erect stems and wiry roots; they are easily recognised by the short, pungent leaves and papery, star-like flowers.

741 **Calectasia grandiflora** Preiss
Blue Tinsel Lily
Perennial herb with short rhizomes; stems erect, wiry, to 40 cm high; leaf blades 5–15 mm long; flowers 2.5–3.5 cm across, changing from deep blue to reddish purple; anthers yellow, ageing brown.
Habitat: sand, sandy loam and gravelly sand, in kwongan, rarely in woodland.
Dist: 17, 21, 22, 23.
C. cyanea has a similar distribution but has smaller flowers and yellow anthers that turn orange or red with age.

742 **Chamaexeros fimbriata** (F.Mueller) Bentham
Tufted perennial; leaves terete to 60 cm long, leaf-bases fringed with pale hairs; inflorescence a panicle, flowers c. 5 mm across, bisexual. *Chamaexeros* is superficially similar to some species of *Lomandra* but differing in having bisexual flowers and leaves with fringed bases.
Habitat: kwongan or shrubland in sand or lateritic gravel.
Dist: 10, 15, 22, 23, 24.

736 *Platytheca galioides*

739 *Hybanthus calycinus*

740 *Hybanthus floribundus*

741 *Calectasia grandiflora*

742 *Chamaexeros fimbriata*

743 Chamaexeros serra

743 **Chamaexeros serra** (Endlicher) Bentham
Little Fringe-leaf
Tufted plant; leaves 6–30 cm long with torn white papery margins; flowers c. 4.5 mm long in clusters at base of plant.
Habitat: clay-loam, sand and laterite in woodland.
Dist: 18, 19, 21, 22, 23.

Dasypogon is a genus of three species confined to south-west WA. Plants are similar to some species of *Xanthorrhoea* but the leaves are flat or inrolled and the flowers are in dense drumstick-like heads.

744 **Dasypogon bromeliifolius** R.Brown
Drumsticks
Tufted perennial with coarse, grass-like leaves 13–37 cm x 2.5–9 mm at base; flower heads 2.5– 3 cm across on a hairy stem up to 40 cm long.
Habitat: sand, in kwongan and woodland.
Dist: 17, 18, 19, 20, 21.

745 **Dasypogon hookeri** Drummond
Pineapple Bush
Arborescent herb to 3 m high; leaves crowded, to 1 m long forming a crown from which several flowering stems arise; flower heads 2–2.5 cm across.
Habitat: sandy clay or gravelly clay in Jarrah forest between Donnybrook and Augusta.
Dist: 19.

746 **Kingia australis** R.Brown
Black Gin

746 Kingia australis

744 Dasypogon bromeliifolius

745 Dasypogon hookeri

Kingia is a genus of one species endemic in south-western WA; it has drumstick flower heads similar to that of Dasypogon but develops a thick, fibrous trunk surrounded by persistent leaf bases through which the roots pass from the crown to the soil. It grows to 8 m tall, occasionally in small clumps. The leaves vary in hairiness.
Habitat: sandy loam and clay loam, in open woodland and kwongan.
Dist: 16, 17, 19, 20, 21.

Lomandra is a genus of 50 species, all native to Australia with two species extending to Papua New Guinea and one of these also in New Caledonia. *Lomandra* is a tussock-forming perennial plant with linear or terete leaves. Male and female inflorescences are on separate plants and are often dissimilar. The large flower spike of *L. hastilis* is unusual in the genus; in most species the inflorescence is shorter than the leaves and is often a loosely branched raceme or a flower cluster close to the base of the plant. Fibre from the leaves of some species was used by the Aborigines for making net bags.

747 ***Lomandra hastilis*** (R.Brown) Ewart
Robust, tussock-forming, dioecious perennial; leaves flat, 30–60 cm long; flower spike about equal in length to the leaves.
Habitat: sand, in near-coastal areas.
Dist: 16, 19, 20, 21.

Xanthorrhoea is a genus of 20 species endemic in Australia with thick, woody stems covered with tightly packed leaf bases; in many species the stems elongate to produce a thick trunk. *Xanthorrhoea* species were used in many ways by the Aborigines. The soft, white leaf bases and young shoots were eaten raw and the large flower spikes could be soaked to produce a sweet drink. Many species are rich in resin which was used as an adhesive in attaching stone tools to a handle or a spear head to a shaft. The resin in the flowering stem was also used as a torch for burning vegetation to aid collection of game and as a light to assist in night fishing. The resin was once extensively harvested as a source of picric acid. Species of *Xanthorrhoea* occur almost throughout Australia, mainly in near-coastal areas, with one species confined to the arid interior.

748 ***Xanthorrhoea gracilis*** Endlicher
Slender Blackboy
Tufted plant without a trunk; scape c. 1.5 m long and 10–20 times as long as the flowering spike.
Habitat: sandy lateritic soil from south of the Avon River to Albany, common in Jarrah forest.
Dist: 17, 18, 19, 20, 23.

747 *Lomandra hastilis*

748 *Xanthorrhoea gracilis*

751 *Tribulus platypterus*

749 *Xanthorrhoea preissii*

749 ***Xanthorrhoea preissii*** Endlicher
Balga, Blackboy
Woody-stemmed perennial, trunk 0.3 to over 3 m tall, covered with closely packed leaf-bases and carrying one or more crowns of dense leaves; flowers densely packed into a thick spike much longer than the stem; regenerates and flowers profusely after fire.
Habitat: widespread and common on a variety of soil types from Jurien Bay to Albany region
Dist: 17, 18, 19, 20.

ZAMIACEAE Zamias

The Zamiaceae is a family of primitive plants similar to palms but not related to them. The family is restricted to warm-temperate and tropical regions of Africa, Australia and North and South America. *Macrozamia* is an Australian endemic genus of 38 species of which 3 are confined to south-west WA. They were an important food source for Aborigines but required processing to leach out the toxins. In the south-west of WA the ripe seeds were gathered and buried in heaps 90–120 cm deep and left for 8 or 9 months, after which they were eaten without further preparation.

750 ***Macrozamia fraseri*** Miquel
Large palm-like dioecious plant usually with a trunk. Crown of 30–100 leaves. Seed cones ovoid 35–45 cm long, 15–17 cm diam. Ripe seeds red.
Habitat: sandy soil in kwongan between Eneabba and Perth.
Dist: 17, 18.

M.riedeli is an understorey plant in jarrah forest from Dwellingup to Albany and west to the coast. It is a smaller plant with fewer fronds and smaller cones. Large zamias in the Esperance district are *M. dyeri*.

ZYGOPHYLLACEAE

The Zygophyllaceae is a family of mainly trees and shrubs which usually have winged or spiny fruits. The family contains c. 240 species world-wide of which c. 33 occur in Australia. They are most common in arid and saline environments. The genus *Tribulus* contains some species that have become troublesome weeds, notably *T. terrestris* (Caltrop). It has a very hard, spiny fruit and an ability to rapidly colonise disturbed ground. The genus *Zygophyllum*, Twin leaf (not illustrated) has yellow flowers and is widespread in dry sands of the inland and some coastal areas.

751 ***Tribulus platypterus*** Bentham
Cork Hopbush
Woody shrub with thick, corky bark on stems; leaves pinnate with two to five pairs of leaflets, each 5–12 mm long; flowers c. 2 cm across; fruit 1.5–2 cm across with five conspicuous orange-brown wings. Habitat: sandy soil in heath or shrubland.
Dist: 8, 12, 13, 14, 15.

750 *Macrozamia fraseri*

Adapted from W.R.Elliot and D.L.Jones, *Encyclopaedia of Australian Plants* (1980—).

achene a small, dry, one-seeded fruit that does not split at maturity, e.g. in *Clematis*, Asteraceae.

acute having a short sharp point.

affinity (aff.) a botanical reference used to denote an undescribed species closely related to an already described one.

alternate borne at different levels in a straight line or in a spiral.

annual a plant that completes its life cycle within 12 months.

anther the pollen-bearing part of a stamen.

apical relative to the apex or top of a structure.

appressed pressed flat against something.

arborescent with a tree-like growth habit.

axil angle formed between adjacent organs in contact; commonly applied to the angle between a leaf and the stem.

axillary borne within an axil.

biennial a plant that completes its life cycle in two years.

bipinnate twice pinnately divided.

bisexual both male and female sexes present.

blade the expanded part of a leaf.

bract leaf-like structure subtending a flower, flower stem or inflorescence.

bracteole a small leaf-like structure on a flower stalk.

c. circa about.

calyx all the sepals.

capsule a dry, dehiscent fruit containing many seeds.

carpel female reproductive organ.

caruncle a fleshy outgrowth of the seed coat near where it is attached.

cauline attached to a stem and usually scattered along it.

chenopod steppe dry vegetation dominated by members of the family Chenopodiaceae (saltbushes and bluebushes).

ciliate with a fringe of hairs like an eyelash.

cm centimetre.

column a fleshy organ in an orchid flower formed by the union of the stigma and stamens.

cordate heart-shaped.

corolla all the petals.

corymb an inflorescence where the branches start at different points but reach about the same height to give a flat-topped effect (adj. corymbose).

crisped very wavy or crumpled, as of leaf margins or hairs.

crustaceous hard, thin and brittle.

cuneate wedge-shaped.

cultivar a variety or form of a plant produced by cultivation.

deciduous falling seasonally, as of leaves of some trees.

decumbent reclining on the ground but with the tips ascending, as of branches.

decurrent running downward beyond the point of attachment, as of leaves, phyllodes, leaflets etc.

decussate opposite leaves in four rows along the stem.

dioecious bearing male and female flowers on separate plants.

dissected deeply divided into segments.

distichous arranged along a stem in two opposite rows and in the same plane.

divaricate spreading at a wide angle.

drupe a fleshy fruit with seed(s) enclosed in a stony endocarp.

elliptic oval and flat with rounded ends.

emarginate having a notch at the apex.

endemic restricted to a particular country, region or area.

endocarp a woody layer surrounding a seed in a fleshy fruit.

entire whole, not toothed or divided in any way.

ephemeral a plant completing its life cycle within a very short period, e.g. 3–6 months.

epiphyte a plant growing on, or attached to, another plant, but not parasitic.

exfoliate to peel off in flakes or scales.

fimbriate fringed with fine hairs.

flexuose having a zig-zag form.

floret the smallest unit of a compound inflorescence such as a daisy.

floriferous bearing many flowers.

follicle a dry fruit formed from a single carpel and which splits along one line when ripe, as in Proteaceae.

forma form (Latin); a taxonomic category below species, usually differentiated by a minor character.

genus a taxonomic group of closely related species.

glabrous without hairs.

glaucous covered with a bloom, giving a bluish lustre.

glutinous covered with a sticky exudation.

habit the general appearance of a plant.

herb a plant that never develops a woody stem.

hybrid progeny resulting from the cross-fertilization of parents belonging to different taxa.

indehiscent not splitting open at maturity.

indumentum the hairy covering on plant parts.

inflorescence the part of a plant bearing flowers.

internode the part of a stem between two nodes.

involucre a cluster of overlapping bracts surrounding a flower head (adj. involucral).

keel a ridge like the base of a boat; in peashaped flowers, the basal part formed by the union of two petals.

kwongan low shrubby vegetation, rich in species, on sandy and gravelly soils of low fertility of south-western Australia; also known as sandplain or sandheath.

labellum a lip; in orchids, the petal in front of the column.

lamina the expanded part of a leaf.

lanceolate lance-shaped; narrowed and tapering towards each end.

lateritic soils formed by weathering of rocks composed chiefly of iron or aluminium hydroxides.

legume a dry fruit formed from one carpel and splitting along two lines when ripe; characteristic of the Fabaceae, Mimosaceae and Caesalpiniaceae.

lignotuber a woody swelling containing dormant buds at the base of a stem; e.g. in mallee eucalypts and many Australian shrubby plants.

ligule a strap-shaped organ; e.g. the enlarged petal (or petals) of a single daisy floret.

linear long and narrow with parallel sides.

m metre.

malesia an area comprising Papua New Guinea, the islands of Indonesia and the Philipines.

mallee a shrubby species of *Eucalyptus* with many stems arising from a swollen basal stem (lignotuber) from which new shoots arise after fire or damage.

membranous thin-textured.

midrib the principal vein that runs full length; as in a leaf.

mm millimetre.

monoecious bearing separate male and female flowers on the one plant.

monotypic a genus containing a single species.

mulga one of several species of *Acacia* (especially *A. aneura*) present as the dominant species in communities of wide occurrence in the arid parts of Australia; cf. mulga woodland, mulga scrub.

nectary a specialized gland that secretes nectar.

nerves the fine veins that traverse the leaf blade.

node a point on the stem where leaves or bracts arise.

NSW New South Wales.

obcordate heart-shaped with the broadest part above the middle.

obovate ovate with the broadest part above the middle.

obloid a 3-dimensional shape with short, parallel sides and rounded ends, as if composed of two hemispheres joined by a very short cylinder.

obtuse blunt or rounded at the apex.

opposite arising on opposite sides but at the same level.

ovary the part of the female flower containing the ovules.

ovate egg-shaped in longitudinal section.

ovule the structure within the ovary that becomes a seed after fertilisation.

panicle a much branched racemose inflorescence.

papillae minute, rounded protruberances.

papillose *of a surface*, bearing papillae.

pappus a tuft of feathery bristles, hairs or scales surmounting the seeds of most of the daisy family (Asteraceae).

parasite a plant growing or living on or in another plant, e.g. mistletoe.

pedicel the stalk of a flower in a compound inflorescence.

pedicellate having a pedicel.

peduncle the main axis of a compound inflorescence or the stalk of a solitary flower.

perennial a plant living for more than two years.

perianth a collective term for all of the petals and sepals of a flower.

persistent remaining attached until mature; not falling prematurely.

petal a segment of the inner perianth whorl or corolla.

petiole the stem or stalk of a leaf.

phyllode a modified petiole acting as a leaf, as in *Acacia*.

pinna a primary segment of a divided leaf.

pinnate once divided with the divisions extending to the midrib.

pinnatifid a leaf lobed with divisions reaching approximately halfway to the midrib.

pinnatisect a leaf approaching the pinnate condition but the divisions from the margins almost or fully reaching the midrib without forming a distinct leaf.

plumose *of hairs or segments*, feather-like.

prostrate lying flat on the ground.

proliferous bearing offshoots and other processes of vegetative propagation.

pubescent covered with short, soft downy hairs.

pungent very sharply pointed; also smelling strongly.

Qld Queensland.

q.v. quod vide (Latin) 'which see'.

raceme a simple unbranched inflorescence with stalked flowers.

receptacle the usually-enlarged tip of a floral stalk bearing the flower(s).

reticulate a net-like arrangement, as of veins.

retrorse turned or directed downwards or backwards.

revolute with the margins rolled backwards.

rhizome an underground stem.

rugose with a wrinkled surface.

SA South Australia.

scabrous rough to the touch.

scape the stem-like flowering stalk of a plant with basal leaves.

serrate toothed with sharp, forward pointing teeth.

sessile without a stalk, pedicel or petiole.

seta a bristle (adj. **setaceous**).

shrub a woody plant that remains low (less than 6 m) and usually with many stems or trunks.

sinuate with a wavy margin.

spathulate spoon-shaped, with a broad top and tapering base.

species a taxonomic group of closely related plants all having a common set of characters which sets them apart from other groups.

spike a simple, unbranched inflorescence with sessile flowers.

stamen the male part of a flower producing pollen, consisting of an anther and filament.

staminal claw a group of stamens having united filaments forming a claw-shaped organ, as in *Calothamnus*.

staminode a sterile stamen often of different form from the fertile ones, e.g. petaloid.

standard the dorsal (uppermost petal) usually applied to flowers of the family Fabaceae.

stigma the usually enlarged area at the tip of the style receptive to pollen.

stipule small, bract-like appendages borne in pairs at the base of a petiole.

stolon a basal stem growing just below the soil surface and rooting at intervals.

stoloniferous bearing stolons, spreading by stolons.

striate marked with narrow lines or ridges.

style part of the female organ of the flower connecting the stigma with the ovary.

subspecies (subsp.) a taxonomic subgroup within a species used to differentiate usually geographically isolated variants.

subtend to stand below or close under as a bract subtending a flower.

succulent fleshy or juicy.

syn. synonym; one of two or more names for the same taxon.

Tas Tasmania.

taxon a term used to describe any taxonomic group, e.g. family, genus, species.

taxonomy the classification of plants or animals.

tepal a term used for the perianth segments when the sepals and petals are alike, e.g. in some Liliaceae.

terete slender and cylindrical.

terminal at the apex or tip.

terrestrial growing in the ground.

tomentose densely covered with short, soft hairs.

trifid divided into three above the middle.

trifoliate a compound leaf with three leaflets.

trigonous triangular in cross section with flat faces.

triquetrous triangular in cross section with concave faces and each corner projected outwards so that the organ has three distinct longitudinal ridges.

tuber a storage organ formed by swelling of an underground stem or root.

tuberous swollen and fleshy resembling a tuber.

umbel an inflorescence in which all the flower stalks arise around the same point and the flowers usually lie at the same level.

undulate wavy.

unisexual of one sex only — staminate or pistillate.

valve a segment of a woody fruit.

vein the conducting tissue of leaves.

venation the pattern formed by veins.

Vic Victoria.

villous covered with long, soft, shaggy hairs.

viscid coated with a sticky or glutinous substance.

WA Western Australia.

whorl three or more segments (leaves, flowers etc.) in a circle at a node.

wing a thin, dry, membranous expansion of an organ; the side petals of flowers of the family Fabaceae.

woolly bearing long, soft, matted hairs.